THE RETU
OF THE M⌐⌐⌐

Purdue Studies in Romance Literatures

Editorial Board

THE RETURN OF THE MOOR

Spanish Responses

to Contemporary

Moroccan Immigration

Daniela Flesler

Purdue University Press
West Lafayette, Indiana

∞ The paper used in this book meets the minimum requirements of
American National Standard for Information Sciences—Permanence of
Paper for Printed Library Materials, ANSI Z39.48-1992.

Printed in the United States of America
Design by Anita Noble

Library of Congress Cataloging-in-Publication Data

Flesler, Daniela, 1971–
     The return of the Moor : Spanish responses to contemporary Moroccan
immigration / by Daniela Flesler.
          p.   cm. — (Purdue studies in Romance literatures ; v. 43)
     Includes bibliographical references and index.
     ISBN 978-1-55753-483-5 (alk. paper)
     1. Spain—Emigration and immigration. 2. Morocco—Emigration and
immigration. 3. Moroccans—Spain. 4. Immigrants—Spain. 5. Spanish
literature—contemporary. 6. Spanish film—contemporary. 7. Spanish
cultural criticism. 8. Spain—social history and criticism. 9. Spanish literature—theory. 10. Spanish film—theory. I. Title. II. Series.
     DP53.M65F54 2008
     305.892'764046—dc22   2008004327

Contents

Acknowledgments

This book would not have been possible without the support and encouragement of many people. I thank the State University of New York at Stony Brook and Dean James V. Staros for a research leave in the spring of 2004 and SUNY/UUP for the Dr. Nuala Mcgann Drescher Award in the spring of 2005, during which I completed writing the manuscript. My thanks also to the Program for Cultural Cooperation between Spain's Ministry of Culture and United States Universities and to the FAHSS Research Fund at Stony Brook for their summer grants to conduct research in Spain. My deepest gratitude goes to Patricia Hart, Purdue Studies in Romance Literatures Editor, for believing in this project, and for giving me the freedom to complete it as I wished. I also thank both Patricia and Susan Y. Clawson, PSRL Production Editor, for their thorough and exquisite editing. Christopher and Teresa Soufas directed the dissertation in which I began to explore some of the ideas that later became part of this book. Their encouragement, advice, and parentlike warmth have been invaluable to me. Lou Charnon-Deutsch, Kathleen Vernon, Román de la Campa, Susan Martin-Márquez, and Jo Labanyi heard or read parts of the manuscript and greatly improved it with their comments and suggestions. Their work has always been a model and an inspiration. Thank you, especially, to Susan, who first introduced me to the work of Juan Goytisolo when I was a graduate student, and who has been extremely generous with her time and expertise ever since. My special thanks to E. Ann Kaplan, and the other members of our Transmission of Cultures Faculty Seminar at the Humanities Institute of Stony Brook: Jane Sugarman, Susan Scheckel, and Katherine Sugg, and to the graduate students in the Department of Hispanic Languages and Literature, with whom I read and discussed many of the works included in the book. My appreciation goes also to Kamal Rahmouni, who suggested materials that became an essential part of the book's argument, and to Carol Lindquist, who edited early drafts. I also wish to thank many people for their friendship and insight, both academic and otherwise: Luz Horne, Valeria Kovadloff, Alejandra Jaramillo, Benigno Trigo, Kelly Oliver, Saïd Messari, Tracey Walters, Eva Woods, Griselda and Santiago Flesler, Darío Contreras, Irene and Silvia Gojman, and my family in Spain,

Mercedes Melgosa González, Adrián, Esther, and José Julio Pérez Melgosa. Leonor and Héctor Flesler taught me to love books, and to strive for what I wanted. I could never thank them enough for their generosity and love. Elsa and Luis Gojman told me stories about the Spanish Civil War, and were always an example of courage. Celia and Natalio Flesler told me stories about immigrants who were forced to leave and forget their homes, and who found new ones. I thank them all for their presence in my life. Finally, I owe thanks to my son Benjamin, for making everything worthwhile, and for kindly waiting to be born until the day after I was finished writing chapter 5. This book is dedicated to my husband, coauthor and colleague, Adrián Pérez Melgosa, for always pushing me to think better and more clearly, for listening to the story and wanting to hear more, for the innumerable ideas and conversations we have had that have found their way here, and for all the ways he shows his support and love.

I am grateful to the editors of the following journals for permission to use portions of my previously published works in this book. Chapter 2 is a revised version of an article that first appeared as "De la inmigración marroquí a la invasión mora: discursos pasados y presentes del (des)encuentro entre España y Marruecos," *Arizona Journal of Hispanic Cultural Studies* 5 (2001): 73–88. Chapter 3 is a revised version of two articles: one first appeared as "Cristianas y moras: la identidad híbrida de España en *Moras y cristianas* de Ángeles de Irisarri y Magdalena Lasala y *El viaje de la reina* de Ángeles de Irisarri," *Revista de Estudios Hispánicos* 37 (2003): 413–35; the second article first appeared as "Battles of Identity, or Playing 'Guest' and 'Host': The Festivals of Moors and Christians in the Context of Moroccan Immigration to Spain," co-authored with Adrián Pérez Melgosa, *Journal of Spanish Cultural Studies* 4.2 (2003): 151–68. For more information, visit http://www. tandf.co.uk/journals. I also thank my coauthor, Adrián Pérez Melgosa, for permission to use the material here. Chapter 4 is a revised version of an article that first appeared as "New Racism, Intercultural Romance, and the Immigration Question in Contemporary Spanish Cinema," *Studies in Hispanic Cinemas* 1.2 (2004): 103–18.

Introduction

European Immigration,
New Racism, and the Case of Spain

> The stranger is both within and without the same
> thing: as the border that determines the necessity
> and impossibility of the difference between one and
> an-other.
>
> Sarah Ahmed
> *Strange Encounters*

On November 10, 1992, in the wake of the 500th anniversary of the Christian conquest of Granada, the Spanish state signed a cooperation agreement with the Islamic communities in Spain, which became Law 26/1992. As explained in the text itself, such agreement was possible because of the profound change in the state's attitude toward religion brought about by the 1978 Constitution, which guaranteed the rights of equality and religious freedom. As an introduction to the description of the protected rights that Muslims and their places of worship would henceforth have in Spain, the agreement states that Islam, which has become "noticeably rooted" in Spanish society, has a "tradición secular en nuestro país, con relevante importancia en la formación de la identidad española" ["secular tradition in our country, with considerable importance in the formation of Spanish identity"] ("Acuerdo"). This matter-of-fact affirmation seems at first to describe something that most people would have no problem agreeing with. Most people have an idea, however vague, that there were Muslims in Spain in the Middle Ages. The statement contains, nevertheless, a contentious truth that still causes enormous rifts in Spain, since there is quite a distance from the idea that there were Muslims in Spain to the idea that Islam is an inextricable part of Spanish identity. The social,

1

political, and cultural ramifications of this belief have very serious consequences in contemporary Spain. Like the "enormous distance" that Jean Loup Herbert finds between this advanced 1992 law and the contents of Spanish school textbooks (12), which still insist on denying the crucial role of Islam in Spanish history, there is an enormous distance between the outward respect for the Muslim community that is recognized in this law and the disastrous conditions in which most Muslim immigrants find themselves. This book argues that, paradoxically, the truth in the affirmation of the importance of Islam in Spanish identity has a lot to do with these disastrous conditions.

Europe's transnational integration and the opening of its internal frontiers have coincided with the closure of its external borders and a return to exclusionary narratives of national identity. As traditional conceptions of citizenship change toward postnational, deterritorialized notions of personal rights, nation and national identities appear articulated in new ways (Soysal 21–24). After decades of sending emigrants to their colonies or former colonies, Western European countries today face the reversal of that migration pattern and the return of the colonized, with postcolonial encounters now taking place "at home" (Brinker-Gabler and Smith 6–8). Western European countries that were themselves exporters of emigrants to Northern Europe, such as Italy and Spain, have transformed themselves into countries of reception. With the intense economic development and accelerated modernization that has been experienced by Spain since the 1970s, especially following its entrance into the European Economic Community in 1986, the country has undergone a rapid inversion in migratory patterns. After being an exporter of economic migrants for almost a century, in the last twenty years Spain has seen itself on the receiving end of immigration. Among these immigrants, North Africans—especially, Moroccans—are the group that focalizes most of the debates over integration and assimilation (Martín Muñoz 32). Because of complex religious, historical, and cultural factors, they have become the immigrant group most ill-regarded by Spaniards (Checa et al. 177–78; Martín Muñoz 32). Statistics show that they are the ones afforded the least preference in facilitating their permanence in Spain, and those who earn the lowest level of acceptance as neighbors (Izquierdo 174). They have also been the main victims of repeated and violent collective attacks, as happened in Terrassa, Barcelona, in July of 1999, and in El Ejido, Almería, in February of 2000. Spaniards' rejection of Moroccan immigrants occurs at several levels, displayed through both subtle and explicit violence and encompassing issues of race, religion, social class, and geopolitical configurations.

This book contends that the current rejection of Moroccan immigrants is related to the fact that they are the one group most directly implicated in the question of Spanish identity in relationship to Africa. Through their characterization as "Moors," they are identified with the Arab and Berber Muslims who colonized the Iberian Peninsula in AD 711 and were responsible for its Arabization and Islamization in the Middle Ages. The historical echoes of this characterization tie current Moroccan migrants to the traditional enemies of Christian Spain, awakening a series of historical ghosts related to their invading and threatening character. Historically, the term *Moors* refers to the North African Muslims of mixed Arab and Berber origin that conquered the Iberian Peninsula in 711. In Spain, the term contains considerable affect. It is extended to signify any Arab or Muslim, and it has highly negative connotations, as the following chapters illustrate. Some of these are associated with the idea of the Moor as attacker or invader, encapsulated in the saying "*hay moros en la costa*" ["Moors on the coast"]. When today's Moroccan immigrants are called "*moros*" ["Moors"] instead of "*marroquíes*" ["Moroccans"], their identity becomes symbolically collapsed with the concept of that attacking enemy.[1] Over the last few years, there has been a double return to the Spanish national imaginary of the figure of the "Moor." On one hand, fictional representations of the historical Moors have multiplied in the culture industry and in popular festivities such as the Festivals of Moors and Christians. On the other hand, the number of Moroccan immigrants in Spain has increased significantly over the last twenty years, constituting today the second-largest national group of resident foreigners.[2] This presence has produced, among other things, new images of the "Moor," this time in the form of representations that attempt to narrate their contemporary immigrant experience. Many of these new representations, as we see in the following chapters, are highly

3

influenced by past ones, as both historical and fictional "Moors" coexist in the same symbolic paradigm in the Spanish cultural imaginary. Contemporary Moroccan immigrants, in turn, often become conceptually collapsed into this category of the imaginary and threatening "Moor."

As in other national contexts, in Spain today there is a clear stratification of immigrants, so that policies and narratives of exclusion do not apply in the same way to all foreigners. As Sarah Ahmed contends, in every encounter there are circumstances in play that result in a situation where "some others are designated as *stranger than other others*" (Ahmed 6; emphasis in the original). In order for a "stranger" to be constituted as such, there needs to be a recognition, and that recognition is dependent upon a prior history of encounters: the recognition of an other as a stranger is constituted through an encounter in the present that reopens past encounters (Ahmed 8, 13, 55). This is precisely what happens with the conflation of the Moroccan immigrant with the historical figure of the "Moor," as we see in chapter 2. Not all foreigners in Spain are, thus, "strangers" in the same sense. This level of "strangeness" and acceptance has little to do with their numbers. Immigrants from other EU countries, which make up 22 percent of foreigners resident in Spain, and from other European countries, constituting 13 percent, are not perceived as "strangers" in the way that Africans, constituting 19.6 percent, are. Latin Americans, in turn, who amount to 38.6 percent of foreign residents, are not perceived to be as much "strangers" as Africans are. The hierarchy of acceptance corresponds, more or less, to a scheme in which Europeans, both from EU countries and not, are at the top of the list, followed by Latin Americans, then Sub-Saharan Africans, with North Africans at the bottom. If, as contemporary critical theory has established, national identities are constituted through the encounter with others, this, however, happens "not simply through or against a generalisable other, but by differentiating between others . . . into familiar (assimilable, touchable) and strange (unassimilable, untouchable)" (Ahmed 100). This differentiation, bounded with conceptions of assimilability, plays a crucial role in the perception and reception of different national groups, as we see in chapter 4.

The Return of the Moor argues that Spain has adopted toward Moroccan immigrants what has been called the European discourse of "new racism," as analyzed in the French and British contexts by Martin Barker, Étienne Balibar, Pierre-André Taguieff, Robert Miles, and Paul Gilroy. This new or differentialist racism replaces the belief in biological inferiority with that of the presumed incompatibility of different cultures, lifestyles, and traditions (Balibar 21), endorsing a conceptualization of the nation as a stable, homogeneous, and isolated cultural entity. This does not mean that "traditional," biological racism does not exist in Spain. It exists, for example, in the form of neo-Nazi groups who explicitly articulate it both in their attacks on immigrants and in interviews in newspapers and magazines. The attention given to these extremist groups both in journalistic reports and in fictional representations, however, masks the reality of the much subtler and more socially widespread culturalist racism that is publicly articulated and accepted in social and political spheres in which "traditional," biological racism would not be. This "new" racism is especially pertinent in the case of Muslim immigrants, whose cultural traditions are seen as "Islamic," and therefore as incompatible with the supposedly democratic, modern, secular values of Western Europe (see Balibar 23–24; Asad 11–17; Ballard 36–40), a view that is shared, in its different national contexts, not only by the right, but by the whole political spectrum (Asad 11–12; see also Nederveen Pieterse 6).[3]

The conceptualization of this particular cultural incompatibility, and the difficulties involved in doing so, are not, in fact, new to Spain. After the Christian conquest of Granada in 1492, those defeated Muslims who stayed in the Peninsula were offered, upon their surrender, religious and cultural freedom.[4] These terms of capitulation were upheld by the first archbishop of Granada, Fray Hernando de Talavera, who set an example of a gradual and nonviolent method to assimilate the *Mudéjares*, as the Muslims under Christian rule were called: he allowed them to keep their own instruments and songs to be used in Christian rituals, permitted the use of Arabic during the Mass, and encouraged clerics and priests to learn it (Fuchs, *Mimesis* 105). Talavera's methods, which later would become common in evangelizing the indigenous peoples of the Americas, were, however, a short-lived exception regarding the *Mudéjares*. Very soon this gradual approach to assimilation was replaced by Fray Francisco Jiménez de Cisneros's forced conversions and cultural repression (Fuchs, *Mimesis* 105; Márquez Villanueva, "El problema" 86–87). As stated by L. P. Harvey, Cisneros's "stubborn intransigence" drove the Muslims of Granada, who had been quite peaceful, to armed insurrection (Harvey, *Islamic* 331). When they rioted against Cisneros's measures, he denounced the minor uprising as a rebellion, which justified the abrogation of their rights under the terms of capitulation and furthered his conversion campaign. The price of a royal pardon for rebellion thus became the acceptance of baptism (Coleman, *Creating* 6). By 1502, when other minor rebellions had also been put down, Muslims were given the "choice" of either conversion or expulsion from Granada and the rest of Castile. The same measure was taken in 1525 in Valencia, the remaining *Mudéjar* enclave, so that by the late 1520s Islam ceased to exist as a public religion in all Spanish kingdoms (Harvey, *Islamic* 333–35; Coleman, *Creating* 6–7).

Although the *Mudéjares* who converted were now legally Christian, the name given to them, *Moriscos*, or "little Moors," underscored their remaining "Muslimness."[5] The *Moriscos*, as baptized Christians, were now under the jurisdiction of the newly established Inquisition, which began surveilling their customs and practices, quickly deemed heretical (Root 122–23). *Moriscos*, like converted Jews, were always suspected of secretly practicing their religion, and, therefore, they were easily accused of religious deviation. By the sixteenth century the status of the *Moriscos* underwent a transformation through which they were reinvented as an internal other. *Moriscos'* lives were heavily regulated and censored in terms of language, clothing, and customs, with increasing levels of prohibitions, so that they would conform to what was deemed to be the current "national norm." Cultural traits and heterodox customs became the vehicles through which to identify their religious deviance (Root 118–19). The biological traces of their Muslim origin, their lack of "purity of blood," could be seen *culturally*. Overwhelmingly, their conversions had been done so quickly that they had not been allowed time for Christian religious instruction, with the result that many *Moriscos* continued, both voluntarily and not, to practice the religion they knew.

One of the early tasks of the Inquisition became to distinguish between what was a matter of faith and what was customary.

One of the problems was the difficulty to clearly differentiate between "purely" Christian and "purely" Muslim practices and between religious and cultural practices. Moorish dress, for example, was customarily used by Christians themselves in the fifteenth and early sixteenth century (Fuchs, *Passing* 6–7), and henna was used for cosmetic and medical purposes by Old Christian women (Root 127; Coleman, *Creating* 63). A whole way of life constructed through centuries of coexistence and contact between Christians, Muslims, and Jews had to be dissected. As explained by Root, in order to solve this issue, "[t]he Inquisition *produced* heresies from the appearance of specific social practices and customs that were determined to deviate from orthodoxy, even if some of these customs were maintained by Old Christians themselves" (Root 124). In order to identify such deviations, the Inquisition moved further and further into the private lives of the community, asking Christians to watch for and denounce *Moriscos* as "crypto-Muslims" not only on the basis of straight religious practices, such as praying in Arabic, making ablutions, turning one's face to the East, or fasting during Ramadan, but also on the basis of cultural practices, such as wearing Moorish clothing and jewelry, a preference for Moorish names, or singing and dancing Moorish songs (Root 125–26). The "heretical" nature of these practices became dogma in the 1567 Edict, which prohibited all "Moorish" customs, and sparked the Alpujarras rebellion of 1568.

As Root explains, the problem of *Moriscos*' (both real and imagined) "dissimulation" was at the heart of what became the "final solution" of their 1609 expulsion from Spain, preceded by their expulsion from Granada in 1569. This measure was unprecedented, since, unlike the Jews expelled in 1492, the *Moriscos* were baptized. The difficulty in determining the sincerity of their orthodoxy, now equated to "Spanishness," meant that having converted and adopted Christian cultural customs were not enough to prove it. The proof increasingly became located in genealogy and "purity of blood":

> The indeterminability of faith apparent in the Inquisition's inability to determine dissimulation, and its effort to circumvent this by continually increasing its demands for proof of orthodoxy, meant the definition of orthodoxy would migrate to genealogy: moriscos were not and could not be "truly"

> Christian because of their ancestry, and they were by defini-
> tion reduced to impenitent heretics and dangerous outsiders.
> A polarity had been constructed that became impossible to
> deal with except by "amputation" and the "casting out" of the
> deviants. (Root 130)

It is through this—again, both real and imagined—"dissimulation" that *Moriscos* embodied the biggest threat for the definition and consolidation of a homogeneous Spanish identity.
Moriscos constituted a problem because they were different—their
Muslim lineage marked them as potential heretics and enemies—
but, at the same time, because they were the same—as converted Christians, without their *Morisco* clothing, language,
and customs, they could be transformed into "real" Spaniards,
they could "pass." They were simultaneously same and other,
Spaniard and foreign. Phenotypically, *Moriscos* were not easily
"distinguishable" from Old Christians. Passing was a common
phenomenon, used both by *Moriscos* and by Christians.[6]

The difficulty of this conceptualization of difference and
the deep ambivalence that it contained was "solved" when, in
1609, *Moriscos* were expelled, first from the Kingdom of Valencia, and then from the rest of Spain. The Edict of Expulsion
itself, however, brought the ambivalence back: as explained by
Georgina Dopico Black, one of the Edict's most controversial
provisions stated that all *Morisco* children under the age of
five were to be left behind in Spain. The age of the children
in question was decided according to the age set by linguistic
theories of the time as that when children achieved language
mastery: after five, *Morisco* children would have a command
of the Arabic language and, through it, enough knowledge of
Muslim culture and religion to constitute a threat to Christian
Spain. The *Morisco* children under five, culturally "innocent"
enough, notwithstanding their "impure" blood, could remain in
Spain and be incorporated into the national body. Most of them
were given to Christian families to be "properly instructed" in
Christianity and became, in fact, virtual slaves (Dopico Black
93–98; see also Harvey, *Muslims* 299–300).

Although one of the main reasons invoked again and again
for their expulsion is the *Moriscos'* alleged cultural and religious inassimilability, there were, in fact, many who were
sincere converts. There was also a high degree of syncretism

between the two religions, as the famous cases of the Mancebo de Arévalo and the Sacromonte lead books ("Plomos") demonstrate (Márquez Villanueva, "El problema" 85–88). The Christianization of the *Moriscos* and their progressive loss of touch with Islam were apparent by the time of the expulsion, when most could no longer read or write in Arabic, used Castilian, and had only a faint grasp of Islamic doctrine (Root 127). Their assimilation, if not complete, was certainly enough for them to be referred to as "Spanish Christians" in North Africa and to suffer persecution and even massacre after taking refuge there (Márquez Villanueva, "El problema" 91).[7]

The *Morisco* "problem" and its successive problematic "solutions" reveal Spain's deep anxiety over the demarcation of national belonging. Today, the responses to Moroccan immigration are still determined by that anxiety. Unlike other Western European nations, Spain is not only experiencing the return of the colonized but also that of its medieval colonizers. While Latin Americans can be seen as the return of the colonized and can be "fixed" in this conceptual category, Moroccans not only embody the return of the colonized but also, especially, and more threateningly, the return of the colonizers or "invaders" of Spain, and thus they cannot easily be "fixed." More acutely than other nations, Spain embodies the deep ambivalence of the politics of postcolonial hospitality. If Spaniards have difficulty in welcoming Moroccan immigrants, it is because they perceive them not only as guests but also as hosts who have come to reclaim what was theirs. Perceived as "Moors," Moroccan immigrants embody the non-European, African, and oriental aspects of Spanish national identity. Moroccans turn into a "problem," then, not because of their cultural differences, as many argue, but because, like the *Moriscos, they are not different enough.* Like Freud's uncanny, or Derrida's specters, Moroccans become for Spaniards the return of the repressed. Spanish responses are permeated with the effort of differentiating and separating, in an attempt to trace clear frontiers between the "Moors" and themselves. The difficulty of doing so is illustrated in Marcelino Menéndez y Pelayo's infamous description of the *Moriscos* in *Historia de los heterodoxos españoles* [*History of Heterodox Spaniards*] as "aquel miembro podrido del cuerpo de la nacionalidad española" ["that rotten member of the Spanish nationality's body"] (628). Parting with this "member" has been extremely difficult because, precisely, it belongs to the body as inextricably as a limb does. *The Return of the Moor* analyzes this particular dynamic between Spaniards and "Moors," which gives a tangible form to contemporary philosophical interrogations that have called into question the possibility of clearly delineating a boundary between self and other, host and guest, and the familiar and the foreign.

The Return of the Moor examines this anxiety over symbolic and literal boundaries, which results in an attempt to establish Spanish identity as unequivocally "European" and set up clear-cut differences with those deemed as outsiders. Through strategies of differentiation and stereotype building, the texts studied attempt to place the Moroccan immigrant into a stable category of otherness but reveal the inherent ambivalence and difficulty that results from trying to do so. The dangerous potential of these stereotypes, as Rey Chow reminds us, is not their conventionality or formulaicness, but their capacity to engender boundaries, and realities, that do not exist. Thus, for example, in the media's account of the migrants' crossing of the Strait of Gibraltar, in semi-fictional testimonies, novels, and in the violent collective attacks against Moroccan workers in Andalusia and Catalonia, the Moroccan immigrant is often collapsed with the figure of the medieval Moorish invader, itself repeated in later figures such as the sixteenth- and seventeenth-century Muslim corsair who attacks the Spanish coast or the twentieth-century Moroccan nationalist mercenary who plunders Spanish villages and towns. The use of the rhetoric of invasion and specific references to medieval or early modern Spain conjures up the stereotype of the violent, invading Moor and thus generates a reality that justifies the rejection of and the violence against Moroccan workers as a form of self-defense.

In other novels, films, and debates—such as those touching on the use of the Muslim headscarf in schools—the figure of the Moroccan immigrant is that of the conservative and oppressive-to-women Muslim man, who cannot possibly be integrated into modern Spanish society. In yet another group of texts, the differentiating construction is that of the Moroccan immigrant as a subaltern to be ethnographically explained and spoken for. The majority of the analyzed texts, ranging from the first chronicles that describe the Moorish invasion of the Iberian Peninsula in 711 to contemporary novels or films that portray the arrival of immigrants in Barcelona or Madrid, articulate a particular sexual violence. In sharp contrast to the gender dynamics articulated in medieval Reconquest texts (see, for example, Mirrer), or in Counter-Reformation texts (see, for example, Mariscal's *Contradictory*), in which Muslims and Jews are represented as effeminate or homosexual in order to set up a contrast with virile Christian men, in these texts of "invasion," Spain is identified with femininity and the Moor/Moroccan immigrant, with masculinity (see, especially, chapters 2 and 4).[8]

The material is analyzed thematically, with literary, visual, and social texts grouped according to the different textual strategies they employ to define the boundary between Spaniards and Moroccans. This means that some materials are analyzed in more than one chapter, from different perspectives. Chapter 1, "Difference Within and Without: Negotiating European, National, and Regional Identities in Spain," explores the specificity of Spanish dynamics of belonging as they relate to the issue of Moroccan immigration, both in the European context and in the internal, regional one. It argues that the specific advantages of Spain's joining the European Economic Community in 1986 were not only political and economic, but also psychological: entrance to the EEC meant official closure to the discourse of Spain's "difference" in Europe, exemplified in the French saying "Africa begins at the Pyrenees." Moroccan immigration reaffirms European belonging, showing Spain as a desirable First World destination, but it also destabilizes it, bringing to the fore the issue of Spanish racial formation. The first part of the chapter analyzes critical moments in different texts that engage the question of Spain's (racial) "difference" in Europe and its relationship to immigration, specifically denouncing what is perceived as the inferior role of Spain as "guardian" of European frontiers and the gap that exists between the image of modern, European Spain and the underdeveloped Spain experienced by immigrants. The second part of the chapter analyzes the intersection of immigration debates and the politics of national and regional identities, in the context of the "Europe of the Regions." While nationalist discourses of an essential "Spanishness" are deployed at the national level, nationalist discourses of self-defense of a seemingly homogeneous Catalan identity are deployed regionally in Catalonia. Focusing on the issue of immigration, the texts studied address anxieties concerning the relationship of Catalonia to the Spanish state. For example, in the case of language, an issue highlighted in the immigration debates in Catalonia, the central concern is whether immigrants will learn to speak Catalan, or will only speak Castilian, mirroring prior debates over Spanish immigration to Catalonia in the 1950s and 1960s.

Chapter 2, "Ghostly Returns: The 'Loss' of Spain, the Invading 'Moor' and the Contemporary Moroccan Immigrant," analyzes the way the Moroccan immigrant is transformed into the threatening figure of the medieval (male) Moorish invader. In the media's account of migrants' crossing of the Strait of Gibraltar and their children's presence in schools, in semi-fictional testimonies like *Dormir al raso* (*Sleeping Unsheltered*, Pasqual Moreno Torregrosa and Mohamed El Gheryb, 1994), in novels like *Las voces del Estrecho* (*Voices from the Strait*, Andrés Sorel, 2000), and in the violent collective attacks against Moroccan workers in Andalusia and Catalonia, the use of the rhetoric of invasion and specific references to medieval Spain conjure up the ghost of the violent invading Moor and thus justify the rejection of and violence against Moroccan workers as a form of self- defense. The analysis of these immigration texts reveals how the figure of the "Moor" continues to haunt the Spanish imaginary, producing slippages between past and present and textually producing Moroccans as Moorish ghosts. Some of the issues discussed include whether Spain's Moorish past survives as an unsolved trauma for Spaniards, whether we can speak of a Spanish cultural trauma in relation to the Moors, passed down through generations, even if it was not historically experienced as such, and the ways this traumatic experience has been marked in gender terms. The contemporary textual productions analyzed in this chapter, collapsing the categories of medieval Moorish invader and contemporary Moroccan immigrant, attempt to demonstrate that all throughout their historical relationship, Spaniards "belong," and Moroccans "invade."

Chapter 3, "Playing Guest and Host: Moors and Christians, Moroccans and Spaniards in Historical Novels and Festive Reenactments," examines the relationship between Moroccan immigration and the current popularity of the figure of the medieval Moor in the culture and tourist industry, focusing on the "boom" of historical novels and the multitudinous *Fiestas de moros y cristianos* (Festivals of Moors and Christians). In both of these cases, the preoccupation with current changes in the racial and ethnic composition of Spanish society is displaced into a distant and safer past, the imaginary space of medieval Spain's "multiculturalism *avant la lettre.*" Both the novels and the festivals are plagued by the anxiety of delimiting, in that past, the concrete space occupied by each group, to ensure that the limits appear well established. The novels *Moras y cristianas (Moorish and Christian Women*, Ángeles de Irisarri and Magdalena Lasala, 1998) and *El viaje de la reina (The Queen's Trip*, Ángeles de Irisarri, 1991) attempt to reconstruct a past in which the domains of thought, activity, and residence of Moorish and Christian women can be clearly delineated. In the same way, the Festivals of Moors and Christians, in which Spaniards reenact Christian triumphs against Muslims in medieval wars and sea attacks, constitute an example of the effort at performatively constructing a clear boundary between the two groups. In both of these cases, the efforts to delimit two clear spaces of separation fail. Moors and Christians become simultaneously guests and hosts in what Homi Bhabha calls a "third space" that is neither one of complete separation nor one of homogenization. These attempts to fix a Moorish other reveal the essential ambivalence of the stereotype in a relationship where the boundaries of belonging are never definitely traced.

Chapter 4, "Impossible Love: The Presumed Incompatibility of Islam and (European) Spain," explores the way the formula of a failed romance between a Spanish woman and an immigrant man functions in fictional narratives to demonstrate the European modernity of Spain as an absolute cultural difference from Moroccan immigrants. In sharp contrast to Spanish colonial narrative and film, in which *mestizaje* served the purpose of "improving the race" and incorporating the other, racial narratives of the 1990s, through the plot of failed intercultural romance, become complicit with the assumptions of differentialist racism, that is, with the belief in the insurmountability of cultural differences and the need to preserve "one's own" identity from racial/cultural contagion and intermixing. The failed

romances studied in this chapter include the films *Tomándote*
(*Two for Tea*, Isabel Gardela, 2000) and *Susanna* (*Susanna*,
Antonio Chavarrías, 1996), and the novels *La cazadora* (*The
Jacket*, Encarna Cabello, 1995) and *La aventura de Saïd* (*Saïd's
Adventure*, Josep Lorman, 1996). In every one of these narratives, a modern, secular, and sexually liberated Spanish woman
becomes romantically involved with a conservative, traditional,
religious, "Islamic" immigrant, a contemporary "Moor" oppressive to women who becomes the opposing image of what Spain
strives to convince itself it has become: a modern, "first-world"
European nation. The chapter also includes a discussion of the
Spanish media's coverage of the case of Fátima Elidrisi, which
spurred a controversy over the use of the traditional Moroccan
headscarf in Spanish schools in February 2002. The coverage
of Fátima Elidrisi's case participates in the same assumptions
about the incompatibility of Islam and modern Europe as do the
impossible romance plots of the novels and films.

Chapter 5, "Testimonies of Immigrant Life: Fact, Fiction,
and the Ethnographic Performance," analyzes the narrative
strategy by which, in attempting to establish clear-cut differences from Moroccans, Spaniards engage in what I call the
ethnographic performance. This performance constructs immigrants as subalterns to be photographed, analyzed, interviewed,
and written about, in an attempt to represent an "accurate picture" of what immigrants' lives are like. Texts like *Dormir al
raso* (*Sleeping Unsheltered*, Pasqual Moreno Torregrosa and
Mohamed El Gheryb, 1994), *Yo, Mohamed: historias de inmigrantes en un país de emigrantes* (*I, Mohamed: Stories of Immigrants in a Country of Emigrants*, Rafael Torres, 1995), *Todo
negro no igual* (*All Blacks Not the Same*, Beatriz Díaz, 1997),
documentary films like *Todos os llamáis Mohamed* (*You Are All
Called Mohamed*, Maximiliano Lemcke, 1997), and novels like
Las voces del Estrecho (*The Voices of the Strait*, Andrés Sorel,
2000) constitute less-than-successful efforts to "give voice"
to the immigrants by using the testimonial genre, which often
results in actually taking away their voices. A similar relationship between fact, fiction, and the construction of subalternity
is also present in sociological studies of immigration that contain "personal testimonies," such as César Manzanos Bilbao's
El grito del otro: arqueología de la marginación racial (*The

Other's Cry: Archaeology of Racial Marginalization, 1999) and Gema Martín Muñoz's *Marroquíes en España: estudio sobre su integración* (*Moroccans in Spain: Study on Their Integration*, 2003). This chapter also analyzes the recurrent fictional character of the Spanish journalist who looks for information about immigrants' lives and, in doing so, reflects upon ethnographic constructions of otherness. This occurs in two short stories of the collection *Por la vía de Tarifa* (*Through the Way of Tarifa*, Nieves García Benito, 1999), in the novel *La aventura de Saïd* (*Saïd's Adventure*, Josep Lorman, 1996), and in the film *Ilegal* (*Illegal*, Ignacio Vilar, 2002). Another focus is what happens when an immigrant refuses to speak, as in the short story "Fátima de los naufragios" ("Fátima of the Shipwrecks," Lourdes Ortiz, 1998).

The strategies of separation and differentiation, of racialization and othering of "Moors" analyzed in this book are not new. Contemporary Moroccan immigrants represent an acute conflict for Spanish society precisely because they embody a very old history of efforts to extricate the "Moorish" from the "Spanish." This was certainly a very difficult endeavor: Menéndez y Pelayo captures some of this difficulty when he concludes his justificatory account of the expulsion of the *Moriscos* by saying: "El nudo no podía desatarse, y hubo que cortarlo" ["The knot could not be untied, so it had to be cut off"] (635). But the difficulty lay not only in disentangling two elements that had become too intertwined. Christians and Muslims, often also Jews, had actually become indistinguishable. As Mark Meyerson remarks, in reference to the medieval and early modern contexts: "One of the paradoxes of Spanish history, it seems to me, is that the legal, literary, and polemical texts in which the 'other' was constructed often were produced because the 'other' had become too familiar and hence too dangerous, because the 'other' was not 'other' at all" (Meyerson, Introduction xiii). Barriers are necessary, then, because in reality there are none. As we will see in the following chapter, these barriers were deemed crucial if Spain wanted to occupy a place in Europe, both yesterday and today.

Difference Within and Without

Negotiating European, National,
and Regional Identities in Spain

> Marruecos es como España. Sólo que España
> está en Europa y Marruecos en África.
>
> [Morocco is like Spain. Only that Spain
> is in Europe and Morocco in Africa.]
>
> Rachid Nini
> *Diario de un ilegal*

This chapter examines the dynamics of Spanish "difference" within Europe and within Spain's own regions as related to the issue of immigration. More specifically, it analyzes how current Moroccan immigration to Spain both destabilizes and reaffirms the notion of Spain's "difference," both internal and external. Spanish attempts to gain acceptance into the European Economic Community began in 1962, when the request was denied because Spain, still under Franco's dictatorship, did not fulfill the required political conditions. In 1977, with the return of democracy, entry was solicited again. After years of negotiations, it was finally granted in June 1985. As for other European nations, the biggest advantage of membership in the EEC was basically an economic one: it guaranteed access to European markets for agricultural exports, to subsidies, and to new technologies (Graham and Sánchez 411). But there were also very specific Spanish circumstances that made belonging to the EEC extremely desirable. During the isolation and repression of the Franco era, from 1939 to 1975, Franco's opposition associated the idea of "Europe" with concepts of modernity, tolerance, and freedom (Montero 319), an association that had existed for liberal thinkers since the eighteenth century. During the transition to democracy, "Europe was seen as an external support system for the emerging democracy, a force for democratic stability, economic growth and social modernization" (Keating, "Minority Nations" 32). This "Europe" was at the time an imaginary monolithic, homogeneous category, and its constructed, "invented" nature was not interrogated.[1] Spaniards saw it "not only as a model to follow, but as a form of insurance policy against any return to authoritarian rule" (Kelly 31). In part because of this, integration into the EEC was the main objective of every Spanish government after the reinstallation of democracy in 1976. Integration was never an element of political breakup or a dividing force for the party system as in the case of other EEC countries (Morán 286–87). Spaniards themselves also accepted their new "European" identity without controversy.[2] In 1987, a year after official integration, more than half of Spaniards considered themselves European as well as Spanish, a percentage somewhat higher than the EC countries' average. Also, the number of those who never considered themselves to be inhabitants of a supranational body, as is Europe, was slightly smaller in Spain than in all other EC countries (Morán 290). These statistics from 1987 are accompanied today by a general belief in and self-assurance with Spain's stable "European" location.

Public and private assurances about this "European" identity speak of two important Spanish realities. One has to do with the fact that a significant number of citizens of the Spanish state prefer to identify themselves as "Europeans" and imagine an identity linked to the concept of the "Europe of the Regions" rather than identifying themselves as "Spaniards," as we will see. As a result of this fact, some have argued that internal enthusiasm for Spain's entrance into the EEC was high because integration was seen by the central government as an antidote to internal fragmentation. Helen Graham and Antonio Sánchez thus argue that "the fundamental appeal of Europe for Spaniards today is that it apparently offers an easy way of unifying an otherwise fragmented and always problematic nationhood" (411).

The second Spanish reality entails an old anxiety about Spain's belonging to Europe, and the efforts at overcoming its "difference," linked in its various historical manifestations to notions of racial impurity, religious fanaticism, underdevelopment, poverty, and a general sense of inferiority in relation to a more-developed Europe. As Jan Nederveen Pieterse has argued, the traditional definition of Europe as a cultural tradition rooted in Judeo-Christian religion, Roman law, and Greek philosophy swiftly ignores the reality of Europe's diversity and heterogeneity both past and present (Nederveen Pieterse 3–4).[3] This notion of "Europeanness" has also systematically excluded many "Europeans" seen as not "developed" enough, especially in Southern and Eastern Europe. Enrique Dussel explains how pervasive Hegel's understanding of European modernity has been. In Hegel's account, modernity belongs to Northwestern Europe, and it began with a German event: the Lutheran reformation, later fully "developed" in the Enlightenment and the French Revolution (Dussel 71–72). Catholic Spain would obviously be excluded from an account that places modernity's origins in the Protestant Reformation, and not in its own watershed date of 1492. Contemporary critics argue that this is the crucial date, since the self-conscious sense of European "modern civilization," and, concomitantly, of Europe's intrinsic superiority, is constituted through the relationship with outsiders that began with the colonization of the Americas (Gilroy 17; Dussel 65). It was later strengthened in the Enlightenment through the justification of colonialism provided by scientific racism (Gilroy 49, 54). In addition, Spain and Portugal's model for the colonization of the New World, itself based on the "Reconquest" of Andalusia, would be the one later applied by the other European colonial powers in Africa and Asia (Dussel 67; Blackburn 156; Mariscal, "The Role" 8). This exclusion of Spain from accounts of modernity is accompanied by its exclusion in theorizations of Western racism. George Mariscal explains how, for English-speaking scholars, still trapped in the discursive heritage of the "Black Legend," "Spanish colonialism serves a double function—because Spain is the most fanatical representative of European expansionism, Spain is the least 'European' of Europe's nations" (Mariscal, "The Role" 7–8). This exclusion was therefore itself "a by-product of Eurocentric practices" (Mariscal, "The Role" 10). As Mariscal argues, excluding Spain's case by analyzing modern racism as if it were only an eighteenth-century phenomenon, or only including Spanish colonialism after 1492 as an extreme case of barbarism—without taking into account the racial, and not merely religious, pre-1492 relationships between Muslims, Christians, and Jews that existed in the Peninsula—produces the effect of detaching Spain from the West (Mariscal, "The Role" 10–11), as does accepting Hegel's point of origin for modernity in the Lutheran Reformation.

This detachment or differentiation of Spain from the rest of Europe is precisely linked to race as an exclusionary category. In early accounts of European views of Spain, there is a long history of accusing Spain of being "impure" in racial, cultural, and religious terms because of its connection to oriental and African elements and the mingling of Christians with Jews and Arabs (Iglesias 394; see also Mariscal; Delgado; Colmeiro; Blackmore and Hutcheson). In the context of Spain's imperial conquests, in the sixteenth century, Germany and the Low Countries spoke of Spaniards and Turks as equally authoritarian and "oriental" cultures that attempted to dominate the entire world (Iglesias 402–04), at a time when "oriental despotism" characterized precisely what Europe posed itself against (Nederveen Pieterse 8). Stereotypes of Spaniards, by this time, as summarized in a French pamphlet, included an inhuman cruelty, tyranny, and lechery, a horrible physical appearance, and a "Satanic moral condition," all characteristics that were associated, again, with their Muslim and Jewish heritages (Iglesias 409). This European discourse about Spanish cruelty, especially the tales of tortures and massacres of indigenous peoples in the Americas—mostly based on Las Casas—will partly inform what has been characterized in Spain as "the Black legend." Spain, in this representation, "served as the negative image of modernity" (Schmidt-Nowara 158), and, therefore, of the way Europe wanted to see itself. [4]

This negative image of Spain as barbaric, uncivilized, and more akin to Africa than to Europe, encompassed in the French saying "Africa begins at the Pyrenees," became for European Romantic travelers an object of unending fascination. They saw in Spain, and especially in Andalusia, a reservoir of exotic culture, "a dream world where time could be slowed, life savored to its fullest, and the disturbances and hypocrisy of the modern, 'civilized' world of large European capitals avoided" (Charnon-Deutsch, *The Spanish Gypsy* 59). Spain's cultural diversity, and especially its Moorish heritage, became a main attraction in a time of orientalist taste, when Spain was perceived as a "close-to-home" Orient. Spain thus became a favorite exotic destination for travel for Europeans, and Spaniards began a deeply ambivalent relationship with this "exotic" and "oriental" conception of themselves (Charnon-Deutsch, "Exoticism" 251).[5] As Charnon-Deutsch and Colmeiro have observed, Spain finds itself in a particular double bind as both a culture that has repressed the "oriental" and Semitic elements of its historical identity, constructing them as its others, and the "close-to-home" Orient to other Europeans (Charnon-Deutsch, "Exoticism" 262; Colmeiro 129).[6]

Spanish thinkers were deeply engaged with these European visions of their nation, agreeing with the notion of Spain's "difference," but interpreting it in different ways, oscillating between the view of "difference" as a shameful inferiority that should be overcome or as a source of national pride, depending on the ideological position of the thinker (see Torrecilla, *El Tiempo* 11–14), and on the changing political circumstances of the triangulation Spain/Europe/Africa. What has remained a constant since the eleventh century, when the Roman Christian rite was imposed over the Mozarabic one, is the idea that what separates Spain from Europe is this religious, racial, cultural, and, later, economic difference that had its origin in Spain's "impure" contact with Africa and Islam. From this perspective, full European membership, in its different historical manifestations, seems the solution to get rid of this "impurity." Even for thinkers who embrace this "difference," there is an understanding that the norm to which Spain should aspire is Europe, and that the connections with Africa and Islam, as opposites of that desired model, should be severed once they are not politically useful anymore. Since the beginning of the so-called "Reconquest," Spain has seen the effort at getting rid of its Arab and Muslim self—that "rotten member of the Spanish body," in Menéndez y Pelayo's phrasing—as a process that goes hand-in-hand with that of reintegrating into Europe. If Europe looked down upon Spain because of its mingling and mixing with Arabs and Jews, the physical and discursive expulsion of that element from the nation would bring it closer to the desired norm.

The nuances of the Europe/Spain/Africa triangulation can be seen in Pedro Antonio de Alarcón's essay "España y los franceses" (1859), which vindicates Spain's African identity as an answer to the French "insult" of "Africa begins at the Pyrenees." He exhorts Spaniards to be proud of not "being able" to be French: "¡nosotros no servimos para franceses . . . ! Si es esto lo que quieren significar al relegarnos al África, ¡sea mil veces enhorabuena! ¡Alegrémonos, queridos compatriotas! ¡Regocijaos, africanos!" ["We are not able to be French! If this is what they mean when they relegate us to Africa, let's congratulate ourselves! Be happy, dear fellow countrymen! Rejoice, Africans!"] (qtd. in Torrecilla, *España exótica* 107). Alarcón's vindication, however, is far from performing a real counter-evaluation of the terms *European* as positive and *African* as negative. He indicates in his article that he completely agrees with France's evaluation of Spain's Africanness as an insult: "entre ser un remedo de los franceses, o unos moros como Dios nos haya criado, preferimos esto último . . . Seremos lo peor con tal de ser la verdad" ["between being a poor imitation of the French, or Moors in the way God wanted it, we prefer this last choice . . . we will be the worst in order to be the truth"] (qtd. in Torrecilla, *España exótica* 107).[7] Alarcón, an example of the exalted patriotism that initially drove many to the 1859–60 Moroccan War, saw this conflict as an opportunity to show Europe that even though Spain seemed in decline, it still counted as an imperial power capable of redeeming an "inferior race." The "Iberian race," he proclaimed in *Diario de un testigo de la Guerra de África*, "subsiste sin haber degenerado, activa y potente, como cuando se extendió por ignorados mundos" ["subsists without having degenerated, active and potent, as when it extended itself through unknown worlds"] (Alarcón 13). This desire to demonstrate to Europe Spain's force is very much related to the effort at defusing a perceived sense of inferiority. As ironically explained by Benito Pérez Galdós at the turn of the twentieth century in *Aita Tettauen*, "[f]ueron los españoles a la Guerra, porque necesitaban gallear un poquito ante Europa, y dar al sentimiento público, en el interior, un alimento sano y reconstituyente" ["The Spaniards went to war because they needed to boast a little in front of Europe, and give public opinion, in the interior, a healthy and nourishing feed"] (Galdós 132).

Both the 1859–60 War and the subsequent Spanish interventions in Morocco can be explained along this effort to demonstrate full European status. By 1908, ten years after the Disaster, when the Spanish army again entered North Morocco and began an occupation that lasted until 1956, it, in fact, did so as a second-class actor in an international obligation. Germany, a new colonial power, had begun to be interested in North Africa, and, as a result, France and Great Britain had had to settle their differences and reach agreement to prevent Germany's expansion. During the negotiations, in which Spain was not invited to participate, Great Britain and France decided to give Spain an area of influence in the north of Morocco. This allowed Great Britain and France to prevent each other from dominating the whole area, since France controlled Algeria, Tunis, and Morocco, and Great Britain wanted to make sure that its ships had continued freedom of movement through the Strait of Gibraltar, the route to India and the Far East. France accepted this "sharing" of Morocco with Spain because it knew its influence would not suffer from the competition, given Spain's weakness (Balfour, *Abrazo* 23–27). Thus, the beginning of the Spanish twentieth-century colonial enterprise, seen by many as a glorious epic that would compensate for the 1898 Disaster, actually underlined Spain's subservient role to the other European powers.[8]

The humiliating defeat of the Disaster and the crisis of modernization of the beginning of the twentieth century encouraged deeply traditional views that intensified a defensive attitude toward "Spanish essential values" and saw any attempt at reform as foreign interference. Miguel de Unamuno, in his 1906 "Sobre la europeización," proudly claims "Africanness" as one of the main values that constitute Spain as outside of Europe. He takes Saint Augustine's African identity as a model of non-European thought, and contrasts "modern European" to "old African," choosing the latter, old African wisdom, in opposition to modern European science, for Spain (925–26). He proclaims Spain's links with the Moors and its Berber identity: "¿Y por qué, si somos berberiscos, no hemos de sentirnos y proclamarnos tales . . . ?" ["And why, if we are Berber, should we not feel and proclaim ourselves so . . . ?"] (Unamuno 936). Instead of lamenting Spain's lagging behind modern European culture, he argues, Spaniards should embrace the impossibility of achieving modernity and their true, non-European, anti-scientific identity (926–27, 936). Instead of attempting to make Spain European, he concludes, Spaniards should make Europe

Spanish, or "españolizar Europa" (Unamuno 936). Ángel Ganivet also championed this idea, and saw Spain as a stoic reservoir of spiritualism and mysticism against the thirst for material riches and "artificial needs" of European civilization (Beneyto 79–81).

The deeply conservative view of Spanish "difference" and its need of isolation from outside contamination adopted by the ideologues of Francoism is related to Unamuno and Ganivet's idea that Spain needed to be proud of its non-Europeanness, and, instead of apologizing for its supposed underdevelopment, to see it as a "spiritual" strength against European materialistic values. For the Francoist champions of the notion of Catholicism as the essence of the true Spain, Spain's mission was "to bring spirituality to an increasingly materialistic world" (Balfour, "The Loss" 30). Spanish "difference," thus, was a positive one:

> In their eyes, it was the northern European nations that had deviated from the true historical path by breaking with Rome and developing a secular, individualistic culture. Franco's self-identification as the "sentinel of the West" was the apotheosis of this conservative view; Catholic Spain was the guarantor of European civilization against the depredations of liberals, freemasons, and communists. (Schmidt-Nowara 152)

This essential religiosity of Spain will serve the purpose of explaining the massive use of Moroccan soldiers on the Nationalist side of the Spanish Civil War. Joaquín Costa had used the rhetoric of *hermandad* ["brotherhood"], underlining Spain's cultural and racial closeness with North Africa, to justify Spain's right to intervene in Morocco and thus have a role in the European colonialist enterprise at the end of the nineteenth century (Martin-Márquez, "Hibridez" 83 and "Here's Spain" 7–8). At the outbreak of the Civil War, this argument constituted the base of an intense propaganda campaign launched to justify the presence of Christianity's traditional enemy within the ranks of its "defenders." The solution to the riddle was found in an appeal to religiosity: Moroccans and "true" Spaniards (those that sided with the Nationalists) had in common the fact that they were "believers," in contrast to the Atheist, "'Godless'

Marxists," and Republicans, who wanted to destroy not only Christianity but religion in general (Madariaga 345–51). In Morocco itself, this propaganda was coupled with measures that supported Muslim religious practices in an attempt to attract new soldiers to the Francoist cause. Thus, for example, in 1937, Franco himself took the initiative of organizing a pilgrimage to Mecca, facilitating the use of an old converted German ship for the pilgrims (347–48). Upon their return, Franco received the Muslim delegation in the Alcazar of Seville, where, in a convenient interpretation of history, he explained to them that "España y el islam han sido siempre los pueblos que mejor se comprendieron" ["Spain and Islam have always been the peoples that best understood each other"] (qtd. in Madariaga 352).[9]

The defense of tradition against modernization and the threat of secularism resulted in the deeply conservative construction of Spanish history as a series of self-defensive acts against outsiders who wanted to impose "foreign" values. Manuel García Morente is a key exponent of this view. In *Idea de la Hispanidad*, based on two lectures he gave in Buenos Aires in 1938, he explains Spain's history as consisting of four moments when Spain was "at the center of world events" (15). The first was the Roman invasion of the Peninsula, fiercely resisted by the Hispanics for two centuries, which resulted in Rome's Hispanization as much as in Spain's Romanization: Spain gave Rome, and, therefore, the world, "men, ideas, intellectual thought, vital and spiritual qualities" that greatly influenced Roman culture and politics (García Morente 16). The second moment was the Arab invasion, miraculously opposed and resisted by a group of "Spaniards" who saved Christianity, and, thus, did a great favor to other European nations by saving "the essence of European culture" (16–17). García Morente emphasizes the foreign nature of the Arabs, explaining the formation of the Spanish national character in absolute opposition to them:

> siempre en dos frentes . . . en negación de lo ajeno y en simultánea afirmación de lo propio, como repulsa de las formas mentales y espirituales oriundas del mundo árabe y como tenaz mantenimiento de las primordiales condiciones y aspiraciones de la naciente nacionalidad. Por eso el espíritu religioso, cristiano, católico, llega a constituir un elemento esencial de la nacionalidad española. Durante ocho siglos no

hay diferencia entre el no ser árabe y el ser cristiano . . . for-
jar su ser . . . contra una convicción religiosa ajena, contraria,
exótica e imposible.

[always on two fronts . . . negating the foreign and simultaneously affirming the self, as repudiation to the mental
and spiritual thought of the Arab world and as tenacious
maintenance of the primordial conditions and aspirations of
the nascent nationality. This is the reason why the religious,
Christian, Catholic spirit comes to constitute an essential element of Spanish nationality. For eight centuries there is no
difference between not being Arab and being Christian . . .
constructing the self . . . against a foreign, contrary, exotic,
impossible religious conviction.] (García Morente 17–18)[10]

The third moment of García Morente's history is the sixteenth
and seventeenth centuries, when Spain "takes in her hands the
direction of world events" expanding outward and teaching
the world three basic ideas "on which modern political life is
founded": the idea of a national state, the model of a national
army, and the theoretical principles and practical implementation of modern imperialism (18–19). According to García
Morente, the fourth historical moment by which destiny placed
Spain at the center of world history was the Spanish Civil War,
which was taking place in Spain while he delivered his lectures
in Argentina. He characterized the democratically elected socialist government of the Spanish Second Republic (1931–36),
against which Franco rebelled, beginning the Civil War, as a
foreign invasion by the communist International, "un ejército
invisible, pero bien organizado . . . [que] resolvió ocupar España, apoderarse de España, destruir la nacionalidad española . . .
y convertir[la] . . . en una provincia de la Unión Soviética" ["an
invisible, but well-organized, army . . . [that] decided to occupy
Spain, capture her, destroy the Spanish nation . . . and convert
her into a province of the Soviet Union"] (García Morente
20–21). He consequently saw Franco's *coup d'etat* as the Spanish nation's defense against this foreign attack, and the then-
current political situation of Spain as a crucial experiment for
the future of the whole world, which would determine whether
"la teoría política y social del comunismo prevalezca sobre la
realidad vital de las nacionalidades y deshaga . . . la división de

la humanidad en naciones" ["the political and social theory of communism might prevail over the vital reality of nationalities and destroy . . . the division of humanity into nations"] (García Morente 21).

García Morente thus takes Unamuno's opposition to the conceptualization of Spain as inferior or underdeveloped in contrast to other European nations and develops it into the idea that Spanish history consisted of a series of favors done by Spain for an ungrateful Europe and world. His view of Spain's defense of Christianity in the face of the threat of Islam is a key moment in his argument, since Spain's resolution to fight against the Arabs is described as a gift that allowed the rest of Europe to dedicate their efforts to other matters: "España, constreñida durante ocho siglos a montar la guardia en el baluarte de Europa, para permitir que el resto de los países europeos vaquen en paz y tranquilidad a sus menesteres interiores" ["Spain, constrained during eight centuries to stand guard in the bastion of Europe, allowed the other European countries to tend to their own internal affairs in peace and tranquility"] (García Morente 17).

On the other side of the political spectrum, the 1898 Disaster brought urgency to the initiatives that sought an approach to a modern norm represented by Europe. The Regenerationist movement called for widespread reforms in education, health, infrastructure, the military, and the electoral process. Its proponents believed the cure for Spain's decline was to be found in a process of modernization that would put it closer to Western Europe (Balfour, "Loss" 25–26). Europe, again, appears in this conceptualization as the opposite of that which Spain wants to escape, Africa. Joaquín Costa became one of the most fervent supporters of the idea that Spain, in order to survive, urgently needed to Europeanize itself, or else, it would become Morocco:

> Todavía se admite diferencia entre nosotros y Marruecos; pero dentro de poco, si nuestro letargo se prolonga, Europa nos mirará desde tan lejos que ya no advertirá diferencia, clasificándonos a las dos como tribus medievales, estorbo en el camino de la civilización.
>
> [There is still a difference between us and Morocco; but soon, if our lethargy continues, Europe will look at us from

so far away that it will not perceive any difference, classify-
ing both of us as medieval tribes, an obstacle in the path of
civilization.] (Costa; qtd. in Beneyto 61–62)

For Costa, thus, Europeanization and reform meant "de-
Africanization." Here we see how the rhetoric of "brotherhood"
with Morocco he also championed was a discursive strategy,
convenient at the time, to claim equal footing with Europe when
what was at stake was a piece of the colonial pie. For Costa,
what Spain really needed to become, was Europe. Thus, different valorizations of Spain's "difference" as positive or negative
still take for granted Europe's superiority, and often betray the
desire to belong to that seemingly superior norm.

The physical persecutions, expulsions, and coerced conversions to Catholicism of Jews and Muslims, as well as the censorship, banning, and burning of cultural artifacts and practices
associated with both cultures that took place in the aftermath
of the Reconquest have been and are even today accompanied
by the refusal to recognize Muslims and Jews as an intrinsic
part of Spanish identity. As we have seen, this conceptualization of Spanish identity is not only the territory of the political
right, and belongs not only to the past. Julián Marías, one of the
ideologues of Spain's transition to democracy in the late 1970s,
argues in *La España inteligible* (1985) that one of Spain's
most prominent national characteristics is that it *decided* to
be European and Western. After eight centuries of Arab influence, by which it could have been completely Islamized, Spain
"chooses" Western European civilization. Spain exists, thus, as
a "fervent will" to be Christian, European, and Western, embracing its Roman and Visigothic past against its Muslim and
Jewish one (Beneyto 259–61).[11]

In his 1997 study about the way Islam is presented in Spanish
school textbooks, Josep María Navarro explains that textbooks
still today deny any profound and meaningful relationship
between the European and African or Middle Eastern cultural
traditions (20). In consequence, he argues, "no debe extrañar
a nadie . . . que en España tratemos de abominar de nuestras
raíces islámicas . . . por cuestiones de prestigio internacional.
¿Cómo vamos a entrar en el club de los 'países VIP' con ese
pasado tan poco europeo?" ["It should not be any surprise . . .
that in Spain we try to abominate our Islamic roots . . . for inter-

national prestige purposes. How are we going to get in the 'VIP countries' club with such an un-European past?"] (Navarro 20). Schools, he affirms, reproduce the discourse of Spanish Europeanness "a partir de una propuesta adulterada de la construcción de España y de la identidad ibérica, una propuesta excluyente con respecto a lo islámico e incluso lo judío" ["from an adulterated model of the construction of Spain and the Iberian identity, a model that excludes Islam and Judaism"] (20–21). In the textbooks' accounts of Muslim Spain, he has observed a constant conceptualization of Muslims as invading foreigners who *were not* European (127; emphasis in the original), and who produced a rupture of Spain from European history (124). Whether understood as a racial and cultural consequence of its Muslim past, or as a general lack of modernization and development, Spain would embark on the process of overcoming its "difference" from Europe as one of the main political objectives of the late twentieth century. This process, however, will not be exempt of the old marks of "inferiority," as we will see in the following pages.

In the last twenty years, one of the consequences of the process of Europeanization has been Spain's reversal from being an exporter of cheap labor to becoming a recipient of economic migrants. The major migration destination for Spaniards from 1887 until the 1960s was Latin America, which received from 60% to 75% of Spanish emigrants in search of work. North Africa became an important migration destination in the 1940s, when Oran and its surrounding area in Algeria and the north of Morocco received from 35% to 41% of the total working force that left Spain. When the European industrial economies began recruiting migrants in the 1960s, 80% of Spanish migrants went to Europe. By the 1970s, it was 91%, more than a million people.[12] Felipe González, who was prime minister for the Socialist Party after the reinstatement of democracy, was a witness to the racism Spanish economic migrants suffered in the booming industrial economies of Germany, Belgium, and Switzerland, and wrote later about how many bars in Brussels displayed signs saying "No entry for Spaniards, Africans and North Africans" (qtd. in Carr 93). It was then, in the late 1970s, that Spain started to receive its first economic migrants, who began to settle in Catalonia when rejected by the newly restrictive EC measures

(López García, *Inmigración* 43–47). Therefore, Spain's current status on the receiving end of migration has a psychological significance—besides a historical and political one—that means more than the issue does to other European countries. Having to deal with the so-called immigration problem becomes an index of Spain's belonging to First-World Europe. As Isabel Santaolalla comments, "In spite of all the problems and difficulties associated with immigration, it is perhaps reassuring for many to see Spain represented no longer as a country of emigrants but as somebody else's Utopia" (Santaolalla, "Ethnic" 62).

Through the Schengen Agreement of 1985, several EC states sought to form a frontier-free area of circulation within Europe. Abolition of internal frontiers through the Schengen Agreement meant that external borders had to be strengthened, and that southern nations had a larger responsibility in guarding their external frontiers, now a "gateway" to Europe. The Agreement, originally signed by France, Germany, and the Benelux nations (Belgium, the Netherlands, and Luxembourg), and, later by Italy, Spain, Portugal and Greece, showed the differences in status of EU members and their unequal inclusion in the Schengen space. Free movement wasn't established until 1988 for Greeks and 1992 for the Spanish and Portuguese (Sassen 125). Several people have analyzed critically the Spanish response to the European demand for strengthening its frontiers and immigration policies. As explained by Kelly, "Spanish politicians rapidly and very avidly took on their new role as custodians of Europe's considerable privileges by endorsing the control as well as the expulsion of illegal migrants" (Kelly 33). In 1985, under the Socialist government of Felipe González, Spain adopted the *Ley de Extranjería* [Foreigners' Law], which many consider to be one of the most restrictive in Europe.[13] The eagerness with which the Spanish government took over the role of guardian of Europe's southern border, in a way similar to the excessive enthusiasm of Spaniards about their "European" identity, betrays an anxiety about Spain's belonging to Europe that is described by Graham and Sánchez as follows:

> Spain, in spite of its own long and painful history of under-development, economic emigration, and otherness, far from recognizing a commonality and attempting to integrate the experience of the marginalized into its own self-proclaimedly

pluralistic culture, has instead assumed the stance of "First
World" Europe. It is almost as if constructing and adopting
the same "others" or outgroups as the rest was considered the
hallmark of Spain's membership of the "club." (415)

This new role of Spain within Europe has already produced a
significant literature of opposition, much of it based on the idea
that the new role was assumed from an old position of subordination. Juan Goytisolo has warned, in several articles, about the
implications of Spaniards' sudden transformation into *nuevos
ricos, nuevos europeos* ["new rich, new Europeans"], who have
eagerly joined Europe as a "club de países ricos con derecho
reservado de admisión" ["club of rich countries with reserved
admission rights"] (Goytisolo, *España* 19, 23).[14] Javier de
Lucas, in his book *Puertas que se cierran: Europa como fortaleza* [*Doors that Close: Europe as Fortress*] argues that "España—la Europa del Sur—tiene un papel claro de miembro de
segunda fila, de guardián de la seguridad, de albergue del ocio
y el descanso de los europeos (más) ricos" ["Spain—Southern
Europe—has a clear role of second class member, of security
guardian, of shelter for the leisure and relaxation of the rich(-er)
Europeans"] (Lucas 11). Rafael Torres, in his "Advertencia" to
a collection of semi-fictional testimonies by immigrants entitled
Yo, Mohamed [*I, Mohamed*], says: "nos hemos convertido . . .
en los cancerberos de Europa, en los porteros míseros, pero
vestidos con levita, chistera y ringorrangos, de Alemania y
Francia, que nos han encontrado colocación al fin lejos de sus
fronteras" ["we have been transformed . . . into the guardians of
Europe, into doorkeepers, wretched but dressed in top hat, tails
and frills, of Germany and France, who have finally found us a
job far away from their frontiers"] (Torres 15). In the also semi-
fictional testimony *Dormir al raso*, Spain is described in very
similar terms: "Europa le ha dado a España la llave de la puerta
de entrada, la ha convertido en el portero que corta las entradas
del cine en tecnicolor que es para los marroquíes la Comunidad
Europea" ["Europe has given Spain the key to the front door,
it has converted it into the doorkeeper who tears the tickets for
the Technicolor cinema that the European Community is for
Moroccans"] (Moreno Torregrosa and El Gheryb 39).

  After centuries of not considering Spain to be truly European,
Europe has welcomed Spain back. Because of the Schengen

Agreement, entrance into Spain now equals, for Third-World economic migrants, entrance into Europe. However, Spain's "difference" hasn't disappeared. We still see it in the tourist industry,[15] and we also see it in fictional representations of recently arrived immigrants. In texts produced in the last ten years, immigrants speak of Spain's difference. They are partly expressing a general disappointment at the Europe of their dreams, which, once they get there, they realize doesn't exist, but they are also expressing a disappointment with Spain in particular as different from that imagined Europe, dismantling the self-congratulatory discourse of Spain in the 1990s under the Partido Popular government. The two examples that follow are comments supposedly made by Moroccan immigrants, although their voices reach us through the heavy mediation of Spaniards. In *Dormir al raso*, several Moroccan immigrants complain about how "España aún no es tan paraíso como otros países europeos" ["Spain isn't yet as paradisiacal as other European countries"] (Moreno Torregrosa and El Gheryb 74). It is important to note the emphasis on "yet." This complaint endorses the belief in Spain's progress toward Europe, in its Europeanization process, and, therefore, in its "not-so-European" past. Comparing it to France or Germany, they find that "nuestros hermanos vuelven a casa con coches cargados de regalos, de muebles y ropa, y nosotros regresamos en el ferry, a pie, con nuestra maleta en una mano y en la otra una bolsa de *El Corte Inglés*" ["Our brothers come home with cars filled with presents, furniture and clothes, and we return in the ferry, on foot, with our suitcase in one hand and in the other one, a shopping bag from *El Corte Inglés*"] (Moreno Torregrosa and El Gheryb 74). When Youssef, one of the Moroccan workers in the greenhouses of Almería, arrives for the first time at the house of his friend, where he has been invited to live, he is shocked to find a house without roof or water. He wonders "¿Y esto es Europa?" ["And this is Europe?"] (22). This same idea is again voiced in the language of geo-political frontiers: "[e]l subdesarrollo de algunas provincias del sur de España, puede hacernos dudar en algún momento, de que las fronteras de la Europa comunitaria se encuentren en el Estrecho, y que puedan estar en realidad, más arriba de lo que figuran en los mapas" ["the underdevelopment of some provinces of Southern Spain can make us doubt at some point, the fact that the frontiers of the European Community are located in the Strait [of Gibraltar], and it can make us think that in reality they could be further up than the maps indicate"] (Moreno Torregrosa and El Gheryb 80).

The significance of this assertion goes further than stating the fact of the scarce economic development of some regions of Southern Spain. Its description of contemporary underdevelopment inevitably echoes the discourse of Europe's exclusion of Spain, the discourse of "Africa begins at the Pyrenees." *Dormir al raso* also explicitly contrasts present Spanish prosperity with its migrant history and impoverished past, an impoverishment that functioned as a transnational equalizer: "España era un país que no ofrecía trabajo. Podías encontrarte compitiendo con los emigrantes españoles en la Renault o en la Citroen, en la construcción o en los invernaderos del Midi" ["Spain was a country that didn't offer jobs. You could find yourself competing with the Spanish emigrants in the Renault or the Citroen, in construction or in the greenhouses of the Midi"] (73). This text also incorporates testimonies of the racism experienced by Spaniards in their migrant journey through Europe, comparing it to that currently experienced by Moroccans in Spain:

> Mis padres emigraron, y ellos me contaron que los españoles teníamos mala fama en Suiza, en Alemania, o en Francia. Que si éramos guarros y no nos lavábamos, que si unos incivilizados salvajes que torturábamos a los animales (lo digo por las corridas de toros), que si teníamos un regimen dictatorial (como si lo hubiésemos elegido nosotros), etcétera. Y a pesar del desprecio y de las opiniones de muchos "europeos," allí tenías al emigrante murciano o de otras provincias . . . buscando el trabajo que aquí le faltaba. ¡La gente ha olvidado cómo nos trataron!

> [My parents emigrated, and they told me that Spaniards had a bad reputation in Switzerland, Germany or France. That we were dirty and did not wash ourselves, that we were uncivilized savages who tortured animals (because of bullfighting), that we had a dictatorial regime (as if we had chosen it), etc. And notwithstanding the contempt and opinions of many "Europeans," there you had the emigrant from Murcia or other provinces . . . looking for the work that he did not have here. People have forgotten how they treated us!] (Moreno Torregrosa and El Gheryb 107)

The film *Poniente* (Chus Gutiérrez, 2002) also explicitly connects the prior emigrant status of Spanish workers and their current position as recipients of immigration, portraying the close friendship between Curro, a Spaniard born in Switzerland after his parents' emigration there, and Adbendi, a Moroccan immigrant who has lived in Almería for several years. The hardships experienced by Spanish emigrants are vividly shown in a scene where Curro watches real-life footage of Spaniards in Switzerland in the sixties, in which the audience can see the emigrants' bodies and faces marked by hunger and impoverishment.[16] However, as Juan Goytisolo has argued, the experience of emigration does not seem to have created a culture of solidarity. In his article "El Ejido, quién te ha visto y quién te ve" ["El Ejido, who has seen you and who sees you now"], published in *El País* in 1998, two years before the xenophobic attacks on Moroccan immigrants, Goytisolo denounced the inhumane work conditions and social discrimination suffered by immigrants there. He argues in this article that the memory of past poverty and forced emigration, instead of creating some kind of compassion or sympathy toward the migrants who are now living in similar situations, has had the opposite effect:

> los moros y negros esclavizados en los invernaderos—necesarios dentro de éstos, pero indeseables fuera—avivan los sentimientos egoístas de superioridad y permiten a los ex emigrantes e hijos de emigrantes saborear la escenificación actual del drama de sus propias vidas, representado hoy por actores distintos, como una venganza ejemplar.

> [the Moors and Blacks enslaved in the greenhouses—needed inside them, but unwanted outside—stir up selfish feelings of superiority and allow former emigrants and their children to enjoy the current enactment of their own lives' drama, now represented by different actors, as in an exemplary revenge.] (Goytisolo, *España* 27–28)

Goytisolo, who was declared *persona non grata* by the municipality of El Ejido after the publication of this article, concludes by saying that there is no excuse for such lack of memory.

A similar lack of memory can be seen in the conflicts between Moroccan immigrants and their Spanish neighbors in various cities of the province of Barcelona, such as Terrassa or Santa Coloma de Gramenet, mostly inhabited by Spanish immigrants and their children, who settled there when looking for better economic opportunities in the 1950s and 1960s. The documentary *Mezquita NO!* [*Mosque NOT!*] by Alberto Aranda and Guillermo Cruz illustrates one of these conflicts in Santa Coloma de Gramenet, a city that grew with the arrival of Andalusian immigrants in the 1960s. In October and November 2004, the opening of a Muslim oratory in the basement of a building in the neighborhood of El Singuerlín sparked protests by neighbors, who did not want a mosque in one of their buildings. Their pretext was that the space did not satisfy the necessary physical conditions to be a place of worship, something that could have been easily fixed, if that was indeed the problem. Instead, they staged such loud protests at the times when people were praying in the oratory that the authorities decided to listen to them and "relocate" the mosque to a semi-industrial lot outside the city. As Taoufik Cheddadi, the spokesman of the El Singuerlín Muslim community, commented, this decision sent the message that it was better to have the Muslims isolated and as far away as possible. His questions, toward the end of the documentary, are poignant: "¿dónde está la integración? ¿qué hay de malo en tener una mezquita en el mismo barrio?" ["Where is the integration? What is wrong with having a mosque in the neighborhood itself?"]. Similar incidents have taken place in other locations in Barcelona, such as the protests in April and May 2002 against the opening of a mosque in a neighborhood of Premià de Mar. These neighborhood-based protests have also taken place in other provinces, such as Almería, where, in 2001, the construction of a Moroccan consulate was stalled three times, in three different neighborhoods, because of protests against it.[17]

The short film *Todos os llamáis Mohamed* (Maximiliano Lemcke, 1997) contains ironic comments about the contradictions of contemporary Spain that are revealed by the presence of current immigrants. In this film (which will be further discussed in chapter 5), there is a clear effort to expose the point of view of the Moroccan immigrant in Spain. In its opening scene, a young Moroccan man arrives in Madrid to meet his friend, who has been living there for a while and has arranged his arrival. The significance of this scene derives from its contrast with the pervasive propaganda, exemplified in the famous comment by former prime minister José María Aznar, "España va bien" ["Spain is going well"]: the ever-present, constant reassurance Spain was giving itself at that time about its modernity, its First-World status, its "Europeanness." This scene presents the perspective of the newly arrived Moroccan immigrant as an instance of confrontation between that propaganda and one of the realities the propaganda completely ignores—that of the immigrants' space. In the scene, two Moroccan men arrive at the outskirts of Madrid. The camera shows us the interior of the taxi, where the two chat in Arabic. A couple of minutes later, while getting out of the car, the one already living in Spain tells the newly arrived one, "Welcome to Spain." The camera then shifts to show us the scene's referent of "Spain," which is a heartbreaking view of overcrowded shantytowns. The phrase "Welcome to Spain," so close semantically to a tourist slogan, acquires all its irony when superimposed onto the immigrants' space, that of the shantytown on the outskirts of Madrid. The same irony is sought in *Dormir al raso*, where the first section of the fifth chapter, dealing with the dreadful work conditions of the immigrant workers in the Andalusian greenhouses, is entitled, "Bienvenidos a la Costa del Sol" ["Welcome to the Costa del Sol"], a tourist slogan for the most popular beaches of Spain.

Difference Within: Immigration and the Regions

Different regions in Spain have had different degrees of real and imaginary attachment to the "impure," non-Christian past of Spain and to European modernity, as well as different migration histories. As Elena Delgado explains, while democratic Spain still tries to reassure itself of its undoubtedly European status, of how it is not "different" from Europe anymore, among some of the regions there is a competition over who is more "European," and, is therefore, superior, to the rest (Delgado, "La nación" 211–12). The essentialist use of "difference," therefore, has shifted from characterizing Spain as a whole to referring to the "peripheral" nationalities as essentially "different" from one another (Delgado, "Settled" 119). In the political context of the European Union, these demonstrations of "difference" and

"Europeanness" aim at the concept of a Europe of the Regions. As Keating explains,

> Europe of the Regions is an ambivalent concept, covering a variety of positions, from support for stronger regional policy measures within the EU, through demands for better representation of regions in Brussels, to recognition of the regions as a third level of government. (Keating, "The Minority Nations" 33)

This is especially the case in Catalonia, which was strongly pro-Europe in the transition to democracy for the same reasons that Spain was, but, in addition, because Europe could provide a new space in which to advance nationality claims (Keating, "The Minority Nations" 30–31). It is not surprising, then, that in a 1994 survey, Catalans scored the highest in terms of identification with Europe, and they were the ones with the most favorable view of Europeans (Keating, "The Minority Nations" 36). Catalonia's Europeanist stance often means a reinforcement of the politics of difference with Spain, seen from this perspective as "different" in the old Francoist sense of atavistically backward, anti-democratic, and anti-modern. Catalan regionalism would then offer itself as a force for the "Europeanist modernization" of Spain (Murphy, Díaz-Varela, and Coluccello 75).

In this configuration, the arrival of the new non-European immigrants to Catalonia produces in Catalonia, as in the rest of Spain, a need to re-evaluate its own identity as separate from that of the newly arrived, but this arrival is furthermore complicated by Catalonia's previous history of reception of immigrants from other regions of Spain. As we will see, the performance of the separation is produced, then, through the cultural identification of new immigrants with those previous Spanish ones, especially in terms of the battles over language use in Catalonia. In this way, current immigration is seen as the contemporary staging of an old struggle by which Catalonia has had to defend its identity from the influence of Spain, an influence that has taken multiple historical forms (African, Muslim, Castilian, anti-modern, anti-democratic) but has always been a quintessentially non-European one.[18]

Thus, the newer set of "otherness" presented by the new immigrants of the 1990s has complicated the various prior internal "othernesses" of Spain as a nation. As David Corkill observes, much of the difficulty arises from the fact that the initial inflow of non-European immigrants, especially Muslim immigrants from North Africa, happened during the 1980s, at the same time that national and regional identities were undergoing major re-configurations during the democratic transition (Corkill 55). In a relatively short period of time, a four-fold process took place: democratization, the political recognition of the Autonomous Regions, European integration, and the arrival of important numbers of non-European immigrants. In part because of this chronological correspondence, it is important to think in parallel of the process of recognition of regional difference by the Spanish state and that of the reception and integration of foreign immigrants, both at the national and regional levels. How do these two processes intersect? Is "foreign otherness" negotiated differently at the national and regional levels? In other words, how do the regional, the national, and the foreign interact in contemporary Spain?

Although Spanish national identity appears today as irreversibly variegated, heterogeneous, and decentered (Jordan 70; Kinder 440), the idea of Spain as an ethnically and culturally homogeneous nation is far from having disappeared. In fact, it still permeates the staging of a defensive reaction toward the foreign: its perceived threat is answered with a return to old discourses of "Spanishness" and centralist nationalism. In the case of Catalonia and the Basque Country, it produces defensive nationalist "anti-Spanish" as well as "anti-foreign" reactions. Each of these cases seems to confirm Étienne Balibar's notion that "the articulation of nationalism and racism cannot be disentangled" (50), whether we are talking about central or peripheral nationalisms. In the case of Spain, we can argue that the articulation of new racism—based on the belief in a homogeneous, essential national identity that becomes threatened by outsiders—is at work in the cases of Basque, Galician, and Catalan national identities as well as in the case of Spanish, or Castilian, national identity.

One of the most interesting elements in this interaction of the regional, the national, and the foreign is the issue of language, popularly considered to be one of the main "obstacles" to the integration of certain immigrant communities in Spain. As noted by Benedict Anderson, language constitutes one of the pillars of nationalism. Anderson explains how language names the nation as that to which one is "naturally" tied, at the same time that languages "appear rooted beyond almost anything else in contemporary societies . . . there is a special kind of contemporaneous community which language alone suggests" (Anderson 145), so that, for example, when people sing *their* national anthem, in *their* language, the effect produced is that of absolute "unisonance . . . the echoed physical realization of the imagined community" (Anderson 145). This link between language and nation is especially strong in Europe, where language became a key element of political legitimacy for the emergent nation-states, most of which came to share their name with their language (Gubbins and Holt 1). We can trace the link between national identity formation and language to the origins of the different nationalisms of the Spanish state. In the case of Castilian national identity, in his 1492 *Prólogo a la gramática de la lengua castellana*, the prologue to the first published grammar of the Castilian language, Antonio de Nebrija explicitly stated the central role of Castilian in the Catholic Monarchs' mission of Empire building. Catalanism was also born together with the consciousness of the fundamental role of language in the creation of national identity. It was this awareness that inspired Valentí Almirall's *particularisme*, the first modern iteration of Catalanist sociopolitical theory, and his founding, in 1879, of *El Diari Català*, the first daily newspaper ever written in Catalan (Harrington 116). Sabino Arana, the father of Basque nationalism, also saw language as the central force in the creation of national solidarity (Harrington 118).

Language is an advantageous point of entrance to immigration texts and debates not only because of its centrality to any nationalism but also because its politics resonate differently at the regional and national levels, constituting one of the issues that was highly conflictive in Spain before there was any preoccupation with foreign immigration. Long before any immigration debates, the relationship and hierarchy among the different languages of Spain were highly contentious issues. In the already-mentioned 1492 prologue to the first Castilian grammar, Nebrija explains how Castilian would help further not only the Spanish Empire's overseas objectives but also

Castile's internal goals of political and cultural hegemony by subjugating the other languages of the peninsula (Harrington 112). In the twentieth century, the Francoist dictatorship revived this logic of subjugation of all manifestations of cultural difference, including the use of languages other than Castilian. These were prohibited in publications, government offices, schools, posters, street signs, shop signs, and advertising. All public uses were banned, and there were efforts to reduce their status as languages, inculcating the idea that they were in fact only "dialects" (Woolard 28). Censorship in this regard partially relaxed by the 1960s, responding to the large number of petitions to "normalize" these languages, especially Catalan. By the time of the 1978 democratic Constitution, Spain's minority languages were declared official, something unthinkable in the previous forty years. A clause of the Constitution's Article 3 stated that "[t]he richness of Spain's different linguistic varieties is a cultural heritage which shall be the object of special respect and protection" (Mar Molinero 337–38). This official status of Catalan, Euskera, and Galician was geographically restricted, though, to their autonomous communities, with the result that, in reality, these languages would always be subordinated to Castilian (Mar Molinero 337). Since the approval of the Constitution in 1978, and since the creation and ratification, between December 1979 and April 1981, of statutes of autonomy for Catalonia, the Basque Country, and Galicia, there has been considerable transfer of power to the regions in terms of education and health care (Harrington 109). Among cultural initiatives, the autonomic governments have made an extraordinary effort to support and promote the use of Catalan, Euskera, and Galician, which had suffered the devastating consequences of being banned from public use.

The regional politics of language appeared in the first Spanish film about African immigration, Montxo Armendáriz's 1990 *Las cartas de Alou* [*Letters from Alou*]. *Cartas* is a film about the process of migration, about movement, travel, and journeys, both transnational and national, in which the process of transportation and its means are highlighted: boats, trucks, buses, trains, cars, planes. It tells the story of a Sub-Saharan immigrant who travels to Spain seeking to better his life. As in other accounts of migration, it begins with the transnational crossing of the Strait of Gibraltar, from Morocco to Spain, and ends with that journey once again, with Alou and his Moroccan friend crossing the Strait to return to Spain after having been deported. But unlike other accounts of immigration, Alou's journey is not only a journey about immigrating to a different country but also one about a subsequent internal immigration through Spain's regions. Alou arrives in Andalusia, travels to Madrid, and then to Catalonia, offering us a view of Spanish regionalism through his experiences. Alou suffers discrimination and hardships in the three regions, but the types of incidents that occur in each of them are quite different: rejection is deployed regionally in different ways, especially when it comes to language.

Alou begins his migrant experience in Almería, where he soon finds work in the greenhouses picking vegetables and spraying the fields with fertilizer. Although he finds a friend who takes him under his protection and provides him with a place to stay and useful advice about work, Alou is constantly misunderstood and unable to interpret his surroundings. The rejection Alou feels is conveyed through language in his friend's continual repetition of the phrase "¿Pero qué dices? ¡Cállate!" ["What are you talking about? Shut up!"]. This happens every time Alou tries to express his frustration about the harsh working conditions of Andalusia, a place where doing anything but slaving in silence is unwelcome. Thus language is an insurpassable obstacle positioned between an uncomprehending, incomprehensible Alou and the space that surrounds him. As soon as he collects his first pay, he leaves and heads north.

When Alou arrives in Madrid, we are presented with the loud and clear announcement of official Castilian itself, in the form of the loudspeaker announcement that wakes Alou up in the train station: "Estación Madrid Atocha. Tren con destino a Valencia. Se encuentra estacionado en vía tercera" ["Madrid Atocha Station. Train traveling to Valencia. Stationed in the third lane"]. Castilian is presented aloud with the qualities of its official function and its supposed neutrality of tone. As Alou awakens to its sound, he realizes his bag has been stolen. Madrid functions from this moment on as the space where Spanish (Castilian) has to be learned. What could be a better place to learn it than the capital of the Spanish state?

Alou embarks on this learning process through a friend he meets while wandering the streets of downtown Madrid. They happen to be from the same country and speak the same language, so his friend takes Alou to the boarding house where he is staying and lends him the necessary money to get by. Here language becomes once again the signifier of rejection. The landlady, hearing Alou and his friend speak their language, warns them: "Aquí se habla en cristiano" ["Here we speak Christian"]. "Christian" is meant here to signify Castilian, but through this equivalency medieval Spain and its notions of language use are superimposed onto the reality of a contemporary, supposedly very different space and time, but a space and time where conceptions of language and national identity are still overdetermined by that past. The symbolic weight of this phrase is due not only to the fact that it conflates the meanings of both "Castilian" and "Christian," negating the possibility of speaking Castilian and not being Christian, and vice versa, and bringing the contemporary setting of the immigration debate back to medieval religious wars, but also to the fact that this same phrase, "*Háblame en cristiano*" ["Talk to me in Christian"], "was the widely utilized insult/response used by Francoist troops with those using or known to favor the use of one of the non-Castilian languages" (Harrington 126; see also Woolard 28). This phrase also remands us, then, to the context of the 1940s and 1950s Francoist repression of the other languages of Spain. After the landlady's comment, Alou's friend starts teaching him Castilian. Alou learns the language together with the survival strategies of selling jewelry and bargaining. Almost miraculously, after a stay in Madrid of no more than a few months, he has learned it perfectly, and he can write to his parents, "I am learning how to understand these people." And, indeed, after Madrid, he speaks Spanish better than any other non-Spaniard in the film. However, his knowledge of Spanish never seems enough for the standards of the Spanish people he encounters, who basically laugh at him and do not take him seriously.

The third region Alou experiences is Catalonia, his original destination, where his friend Mulai lives with Rosa, his Spanish wife, and their baby. With Alou's arrival in Barcelona, then, language is again introduced via the announcement in Catalan of the train's arrival in the Barcelona-Sans Station, followed by a fading one in Castilian. However, after this announcement, which reminds us of the parallel one in Castilian upon Alou's entrance to Madrid, Catalan almost disappears as a language.

We re-encounter it only when Alou enters a bar on his way to Lérida and his Castilian is rendered useless. The other clients at the bar use a familiar tone and speak Catalan to the bartender, and when Alou asks in his clear and correct Castilian for a Coca-Cola, he gets silence in return. The bartender refuses to answer him and acts as if he does not see or hear him. After asking for the Coke several times, Alou takes one himself, pays for it, and heads out of the bar, while the bartender shows his anger. This almost silent confrontation at the bar is not only a clash between native Catalonians and a foreign immigrant but also one between Catalan and Castilian. Alou learns then that his recently acquired fluency in Castilian isn't nearly enough to fit in in Catalonia. However, the film silences Catalan from this moment on, except in two scenes in Barcelona, when it is still symbolically silenced, since only the television speaks it, while the people watching the television, mostly immigrants, speak among themselves in Castilian or their native language. The first of these scenes happens at a bar where the clients are watching a soccer game. The second scene takes place at Mulai and Rosa's apartment. In this scene, the disjuncture between the television's message and the circumstances of its audience is further reinforced by the weather outside: while the television speaks Catalan and they speak Castilian, the television shows a beautiful summer day, and in Barcelona it is extremely cold and snowing. *Letters from Alou* thus seems to propose that immigrants' language is, undoubtedly, Castilian, and that Catalan is just for "Catalans," implying, then, that these identities cannot be combined.

This same idea is conveyed in a very different film from 2000, Isabel Gardela's *Tomándote*, which shows a multicultural Barcelona as the place where the seduction game of differences and similarities with immigrants of the opposite sex takes place (analyzed in more detail in chapter 4). Its protagonist, Gabi, is a liberated young Catalan writer who has won the erotic literature Sonrisa Vertical prize for her first novel. She falls in love with Jalil, a conservative Muslim Indian who works at a flower shop in Barcelona. We can see the interaction of the foreign in the national/regional dispute between Catalan and Castilian very clearly in this film where Catalan is the main language, except, once again, when it comes to talking with immigrants. Gabi meets Jalil when she asks him to take care of her motorcycle, in Catalan, and he answers in Castilian. From their second encounter on, they communicate in Castilian. The film alternates between Gabi's regular life with family and friends, which all happens in Catalan, and her dates with Jalil, when Castilian is spoken. This tension between the "normal" and the "strange," which replicates the cultural tension that develops between her liberal lifestyle and Jalil's conservative values, is made explicit in a visit with Gabi's grandmother, Aurora. After introducing Jalil to her, Gabi instructs her grandmother to speak Castilian to Jalil. The dynamic that emerges in the visit consists then of Aurora asking Jalil questions in Castilian, while still speaking Catalan to Gabi. The irony is that, as happens with many films in Catalan, the video of *Tomándote* that was released for the national market was dubbed in Castilian (a practice from Francoist times that is still in place) so that this language dynamic between Catalan and Castilian that takes place in the original format completely disappears in the dubbed version.

The language dynamic presented in these two films is very much related to current debates about how immigration affects notions of language at the national and regional levels. As happens in the two films, the issue at stake for both the central and Catalan governments is the prevalence of Castilian Spanish. In the centralist news, language is frequently mentioned as one of the major obstacles to the integration of immigrants. Learning Castilian becomes a sign of willingness to participate in Spanish society, and those migrants, such as Latin Americans, who have the language advantage, are perceived as much easier to assimilate. On the contrary, in Catalonia, the use of Castilian by large numbers of immigrants is perceived as a threat to Catalan identity. This perception is reflected in current debates over whether immigrant children should be taught in Catalan or Castilian at school. It was also one of the main issues in the controversy that followed the comments of Marta Ferrusola, the wife of Jordi Pujol, the former president of the Generalitat, in February 2001, in Girona. Ferrusola explained that when her children were little, they could not play with other kids in the park because "all of them spoke Castilian" instead of Catalan, and that now, with the arrival of North African migrants, characterized by her as "esta gente que no sabe lo que es Cataluña" ["these people who do not know what Catalonia is"], things had worsened. According to Ferrusola, they do not learn Catalan but Castilian, and instead of learning local manners, they want to impose their own. The scandal was made worse by the later justification of her comments by the two highest authorities in Catalonia, Artur Mas and Jordi Pujol. In addition, around the same time, Heribert Barrera, the eminent nationalist politician of *Esquerra Republicana* who presided for many years over the Catalan Parliament, declared that Catalonia was under threat of disappearance because of immigrants, especially if they were not forced to learn Catalan.

As these declarations show, the issue at stake for Catalonia is not only about the foreign but about the regional and the national, about Castilian and Catalan, as it is portrayed in immigration films, where no immigrant is shown speaking Catalan because, instead, they are speaking Castilian. Many critics have pointed out the relationship between this new preoccupation with foreign immigrants and a prior preoccupation with the arrival in Catalonia of Spanish-speaking migrants from other parts of Spain, an arrival that was also perceived, especially by nationalist politicians and commentators, as a threat to the Catalan language and identity. This new migration, of real "foreign" migrants, thus encounters a previously constructed imaginary about the invasion and "Spanishization" of Catalonia through domestic migration. These migrants were attracted to the jobs that opened up as a result of the development of Catalonian industry in the late nineteenth century. After two initial migration movements in 1888 and 1929, coinciding with Barcelona's Universal Exhibitions, a more numerous one occurred in the 1950s and 1960s. It is estimated that 1.4 million people settled in Catalonia between 1950 and 1975 (Woolard 30). Most politicians and intellectuals at the beginning of the twentieth century saw this migration as a threat to public order, health, and national integrity, and demographers voiced concerns that the Catalan nation might eventually be "engulfed by immigrants" and lose its national character (Pujolar i Cos 141–42). As explained by Jacqueline Hall, the way immigration is seen in Catalonia has been highly influenced by the work of Josep Vandellós, who, in the 1930s, argued that immigrants were a demographic threat, because of the lower birth rates of the Catalan people, and a cultural one, because of their radically different "mentality" (Jacqueline Hall 99–100). In this way, Pujol argued in 1958 that, through immigration, Castile was trying to destroy Catalonia, introducing values and a totally different mentality (Jacqueline Hall 102), and, as late as the 1980s, Miquel Strubell spoke of the danger of Catalan speakers becoming a minority because of their low birth rates (Pujolar i Cos 148). Politicians, demographers, and sociolinguists worried about the low birth rate of Catalans as opposed to that of immigrants, and, especially, about their role in the reproduction of the Spanish language at the expense of Catalan. They carried out studies that produced alarmist results about Catalans becoming a minority in their own nation and Spanish replacing Catalan as the everyday language of Catalonia (see Pujolar i Cos).[19]

This preoccupation with language is tied to cultural and political factors. One has to do with the currency, in the 1960s, of a series of nationalist romantic theories about land and language as the essence of a nation. These theories justified the position that the survival of the Catalan nation was dependent upon the survival of the Catalan language, and that the "Catalan personality" was only able to manifest itself in Catalan (Jacqueline Hall 105). This meant that the "defense" of the Catalan language was non-negotiable (Jacqueline Hall 107). Another crucial factor at play was, of course, the Francoist political and cultural oppression of Catalonia, and its banning of Catalan from public use. It was because of this repression that Catalan needed to be "defended," and, as explained by Manuel Cruells, this defense justified making every effort, even those seen as aggressive ones, in order to impose it [on Spanish-speaking migrants], since the Francoist imposition of Spanish on Catalan speakers was also seen as an aggression (Jacqueline Hall 104). Immigration in the 1960s is thus, at least initially, understood by Catalan nationalists as another form of persecution by the Francoist State, by which the essence of their identity—the Catalan language and "mentality"—was being attacked.[20] Although much of this thinking about the intrinsic differences between Catalans and Spanish immigrants—especially its more overtly racist overtones—has now been discredited, and Catalonia prides itself on being in the avant-garde of tolerance and respect for others, there persists an unofficial understanding about language, in which the use of Catalan is the main vehicle through which a person is thought of as a "real" Catalan. As explained by Joan Pujolar i Cos,

> In actual everyday life . . . [t]he key criterion for categorizing somebody [as "Catalan" or "immigrant"] is whether or not that person uses predominantly the Catalan language with friends and relatives. "Castilians" or "immigrants" (that is, speakers of Spanish) are expected to "integrate" into Catalan society, to become fully Catalan. And this is to be achieved by learning and adopting the language in their everyday lives. (Pujolar i Cos 144)

Thus, sociolinguistic studies that attempt to evaluate the linguistic situation of Catalonia, including the consequences of the Francoist repression of Catalan and the linguistic integration of native Spanish speakers, have as their object of study, as put by Pujolar i Cos, "the political 'hot potato' by excellence" (145). Language specialists such as Francesc Vallverdú, Kathryn Woolard, Miquel Strubell, and Carles de Roselló i Peralta have argued that the extensive use of Castilian by Spanish migrants during the period of repression of Catalan was a major source of pressure on that language, which had the result that, by 1986, 36 percent of the population of Catalonia could not speak it (Newman).[21] Nevertheless, Catalan did not disappear. Catalonia is the region where the most successful language promotion programs have occurred, with most schools offering some or much of their curriculum in Catalan, and newspapers, television, radio stations, theater, cinema, and literature in Catalan. This success has occurred partly because Catalan "has always been the language of the whole Catalan population including, significantly, the upper and middle classes . . . [so that it serves] as a symbol of social mobility and acceptance" (Mar Molinero 339). The influx of Spanish speakers did not, then, lead to an abandonment of the language by Catalan speakers, and Catalan is today considered to be a "success story" in efforts to reverse language shift (Newman).

So, what is the linguistic situation of today's foreign immigrants, and their children, in Catalonia? Except for Latin Americans in relation to Castilian, the new immigrants of the 1990s do not necessarily know either language, as is the case of Alou in Armendáriz's film. It is partly because of this that immigrants seem to focus attention on the preeminence of one language over the other. As Michael Newman indicates, initial anecdotal evidence suggests that in the metropolitan area of Barcelona, where there are large numbers of Spanish speakers, the tendency is to adopt Spanish. Elsewhere in Catalonia, immigrants appear to orient toward Catalan. The young ones, however, learn Catalan in school, as Catalan-dominant bilingual education is now the norm in Catalonia. This means that even though Spanish might seem the dominant language among immigrants in Barcelona, Catalan is also known and used when necessary, especially by young ones (Newman). Which language these second generations choose, and in which circumstances, has become the focus of new sociolinguistic studies today.

This fear of invasion and the need to protect a presumably uncontaminated identity from immigrants can also be seen in the Basque country. As in Catalonia, the Basque country's late nineteenth-century industrialization brought large-scale immigration from other parts of Spain, and tensions between native and immigrant workers fed nationalist movements (Keating, *State* 60). As was also the case in Catalonia, Franco's cultural repression and Spanish-speaking migrants exerted great pressure on the use of Euskera, reducing its use to a third of the population by 1981, with perhaps only a quarter of the population, concentrated in rural areas, using it as their regular means of communication (Keating, *State* 216). The problematic of language is thus more delicate in the Basque country than in Catalonia, for a much smaller percentage of the population speaks Euskera, which is also a much less accessible language to learn for Spanish speakers. In part because of this language difficulty, there was always a greater separation between immigrant workers and the Basque-speaking population than there was between immigrants and Catalan speakers (Keating, *State* 216). There is also the issue of Euskera's symbolic status in connection to separatist groups like ETA. The anti-Spanish sentiment engendered by this extreme brand of nationalism is humorously represented in the collection of testimonies *Todo negro no igual* by Beatriz Díaz, which is analyzed in more detail in chapter 5. The collection contains a section dedicated to language issues. One of these texts is a story told by someone

named Djili, from Gambia, entitled "¿También sabes euskara?"
["You also know Euskera?"]:

> Yo estaba en un bar de Hendaya, y le digo a un señor:
> —Oye, cómprame algo . . .
> Él me responde en francés:
> —Ici on ne parle pas espagnol, ce n'est pas l'Espagne!
> (Aquí no se habla español, esto no es España!)
> Así que le digo en francés:
> —Tu n'aimes pas ce que je vends . . . ? (¿No te gusta lo
> que vendo . . . ?)
> Pero él cambió al euskara:
> — . . . Euskal Herrian gaude! (Estamos en Euskal
> Herria!)
> Yo sigue diciendo en euskara:
> —Ona, polita, merke merkea. . . (Bueno, bonito, barato . . .)
> Y entonces me responde en español:
> —Cabrón!, ¿también sabes euskara?

> [I was in a bar in Hendaya, and I say to a man:
> —Listen, buy something from me [in Castilian in the
> original]
> He answers me in French:
> —Here we do not speak Spanish, this is not Spain! [in
> French in the original]
> So I tell him in French:
> —You don't like what I sell? [in French in the original]
> But he switches to Euskera:
> —We are in the Basque Country! [in Euskera in the
> original]
> I continue in Euskera:
> —Good, nice, cheap . . . [in Euskera in the original]
> And then he answers me in Spanish:
> —Son of a bitch! You also know Euskera? [in Castilian
> in the original]] (Díaz 146)

The same anxieties that we have seen in the cases of Madrid or
Barcelona regarding language use are humorously portrayed in
this exchange, where the conflict arises because Djili doesn't
participate in the internal politics of one language's precedence
over others, but uses them without care for their hierarchy, for
communication and commercial purposes only.

The Basque country has not been the focus of much discussion regarding immigration partly because its numbers are much

lower than those of Madrid, Catalonia or Andalusia (Ormazabal and Camacho). In 1998, however, a publicity campaign by the Basque Department of Justice resulted in a great controversy that had to be resolved through the arbitration of the nonprofit organization SOS Racism. The ad in question read in its Spanish version:

> He nacido blanco, soy vasco y soy europeo. Una cuestión de azar, pero también de suerte, porque hoy por hoy el origen de los seres humanos marca definitivamente el futuro. Muchas veces me pregunto hasta cuándo tendrá que ser así.

> [I was born white, I am Basque and European. A question of chance, but also of good luck, because today the origin of human beings definitely marks the future. I often wonder how long this will be the case.]

As analyzed by Elena Delgado, the ad assumed an obsolete premise of gender, race, ethnicity, and geographic location as essentialist and exclusivist spaces of privilege. It also prevented the possibility of imagining possible other *combinations* of these characteristics: "female Basque," "Black Basque," even "Spanish Basque" subjects are excluded in this representation that, ironically, was part of a series commemorating the 50th anniversary of the Declaration of Human Rights (Delgado, "Settled" 123).

An important corollary of these controversies and representations is that they make explicit and bring into the open the similarity of concerns regarding immigration that are shared by Madrid, Catalonia, and the Basque country. Étienne Balibar explains how difficult it is to unravel the category of nationalism when taking into account "the antithetical nature of the historical situations in which nationalist movements and policies arise" (Balibar 45). In the same way, Keating warns that we should

> distinguish between movements for the creation of unitary nations and movements of the periphery formed precisely to resist this. Both . . . may call themselves nationalist, but paradoxically many of the regional "nationalists" are anti-nationalist in the classic sense of the term. (Keating, *State* 9)

However, as Balibar points out, there are numerous examples in history of the uncanny parallels developed between different nationalisms, where nationalisms of "liberation" are transformed into ones of "domination" and racist exclusion (Balibar 46). In the cases of the different nationalisms in Spain, they seem to operate under very similar assumptions when confronted with the "foreign." In his study about the historical representations of Moroccans in Spain, Eloy Martín Corrales asserts: "En la imagen de los musulmanes y marroquíes en España no existen diferencias [regionales]: la valoración peyorativa fue compartida mayoritariamente por todos los españoles" ["In the image of Muslims and Moroccans in Spain there are not [regional] differences: the pejorative evaluation was mostly shared by all Spaniards"] (Martín Corrales 28). Nationalist Catalan commentators explain the fear and sense of invasion of Catalonia by comparing it to that felt in other regions of Spain, downplaying regional differences. Joan B. Culla i Clarà explains how racism is felt in the same way by the "national," whether Catalan or Spanish:

> ¿Qué sucederá si mañana unos inmigrantes de los hasta ahora encerrados alquilan el piso de al lado, y más tarde otros hacen lo propio con el de arriba, y poco a poco van impregnando la finca entera, la calle, el barrio con sus formas de vida, sus olores y sus sonidos? ¿Subsistirán entonces la solidaridad y la simpatía o el *nacional*—que se considere catalán o español será lo de menos—reaccionará con el miedo y el complejo de invadido que son la base de cualquier racismo?
>
> [What will happen if tomorrow some of those immigrants who up until now have been enclosed rent the apartment next door, and later others do the same with the apartment above, and little by little they start to impregnate the whole building, the street, the neighborhood with their ways of life, their smells and their sounds? Will solidarity and empathy still survive or will the *national*—Catalan or Spaniard, it makes no difference—react with the fear and the invasion complex that are the basis of any racism?]. (Culla i Clarà)

In a similar way, Javier Galparsoro, president of the Basque Country's CEAR (Spanish Comission for the Help of Refugees), says: "A mí me gustaría saber qué pasaría si todos los días llegasen [al País Vasco] pateras con 200 pasajeros o un barco con 600 kurdos" ["I myself would like to know what would happen if boats with 200 immigrants or a ship with 600 Kurds arrived every day [in the Basque Country]"] (Ormazabal and Camacho), implying that, very possibly, people's reactions in the Basque Country would be the same as those in the rest of Spain, where these arrivals produce the utmost alarm.

These similarities might exist because, as Harrington argues, "each of the four primary movements of national identity within the Spanish state . . . has been deeply and fundamentally imbued with the logic of historicist essentialism" (Harrington 110). The religious imperatives and messianic thrust that imbued Nebrija's vision of the Spanish Empire's mission through the Castilian language and its community of users is not exclusive to Castilian nationalism. Conservative politics and militant Catholicism are, in fact, common denominators in the development of all four peninsular nationalisms. The Catalanists of the late 1880s and early 1890s (Enric Prat de la Riba, Francesc Cambó, Josep Puig i Cadafalch, and Josep Torras i Bages) were, like their Castilian counterparts, conservative and Catholic, and they sought to give expression to the "essential," *spiritually inspired* elements of Catalan identity (Harrington 118; emphasis in the original). The first formulations of Basque national identity, generated by Sabino Arana during the same decade, "grew out of a similar social and religious environment" (Harrington 118), with an emphasis on Catholicism, racial exclusiveness, and social conservatism (Keating, *State* 101). Catholicism plays a crucial role here: as Keating points out, it was the major unifying factor at the cultural level among the regions (Keating, *State* 38). The more or less covert religious content of much of the rejection of Muslim immigrants today shows us how, not only in the case of the Spanish state, but also in that of the peripheral nationalities, "the bundled discursive relationship between faith and national identity developed in the time of Nebrija was never seriously challenged" (Harrington 115).[22]

There is an inherent slippage present, however, every time we criticize the trappings or racism of Catalan and Basque nationalisms. As happened with the scandals brought about by Marta Ferrusola's comments and by the Basque government's ad, the Madrid press and the then-ruling Partido Popular showed an indignation that "conceals an agenda that has little or nothing to do with sensitivity to racism and much to do with their opposition to Basque [or Catalan] self-determination" (Delgado, "Settled" 123). Joseba Gabilondo analyzed the smashing success of Jon Juaristi's *El bucle meláncolico: historias de nacionalistas vascos* and concluded that the resonance of Juaristi's book precisely at a moment "when the Spanish state [was] set on a course of Europeanization and globalization" (Gabilondo, "Jon Juaristi" 541) could be explained in part because Juaristi, the ultimate Basque insider, offered Spanish nationalism the means to safely criticize Basque nationalism, therefore implicitly justifying the state's attempts to control and reduce it (Gabilondo, "Jon Juaristi" 552). In the same way, Harrington notes that the representatives of the Partido Popular government in Madrid enthusiastically receive the self-criticism of Basque or Catalan nationalists, but they themselves "do nothing to encourage a similar analysis of Castilianism's ample tradition of historicistically-justified exclusivity" (Harrington 131). Because we cannot afford not to see the parallels, these questions of racism and nationalist exclusion should be perceived at the level of what Gabilondo calls "the Spanish state and its nationalist system," including both Spanish and peripheral nationalisms (Gabilondo, "Uncanny Identity" 267), and not forgetting the differential relationships of power and subordination that exist among the regions.

However, together with the persistence of exclusivist nationalist discourses and practices, there exists a reality of heterogeneous identities all over Spain, both among and within regions, where bilingualism and trilingualism are common practices of the everyday. It is useful in this sense to remember Anderson's words on how nations can always be joined: "If nationalness has about it an aura of fatality, it is nonetheless a fatality embedded in *history* . . . one could be 'invited into' the imagined community" (Anderson 145; emphasis in the original). If two of every three Catalans have parents or grandparents born outside of Catalonia (Núñez Ruiz 268), it is very much possible to imagine that which the films *Las cartas de Alou* and *Tomándote* have not yet been able to imagine, which is a Spanish, Catalan, or Basque person born in Morocco, India, or Senegal. These people not only already exist, but they are also writing their stories in their second or third languages, as is the case of *El Diablo de Yudis* written by Moroccan Ahmed Daoudi in Spanish; *Jo també sóc catalana* by Moroccan Najat El Hachmi, written in Catalan; and *Calella sen Saída* by Víctor Omgbá from Cameroon, written in Galician.

The immigrants' presence, especially Moroccan immigrants' presence, both underlines and questions Spain's belonging to Europe, and Catalonia's belonging to both Europe and Spain. It affirms that belonging insofar as migrants come because of the opportunities offered by the "Europeanness" of Spain, because Africa doesn't begin at the Pyrenees anymore. But it also underlines Spanish "difference" within and without, its recent migration history, both outside and inside its borders, and notices and points to Third-World spaces inside a First-World package, to that in Spain which is still "not yet," to mixed and unstable identities and locations. It also awakens old ghosts of Spanish closeness with North Africa, and the long-repressed memory of trauma, as we will see in the following chapter.

Ghostly Returns

The "Loss" of Spain, the Invading "Moor," and the Contemporary Moroccan Immigrant

En algunos de esos pueblos remotos a cuyos campos fuimos a trabajar, la gente apenas sabía nada de
los marroquíes. Todo lo que sabían se remontaba
a antiguas leyendas sobre los moros que habían
ocupado su tierra. Y a los que habían expulsado de
mala manera. Leyendas transmitidas de padres a
hijos que cuentan una historia fantástica repleta de
falsificaciones.

[In some of those remote towns where we went to
work on their farms, people hardly knew anything
about Moroccans. All they knew went back to old
legends about the Moors who had occupied their
land. And whom they had brutally expelled. Legends transmitted from parents to children, that tell a
fantastic tale full of falsifications.]

Rachid Nini
Diario de un ilegal

One of the most troubling aspects of the current relationship
of Spaniards as hosts and Moroccans as guests is a slippage by
which Moroccans are transformed from immigrants who have
come in search of economic opportunities to invaders who have
come to reclaim what was once theirs. Derrida states in *Specters of Marx* that "haunting is historical" (4). The presence of
a ghost tells us that the past is not closed and solved, but that
the present "is still haunted by the symptomatic traces of its
productions and exclusions" (Gordon 17), by that which has
been rendered ghostly (Gordon 18), excluded, or marginalized.
As in the case of Marx's ghosts analyzed by Derrida, in which

no disavowal has been able to make them completely disappear (Derrida, *Specters* 37), Spaniards' difficulties with Moroccan immigrants, and their perception of them as "Moors," becomes a symptom of the ghostly slippage between the present and past they produce, and the unsolved historical trauma they awake.[1] Derrida maintains, quoting Hamlet's phrase, "The time is out of joint," that ghosts happen in a "disjointed or disadjusted now . . . that always risks maintaining nothing together in the assured conjunction of some context whose border would still be determinable" (Derrida, *Specters* 3). The ghost of the Moor inhabits precisely that "disadjusted now," a space deeply infiltrated by a past and inextricably entangled with it.

This past, in the case of the ghostly returns of the "Moor," is medieval al-Andalus. The rhetoric of reclaiming contemporary Spain as the lost al-Andalus was made infamously current by Osama bin Laden, who presumably referred, after the September 11 attacks in the US, to a desire to recover the lost splendor of Muslim al-Andalus. In a similar manner, a video found in the apartment blown up in Leganés, the Madrid suburb where, it seems, several of those responsible for the March 11, 2004, Atocha attack were living, also contained, together with references to the Crusades and the Inquisition, an allusion to Spain as al-Andalus, the land of Tarik ben Ziyad.[2] We could dismiss these claims to a lost Muslim Spain as one more in a series of irrational, fanatical actions by extremist groups. They are, however, part of an anachronistic rhetoric of confrontation that does not belong exclusively to Muslim extremists. José María Aznar, in a lecture given at Georgetown University, exposed the same type of anachronism when he affirmed that "Spain's problem with Al-Quaeda and Islamic terrorism . . . begins more than 1,300 years ago, in the eighth century, when Spain, invaded by the Moors, refuses to become one more piece of the Islamic world, and begins a long battle to recover its identity."[3]

This rhetoric has also permeated more moderate voices in the relationship between Spain and Morocco, on both sides of the border. In the specific context of Moroccan immigration to Spain, what we find is a mechanism by which immigrants are seen as the return of the imaginary invading Moor who was the "owner" of al-Andalus, in an extension of the beliefs voiced by bin Laden and the speaker in the video found in Leganés to

...oroccan immigrants in general. This slippage between past and present can be seen in many fictional and social texts related to Moroccan immigration, as we will see in this chapter. The basic consequence of seeing current immigrants as Moorish invaders is that the language of hospitality quickly turns into a language of military defense against a potential enemy. This vision, exposed by José María Aznar in his Georgetown discourse, in which "Moors" are to be seen as a constant threat to Spain's sovereignty and unity, is based on the interpretation of the events of AD 711 as a violent invasion of Spain by the Moors. It has, of course, a very long history, which permeates current Spanish views of Moroccan immigrants.

The AD 711 Arab and Berber invasion has thus long been seen as the origin of Spain's historical trauma. Spaniards have been persuaded by a long tradition of nationalist historiography that the invasion and ensuing Muslim presence was, in fact, traumatic, and that Christians (identified as "Spaniards" in these accounts, introducing a doubt as to whether Muslims and Jews were genuinely Spaniards as well) were finally able to "recover" their true identity and way of life after the expulsion of the infidels. In spite of the fact that Spain is, and has always been, a heterogeneous nation, the notion of a society ethnically, culturally, and religiously homogeneous continues to make frequent appearances in discourses aiming at justifying its identity as a nation. This homogenizing discourse has become a frequent response to the perceived threat that immigration poses to national integrity. In this context, old binary oppositions such as that of the Moor as "invader" versus the Christian as "invaded" have reemerged. Inasmuch as the more than eight centuries of Muslim presence in the Iberian Peninsula are perceived as a breach of the Christian continuum, they constitute a cultural or historical trauma. Ann Kaplan explains how trauma originates in a series of events that render an individual, or a social group, unable to process the experience cognitively: "cultures too can be traumatized by events not cognitively processed and which intrude persistently . . . Cultures repeat and repeat traumas too problematic to confront directly" (Kaplan, "Trauma" 308). A "historical trauma," says Kaja Silverman, is a specific historical disruption that "manages to *interrupt* or even *deconstitute* what a society assumes to be its master narratives and immanent

Necessity" (qtd. in Kaplan, "Melodrama" 203–04). Among the master narratives of a nation, one acquires a central role. Silverman, following Jacques Rancière, identifies this preeminent narrative as the dominant fiction of a society: a dominant fiction "neutralizes the contradictions which organize the social formation by fostering collective identifications and desires . . . Social formations consequently depend upon their dominant fictions for their sense of unity and identity" (Silverman 54). In the Spanish case, the historical trauma, supposedly represented by the Moorish presence, disrupts the dominant national fiction of a pure and uncontaminated "Spanish" origin, both at the personal and the social levels, where the concept of "Spanishness" is associated and identified with Christianity. Manuel García Morente is representative of this position, as we saw in chapter 1. In a similar line of thought, Claudio Sánchez Albornoz views Muslim Spain as an "interruption" to a "Spanish" [Christian] continuum. He understands this historical period as a "brutal contortion" that "broke apart the Hispanic unity and interrupted its normal evolutionary process" (Sánchez Albornoz, *El Islam* 32). His works are dedicated to trying to demonstrate "the preservation of the pre-Muslim Hispanic in Muslim Spain," where "millions of Spaniards . . . maintained the temperamental inheritance of their millenary grandparents" (Sánchez Albornoz, *Ensayos* 20).[4] Today, historians allied with the ideas of José María Aznar—like César Vidal in his *España frente al Islam* and Serafín Fanjul in his *La quimera de al-Andalus* and *Al-Andalus contra España: la forja del mito*—have continued this tradition.

The "Invasion" of AD 711

Symptomatically, there is a long tradition of writing going back to medieval chronicles that attempts to explain how it was that the Arabs and Berbers were able to conquer Spain. This basic narrative portrays the invasion as a tragic event (often a punishment from God) that resulted in the "loss of Spain" to the Muslims and the desire to "recover" it for Christianity. The so-called Loss of Spain Legend names the invasion in an evident ideological positioning with regard to those who were the "real owners" of the territory (the Christian Visigoths) and those who were the usurpers (the Muslim Arabs and Berbers). Its basic elements consist of the seduction and rape of la Cava by Visigoth king Rodrigo and the subsequent revenge of her father, don Julián, governor of Ceuta, who collaborated with the Muslims by "opening" the gates of Spain. This narrative, which has been told and retold for centuries, represents for the Spanish nation one of its most important foundational myths. The mere fact of its widespread interest for so many writers across the centuries testifies to its importance in the construction of national identity. This basic story of national loss was written and rewritten in several medieval chronicles, in romances, seventeenth-century works by Lope de Vega, Fray Luis de León, and de Saavedra Fajardo, eighteenth-century narratives by Feijóo, de Vela, Cadalso, Concha, Montengón, and Gálvez, and nineteenth-century ones by Rivas, Espronceda, and Zorrilla, to culminate in its rewriting by Goytisolo in 1970 (*Reivindicación del conde don Julián*). Kaplan argues that "[t]he repetition of certain stories may betray a traumatic cultural symptom" (Kaplan, "Melodrama" 203). For each one of these writers, the AD 711 invasion is one of those traumatic episodes of the past that a culture needs to rewrite in order to understand its present, since, as Hayden White points out, "the greatest historians have always dealt with those events in the histories of their cultures which are 'traumatic' in nature and the meaning of which is either problematical or overdetermined in the significance that they still have for current life" (White 87).

But, was the Arab and Berber invasion a truly traumatic event at the time or only constructed as such later on? This is a contentious issue, not only because there are few surviving sources about this period, but also because an assessment of the AD 711 conquest involves an ideological position regarding one of the most sensitive aspects of Spanish racial, religious, and cultural identity, an issue that encompasses such emotionally charged issues as whether Spain has more in common with North Africa than with Europe. Far from having had a separate history from North Africa, by which it was suddenly invaded in AD 711, Spain has always shared different waves of peoples and political regimes with that region, in a pattern "that can be traced from Antiquity to the present" (Collins 21). Iberians probably originated in northern Africa, for Carthage attempted to dominate the peninsula, and early Spanish Christianity had a strong African influence (Collins 20–21). Both shores of the Strait of Gibraltar were colonized by Phoenicians, Romans, Goths, and Arabs. Both shores were pagan, until Christianity arrived through the Roman Empire in the third century.[5] When the barbarian Germanic peoples invaded the Roman Empire at the beginning of the fifth century, one of these groups, the Western Goths, invaded both the Iberian Peninsula and North Africa.[6] In the same way, at the beginning of the eighth century, the Arabs conquered both North Africa and the Iberian Peninsula, aided in this later conquest by the indigenous inhabitants of Morocco, the Berbers, who had by then converted to Islam. So there was not anything intrinsically different about the Arab invasion in comparison to any prior conquest that had been experienced on both shores of the Strait of Gibraltar. As far as religion is concerned, the greatest challenge to the Catholic Church at the time was Christian heterodoxy. At the time of their invasion of the Roman Empire, the Visigoths were Christians, but they belonged to the Arian sect, considered heretical by the Catholic Church, since they did not believe in the divinity of Christ. They were thus seen as foreign invaders of Catholic, Roman Spain, until, in AD 589, Visigoth King Recaredo convened the Third Council of Toledo, repudiated Arianism, and converted to Roman Catholicism. This conversion allowed Christian historiographers such as John of Biclaro (c. AD 590) and Isidore of Seville (c. AD 625) to regard them as the legitimate heirs of Christian imperial rule in Spain (Wolf, *Conquerors* xvii).

A careful reading of sources contemporaneous to the events reveals that the Arab invasion was not considered a religious threat at the time, but was only constructed as such later on. The anonymous *Crónica mozárabe de 754*, written in Latin as a continuation of the chronicles of John of Biclaro and Isidore of Seville, is considered a very reliable account of early eighth-century Spain because of its temporal proximity to the events it narrates (Collins 26–28; de la Serna 57–58). Its author was a Mozarab; that is, a Christian who stayed in the land now ruled by Muslims.[7] Because of his many informed references to Iberian churchmen and to political events in Muslim Spain, some critics believe he was probably an ecclesiastic with close ties to the Cordoban court (Wolf, *Conquerors* 26–27).[8] His text reveals the ambivalence of early eighth-century Mozarabs, who lived between two traditions. The chronicle contains both: modeled as a continuation of Christian chronicles that celebrate Spain as a Christian kingdom, it describes Spain through literary Arabic conventions as a "pomegranate," and combines Christian-imperial dating schemes with Islamic chronologies (Wolf, *Conquerors* 26–27). In judging Visigoth and Muslim rulers, it does so within the same political parameters, according to their effectiveness at promoting peace and justice, not by their religious affiliation (Wolf, *Conquerors* 33).[9] In fact, this chronicle does not represent the conquerors as a religious threat: in it, there is no information given about their religious identity, even though the author is interested in describing religious developments and Catholic deviance—something that worried the Spanish Church more than the supposed religious threat of Islam (Wolf, *Conquerors* 35–39).[10] Having available the models provided by the historical books of the Old Testament, where foreign invasions are interpreted as scourges sent by God, the author of the chronicle chooses not to follow them. Instead, his chronicle treats the conquest politically (Wolf, *Conquerors* 31–33).

Thus, his lament for the violence that ensues during the invasion[11] is accompanied by a statement describing the devastation of Spain at the hands of fighting Visigothic political factions, prior to AD 711, over the succession to the throne: "España . . . se sentía duramente agredida no sólo por la ira del enemigo extranjero, sino también por sus luchas intestinas" (*Crónica* 71); "Spain . . . was greatly afflicted not only by the enemy but also by domestic strife" (Wolf, *Conquerors* 132). Later chronicles produced by the defeated king's faction put a lot of effort into rescuing and mythologizing Rodrigo as a heroic tragic figure. The *Crónica mozárabe*, however, leaves the issue of his illegitimate ascent to the throne clear when it states, "ocupa Rodrigo el trono en virtud de una revuelta" (69); "Roderic rebelliously seized the kingdom" (Wolf, *Conquerors* 131). Archeological records also indicate political strife: at this time coins corresponding to two different kings were made (Collins 32; de la Serna 58). King Vitiza had died in AD 709 but none of his sons gained enough support to claim the throne, and thus Rodrigo occupied it. The Berber invasion, then, very possibly counted on the support of Vitiza's sons, who wanted to remove

Rodrigo from the throne (many historians actually believe they invited the invaders). The invasion then became part of this political struggle between different factions of the Visigothic kingdom, a struggle that seems to have taken the form of a civil war. The *Crónica mozárabe* certainly points in this direction when it speaks of Spain having been "injustamente destrozada desde tiempo atrás" (*Crónica* 71); "long plundered" (Wolf, *Conquerors* 132) at the time Muza invades it.

In the same way that the *Crónica mozárabe* does not describe Christians and Muslims as religious antagonists (Wolf, *Conquerors* 37), it is very difficult to assert the unequivocal belonging of chronicles such as this one to either Muslim or Christian sources. They are marked, as was every aspect of daily life in the Peninsula, by deep interrelations between the two. The use of both Latin and Arab sources in this Latin chronicle sets up a model that characterizes all subsequent chronicles. The Egyptian historian Ben Abdelhákem, in the ninth century, greatly influenced the development of Rodrigo's legend, introducing the element of the enchanted palace, taken from classic Arab literature. The Christian archbishop El Toledano based his version on Ben Abdelhákem, as did the Christian King Alfonso el Sabio for his *Historia de España*. The Arab work of Al-razi or "el moro Rasís," included in the Christian *Crónica de 1344*, is the main source for the *Refundición de la crónica de 1344*, by a Jewish converso from Toledo, and for the famous *Crónica sarracina* by Pedro del Corral (1430) (Menéndez Pidal xliv–lxxx). In his turn, the *Morisco* Miguel de Luna rewrote the *Sarracina* in a particular way, when his *Verdadera historia del rey don Rodrigo* was published in 1592 and 1600, where he depicted Visigothic Spain as "a nightmare which is providentially ended by the Arab invasion" (Márquez Villanueva, "La voluntad" 363).

The beginnings of a nationalist construction of the AD 711 Arab and Berber conquest as God's punishment for the sins of its Christian rulers can be traced to the Asturias kingdom, in the mountainous northern tip of the peninsula. The *Chronicle of Alfonso III* dates from some time during the reign of this Asturian king (AD 866–910). As a continuation of Isidore's work, the narrator incorporated this kingdom's history into the history of the Goths, establishing through his narration the Asturian dynasty as the legitimate heirs of Christian Spain. To this end, the *Chronicle of Alfonso III* detailed the sinful nature of the last four Visigothic kings, who offended God and thus suffered the consequences, and the close relationship that Pelayo, the first Asturian king (AD 718–37), had had with them. The narrator made a great effort to demonstrate this closeness, trying to create a continuity that in reality did not exist between the two monarchies (Wolf, *Conquerors* 43–49; de la Serna 74–75). The chronicler dedicates most of his narration to the mythical story of Pelayo's resistance to the Muslims at Covadonga. The first Asturian king is thus inscribed as the one "hand-picked by God to begin the restoration of Gothic Spain" (Wolf, *Conquerors* 50). The ideas of Pelayo as a rebel who resists occupation and thus begins the "Reconquest" and Asturias as having been exempt from Arab domination, defended by a long tradition of nationalist historiographers such as Claudio Sánchez Albornoz, have long been questioned. Pelayo, as did most of the Visigothic nobility, had to negotiate with the Arabs and submit to their authority (Márquez Villanueva, *Santiago* 60–61). The linkage of the Astures dynasty to the Visigothic past, together with Pelayo's mythical victory against the invaders in Covadonga, were more reflections of late ninth-century intent than descriptions of eighth-century events (Collins 146–48). Covadonga, especially, was not nearly as significant as these chronicles suggest, and historians agree that to view it as the beginning of the ideology of Reconquest would actually be quite anachronistic (Collins 148–49).

In order to legitimize their claim as rightful heirs to the Christian legacy of the Peninsula, the chroniclers of the newly formed kingdom of Asturias had to demonstrate not only their connection to the defeated monarchy but also enough of their difference when it came to committing deadly sins. We can trace here the beginning of a discourse on the "saintly" nature of these new Christian kings: if the Visigoths were punished by God because of their (mostly sexual) sins, Spain's restorers would be characterized by their asceticism and chastity. The chroniclers also needed to establish that the invasion of AD 711 was not just a political change of authority but a divine scourge. Scourges, in the historical books of the Old Testament, were "temporary punishments inflicted to correct the sins of a chosen people. They were to be lifted when the price for the transgression had been paid" (Wolf, *Conquerors* 40). The triumph of Covadonga is thus described in the *Chronicle of Alfonso III* as a sign of God's favor, a favor that implied that the scourge was over. The merit of Pelayo's triumph is thus mostly God's:

> the 63,000 [Muslims] who were left alive ascended to the summit of Mt. Auseva . . . But they could not escape the vengeance of the lord. For when they had reached the summit of the mountain . . . it happened, by a judgement of God, that the mountain, quaking from its very base, hurled the 63,000 men into the river and crushed them all. (Wolf, *Conquerors* 168–69)

By inscribing the AD 711 invasion in the rhetorical model of a divine scourge, this chronicle also inaugurates a long line of interpretation that emphasizes the destructive nature of the conquest, and, in consequence, the evil nature of the conquerors. The Arabs and Berbers thus caused the "loss" of a kingdom that had to be "recovered" through the Reconquest. More and more, then, the AD 711 conquest appeared in Christian chronicles as an event of apocalyptic proportions. As explained by José Antonio Conde in the prologue to his 1874 edition of Arab manuscripts:

> nuestras antiguas crónicas . . . se deben considerar como relaciones sospechosas de enemigos que escribían cuando el odio era más vehemente . . . [d]e aquí proviene que se crea comunmente que los Moros, cuando hicieron la entrada en España, eran innumerables y no tanto guerreros valientes y afortunados, cuanto bárbaros crueles, sin cultura ni policía alguna. Que todo lo llevaban a sangre y fuego; e inhumanos y sin género alguno de piedad no perdonaban edad ni sexo, ni dejaban piedra sobre piedra en las poblaciones.

> [our old chronicles . . . should be considered dubious accounts by enemies who wrote them when hate was at its strongest . . . it is because of that that it is commonly believed that when the Moors entered Spain, they were innumerable and not brave and fortunate warriors but cruel barbarians, without culture or rules whatsoever. That they laid waste to everything with blood and fire, that being inhuman and without any kind of mercy they forgave neither age nor sex, nor did they leave any stone unturned in the towns.] (Conde 4)

As Conde indicates, some sources actually show that the "tragedy" of the invasion was not exactly so:

> las condiciones que imponían a los vencidos eran tales, que
> los pueblos en vez de opresión hallaban comodidad en ellas;
> y si comparaban su suerte con la que antes tenían se consi-
> deraban harto venturosos. El libre ejercicio de su religión, la
> conservación de sus templos, y la seguridad de sus personas,
> bienes y posesiones, recompensaba la sumisión y el tributo
> que debían pagar a los vencedores.

> [the conditions imposed on the defeated were such that,
> instead of oppression, people found comfort in them; and if
> they compared their situation with what they had before they
> considered themselves extremely lucky. The free exercise
> of their religion, the preservation of their temples, and the
> safety of their people, goods and possessions, compensated
> for their submission and the tribute that they had to pay the
> conquerors.] (Conde 4)

One of the remarkable facts about the conquest was its ex-traordinary swiftness. While the Arabs took about seventy years to conquer North Africa, they (with an army basically com-posed of Berber warriors) only took three years to reach north-western Spain (de la Serna 60). The reason, as Conde indicates, was that open battle quickly turned into peace treaties with the Peninsula's inhabitants. As administrative records show (the actual text of one of these treaties has survived), the treaties exchanged submission for personal safety, and Christians and Jews, as *dhimmis*, or "People of the Book," were able to keep their faith, their religious laws, their communal authorities, and their property. In return for this protection, Christians and Jews paid a special, additional tax (Fletcher 18–19; de la Serna 64; Collins 39–40; García Arenal 803). The treaties permitted the Arab/Berber army to advance without need to worry about garrison duties behind the front, and they produced very little change in the lives of people at the local level: "people tilled their fields and tended their olives and paid their taxes as they had done before: only the management was different" (Fletcher 19). Both Christians and Jews found all kinds of opportunities under this "new management." Since *dhimmis* "had no legal limitations in the choice and exercise of professions . . . they could be highly successful; and in al-Andalus, as well as in

Egypt and Syria, they could legally hold positions that in fact imply considerable power, such as court physician or ambassador" (García Arenal 803). By the ninth century, "Christians and Jews were regularly employed by the emirs as tax collectors, ministers, and even bodyguards" (Wolf, "Christian" 92). This information contributes to the hypothesis that, for many people, the AD 711 conquest was not a particularly traumatic event *per se*, but was constructed as such *a posteriori*.

There is also a religious explanation for the rapid advance of Muslim troops and influence. Far from seeing the Muslim invaders as a religious enemy, this theory suggests that the remaining Arian Goths saw them as fellow monotheists in contrast to the relatively new, Trinitarian, Orthodox Catholic establishment of the Visigothic court, represented by Rodrigo. This theory supposes that a century after Recaredo converted to Roman Catholicism in AD 587, religious unification was not complete, and that the Arian Christian belief, which was previously the official religion of the Visigothic monarchy, still pervaded. Many Arians, who had faced persecution and seen their texts destroyed by Recaredo, did not understand as monotheist the Roman Catholic belief in the Holy Trinity (de la Serna 61). Under this hypothesis, then, not only Jews but also Arian Christians would have seen the arrival of Muslims as a protection against religious intolerance. In fact, some sources suggest that Vitiza's sons' alliance with the Berbers came about because they were Arians who wanted to replace Catholic Rodrigo. Thus, Arian factions would actually have fought on the side of the Berbers against the king.

The embracing of Islam by the inhabitants of the Iberian Peninsula can be seen in the gradual but steady conversion of the population to this religion: by the middle of the ninth century, about 12.5% of the population had become Muslims. By about AD 900 it was 25%, and by the year AD 1000 it had reached 75% of the population. This conversion had no traces of force behind it. The Berber conquerors were only partly "Islamicized" themselves at this time, and they had no interest in converting Christians and Jews, who paid the highest taxes because of their status as non-Muslims. The conversions, instead, were probably due to reasons such as career opportunities, higher social status, and the perception of Arabic culture as superior (Fletcher

35–38). By the mid-ninth century, the level of Islamization was such that a group of Christian intellectuals began to feel they had to take action to prevent the further flight of young Christians toward Arab culture. They were especially worried about young Christians' "abandonment" of Latin culture and their attraction to Arabic poetry and books. The perceived decline of Christian faith was answered through self-sought "martyrdom": by publicly denouncing Islam and cursing Mohammed this group of zealots accomplished what they desired, since this public offence carried the death penalty.

Attempting to justify these martyrdoms (which were condemned by Bishop Recafredo of Seville), Eulogius and Alvarus of Córdoba shed light on the fluid connections between Muslims, Jews, and Christians that they saw as disastrous; the high number of mixed marriages, the frequent conversions and borrowings from one faith to another, the differing beliefs in a single family, and the generalized use of Arabic as learned language (Fletcher 38–40; de la Serna 68–69; Menocal 66–70). It was at this moment, with Eulogius's defense of the Cordoban Christian martyrs, that the first attempt to emphasize Islam's differences from Christianity occurred. Up to this moment, as we have seen in the *Crónica mozárabe de 754*, Christian clerics were much more concerned with religious heterodoxy inside Christianity and with the threat of contagion from Jewish practices. The Cordoban-martyrs episode reveals the extent of the assimilation of many Christian Cordobans, who asked Eulogius how the martyrdom of these Christians could be considered legitimate when they had "suffered at the hands of men who venerated both God and a law." It is through this attempt to understand the actions of the martyrs that the earliest reference to Islam as a separate religion occurs, with Muslims seen as "monotheists who worshiped the same God as they, though on the basis of a distinct, revealed law" (Wolf, "Christians" 96, 107). As Wolf indicates, this religious closeness justified for Cordoban Christians their cooperation and interrelationships with the Muslims (Wolf, "Christians" 96).

Eulogius and Alvarus were not the only ones who were worried about the close relationships between Christians and Muslims. Almost a century earlier, in a AD 782 letter to his representative in Spain, Pope Hadrian I had explicitly condemned any form of intermarriage between Christians, Muslims, and Jews. His representative, it seems, had found the Spanish Church "dangerously open to the influence of Islamic and Jewish ideas and practices" (Collins 221). One of the most important Christian controversies of the eighth century, Adoptionism, also attests to the initial degree of convergence of the two faiths in Spain. Counter to the idea that Spain was destroyed by the Arab invasion is the fact that the Christian Church persisted almost untouched by the change in political authority. The post-Visigothic, Mozarab Church adapted to the new circumstances, and it was concerned about the accusation of polytheism by the Muslims. Trying to find a middle ground with Muslim doctrine, the Archbishop of Toledo and top ecclesiastic authority in Spain at the moment, Elipando (717–808?), proposed the idea that Christ was not God's natural son, but an adoptive one, showing thus that Catholicism, like Islam, also had just one God. It was at this juncture that one of the first strong voices against religious coexistence appeared. From an Asturian monastery, the monk known as the Beato de Liébana defied Elipando's authority, denouncing what he saw as "collaborationism" with the invaders, in the same way that almost a century later Eulogius and Alvarus defended the martyrs of Córdoba. Eventually, the vision that prevailed and sustained the Reconquest was that of confrontation, as proposed by the Beato, not that of Elipando (Márquez Villanueva, *Santiago* 62–69). However, this controversy, like that concerning the Cordoban martyrs, seems to indicate that, even in religious terms, Muslims were not considered to be a threat. As the alarmed writings of the Beato, Eulogius, and Alvarus testify, people had accommodated themselves to living with the new authorities and were engaged in productive relationships with them.

Therefore, even though many historians today believe that the "invasion" of AD 711 was neither truly an "invasion" nor a traumatic event *per se*, there is such a long historiographic tradition of interpreting it this way that the belief in its intrinsically violent, disruptive, and, therefore, traumatic nature has become commonplace.[12] The status of "truth" in assessing historical events, however, has become highly discredited as an analytical tool to understand the past. The also-contentious issue of the "truth" of trauma claims is at the center of contemporary debates over the handling of post-traumatic-stress-disorder cases. Cathy Caruth explains that the problem of post-traumatic-stress-disorder and truth arises "not only in regard to those who listen to the traumatized, not knowing how to establish the reality of their hallucinations and dreams; it occurs rather and most disturbingly often within the very knowledge and experience of the traumatized themselves" (Caruth 5). Trauma exposes a crisis of truth that occurs because there is no easy access "to our own historical experience" (Caruth 6). What matters in these cases, says Caruth, is not the evaluation of the event itself, but its reception—how it is that those affected can never really escape it:

> The pathology cannot be defined either by the event itself— which may or may not be catastrophic, and may not traumatize everyone equally—nor can it be defined in terms of a *distortion* of the event, achieving its haunting power as a result of distorting personal significances attached to it. The pathology consists, rather, solely in the *structure of its experience* or reception: the event is not assimilated or experienced fully at the time, but only belatedly, in its repeated *possession* of the one who experiences it. To be traumatized is precisely to be possessed by an image or event. (Caruth 4–5; emphasis in the original)

Whether the AD 711 invasion was a truly traumatic event *per se* or not, there is no doubt that its consequent historiographical interpretation and, therefore, its consequent historical reception, in the context of the extended "Reconquest" period, became a traumatic one. The symptom of this trauma is the compulsion to repeat: in this case, the narrative of how Spain was lost to the Moors "possesses" Spanish culture. Kaplan explains how "at certain historical moments aesthetic forms emerge to accommodate fears and fantasies related to suppressed historical events" (Kaplan, "Melodrama" 203). The long history of writing and re-writing this story, in the form of the "Loss of Spain" Legend, betrays a compulsion to repeat that becomes the symptom of an unsolved trauma, as the repetition ensures that the AD 711 "invasion" is increasingly interpreted (and therefore vicariously re-experienced through the centuries) as such.

The Compulsion to Repeat
and the Legend of the "Loss" of Spain

In order to explain the notion of trauma, in *Beyond the Pleasure Principle* Freud expands his prior observations from "Psycho-Analysis and War Neuroses," in which, studying the consequences of World War I, he had contemplated the possibility that a trauma occurs as a response to a threat or danger outside the ego (Freud, "Psychoanalysis" 210). He characterizes as traumatic "any excitations from outside which are powerful enough to break through the protective shield" (Freud, *Beyond* 29). The compulsion to repeat, frequently in the form of recurring dreams that bring the patient back, again and again, into the traumatic event, reveals the existence of a traumatic neurosis (Freud, *Beyond* 32). Freud attempts to explain this repetitive impulse that characterizes the traumatized condition. This re-experience of the trauma in repetitive dreams forces him to conclude that not all dreams are guided by desire or wish fulfillment and, therefore, to postulate the existence of principles, such as the compulsion to repeat, which go beyond the pleasure principle (Freud, *Beyond* 13, 17, 20). Freud uses the example of children's play to illustrate this point: he analyzes the way a one-and-a-half-year-old boy found great pleasure in throwing his toys far away from himself and later finding them. Freud understood this game as one in which the child staged his daily drama of instinctual renunciation of letting his mother go away without complaining. The principle guiding the repetition of the game, he concluded, was not one of pleasure, but of mastery: if in the initial unpleasurable experience of his mother's abandonment he had a passive role, then in his own repetition through play he took on an active one and could control it (Freud, *Beyond* 14–16).

Through a similar mechanism, in the "Loss of Spain" Legend's repetition, one of the features that strikingly stands out is the systematic structuring of the narrative so as to have Rodrigo or Julián as the protagonist. This particular interpretation of the invasion places the responsibility of the conquest in individual hands. As Kaplan explains, "public traumas . . . are displaced into dramas about the domestic sphere, where traumas could be shown as caused by individual error" (Kaplan, "Trauma" 308–09). The particular interpretation of events by the legend also displaces its historical protagonists, the Arabs and Berbers, and transforms the narrative into one about the predestined tragedy of the Visigoths, with either Rodrigo or Julián at its center. In most versions, the narrative begins with Rodrigo forcing open an enchanted palace (or house of Hercules) that each king before him had helped to keep closed. Guided by greed and looking for treasure, Rodrigo finds instead an ark containing Arab warriors painted on a cloth and, written on it, an old prophecy warning that whoever unlocked the closed palace doors would bring about the destruction of the kingdom. This first transgression or error is followed by a parallel violation of a sacred space when the king seduces and rapes Cava, or Florinda, the daughter of Count don Julián, the governor of Ceuta. Julián then avenges his daughter's honor by helping Muza cross the Strait of Gibraltar through Ceuta, provoking the AD 711 invasion.

The defeat of the Visigoths is thus explained through Rodrigo's moral transgressions or Julián's wrath and treason, depending upon which side the chronicler situates himself. However, the true responsibility stays in Christian hands: the invasion is due to Rodrigo's and Julián's actions, and not to the political or tactical superiority of the conquerors. Curiously, this explanation appealed to both Muslim and Christian chroniclers, who found through this narrative an exculpation of their role in the invasion and subsequent conquest of the Peninsula. For Muslims, placing the blame on Rodrigo/Julián meant they had been "invited" to the Peninsula. The centrality in their versions of the House of Hercules / enchanted palace episode, with the prophecy that announces the invasion, can be thus understood as a further justification: external forces contributed to their arrival, not just their own military or political will. For Christians, the legend provided exculpation for having actually allowed the invasion and their subsequent coexistence with the Muslims. As noted previously, the full meaning of this exculpation is found in a religious perspective that interprets the destruction of the kingdom as God's punishment for their sins. The vision of the AD 711 invasion as a fall and the construction of a supposed beginning of the Reconquest with Pelayo, as presented in the *Chronicle of Alfonso III*, became a discursive ally in the advance of the military "Reconquest" of Muslim territory. This is the case of the work of Rodrigo Ximénez de Rada, El Toledano,

(AD 1170–1247), Archbishop of Toledo under Fernando III (AD 1217–30). El Toledano can be considered "the chief ideologist of Fernando's court—that is, of the self-confident and expansionist Castile that, having won the decisive battle of Las Navas de Tolosa in 1212, swept on to conquer most of Andalusia" (Deyermond 347). Alfonso X el Sabio's (AD 1252–84) adoption of El Toledano's views consolidates and popularizes this interpretation of the conquest, utilizing the medieval model of moral fall and redemption. As Alfonso III's chronicle tried to justify the legitimacy of the Astures dynasty's origins in the Visigothic one, Alfonso X justifies through his chronicle his own legitimacy as heir to the kingdom inaugurated by Pelayo. The view of an unbroken succession of monarchs from Pelayo to himself was reinforced by his introduction of the numbering of kings (Deyermond 345–46).

Alfonso X thus explained in his *History of Spain* how Spain's fall into sin, like the biblical Fall, was prompted by the Devil, "enemigo dell humanal linnage" ["enemy of the human lineage"]: "el diablo . . . sembro la su mala simient et negra en el regno de Espanna, e metio en los poderosos soberuia . . . e en ricos et abondados luxuria et muchodumbre de peccados . . . por esta guisa . . . fue el regno de los godos de Espanna destroydo" ["the Devil . . . planted his bad black seed in the kingdom of Spain, and put arrogance in the powerful . . . and lechery and many sins in the rich and wealthy . . . because of this . . . the kingdom of Spain was destroyed"] (305). This interpretation of the legend prevailed, with Lope de Vega, for example, writing *El último godo* (1600–15) as a Christian allegory of the loss of Paradise, exploring issues of temptation, transgression, and salvation through sacrifice (Niehoff 261–62). After his troops' defeat, Rodrigo understands that "[d]el cielo ha sido el castigo" ["the punishment has come from heaven"] (Vega Carpio 655), and, in the third act, when Pelayo triumphantly undertakes the Reconquest, he also interprets his triumph as God's: "[a] vos, Señor, que no al hombre, / se debe el triunfo y la gloria" ["to you, Lord, not to man, / we owe the triumph and the glory"] (Vega Carpio 664). Contemporary with the *Moriscos*' 1609 expulsion, this play participated in what was seen as the final stage of that redemption. In the same way, Diego de Saavedra Fajardo explained in 1645 that the invaders were accompanied by "el brazo enojado de Dios, que disponía la ruina de España" ["God's angry hand, that arranged Spain's ruin"] (Saavedra Fajardo 377). Like the authors of the previous works, Saavadra Fajardo wrote his *Corona gótica, castellana y austríaca* for the Spanish prince, tracing a connection between his intended royal reader and the Visigothic kings, "sus gloriosos progenitores" ["your glorious progenitors"] (Saavedra Fajardo 373). This chronicle ideologically accompanied the recent expulsion of the *Moriscos* by reinscribing a Christian continuum in the Peninsula, where its present Christian inhabitants were descendants of the Visigoths, and, particularly, by constructing the Moors and, therefore, the *Moriscos*, as a strange, outsider presence. For this purpose, the AD 711 invasion is described as an animal plague: "África, la cual soltó luego por España sus sierpes, inundándola con nuevos diluvios de gente" ["Africa, which later unleashed through Spain its serpents, flooding it with new torrents of people"] (Saavedra Fajardo 378). Characterizing the invasion as a flood, with resonances of a biblical plague, Saavedra Fajardo participates in the myth that tries to justify Spain's Islamization by affirming that there was a demographically dramatic influx of Muslims with the invasion, and that they were the ones who were expelled nine centuries later, having been kept neatly separated from the Christian population. This characterization of Africans as animals also anticipates the racial dynamic that will become an essential component of their disqualification as not "fully human."

Like the small child in Freud's analysis, who repeated the scenario of his mother's leaving, but displaced it onto his toys in order to have control over its development and outcome, the multiple versions of the "Loss of Spain" legend attempted to master the story of how the invasion happened, positioning the Visigoths as the ones who precipitated it, but making God ultimately responsible for it. Instead of trying to become active protagonists in a traumatic event in which they were passive sufferers, like the child in Freud's story, Muslims and Christians found in this version of events an exculpation for the people on both sides who were responsible for either conquering the new territory or accepting the new rulers.

The Christian characterization of the AD 711 invasion as a fall from Paradise was dependent upon an apocalyptic description of the destruction caused by the conquerors. According to Alfonso X el Sabio:

> Toda la tierra desgastaron los enemigos, las casas hermaron, los omnes mataron, las cibdades quemaron, los arbores, las uinnas et quanto fallaron uerde cortaron. Tanto puio esta pestilencia et esta cueta que non finco en toda Espanna Buena uilla nin cibdad o obispo ouiesse que non fuesse quemada o derribada o retenida de moros. (Alfonso 313)

> [Our enemies wasted the whole land, razed dwellings, killed people, burned cities, and cut down trees and vineyards and everything else they found. So widely did this pestilence and destruction spread that there did not remain in all Spain a single Episcopal city that was not burned or razed or occupied by the Moors.] (Smith 21)

Alfonso continued, explaining that it was through trickery that the conquerors were able to secure the collaboration of and coexistence with the Christian inhabitants of the Peninsula:

> ca las cibdades que los alaraues non pudieron conquerir, engannaron las et conquiriron las por falsas pleytesias . . . Et por tal encubierta fueron los omnes engannados, e dieron los castiellos et las fortalezas de las uillas; et fincaron los cristianos mezclados con los alaraues, et aquellos ouieron nombre dalli delante moçaraues por que uiuien de buelta con ellos. (Alfonso 313)

> [for the cities which the Arabs were not able to capture, they deceived and took over by false terms of capitulation . . . By this trick men were deceived, and handed over the castles and the fortified positions inside the towns. The Christians mingled with the Arabs, and thenceforth acquired the name of Mozarabs because they lived among them.] (Smith 22–23)

This characterization of the conquest also constructs the figure of the invading Moor as threatening, violent, malicious, and racialized, in addition, however, to a certain ambivalence:

> Los moros de la hueste todos uestidos del sirgo et de los pannos de color que ganaran, las riendas de los sus cauallos tales eran como de fuego, las sus caras dellos negras como la pez,

el mas fremoso dellos era negro como la olla, assi luzien sus
oios como candelas; el su cauallo dellos ligero como leopar-
do, e el su cauallero mucho mas cruel et mas dannoso que es
el lobo en la grey de las ouejas en la noche. (Alfonso 312)

[The Moors of the host wore silks and colorful clothes which
they had taken as booty, their horses' reins were like fire,
their faces were black as pitch, the handsomest among them
was black as a cooking pot, and their eyes blazed like fire;
their horses as swift as leopards, their horsemen more cruel
and hurtful than the wolf that comes at night to the flock of
sheep.] (Smith 19)

Alfonso's comparisons of the Moors to fire, leopards, and
wolves combines horror at their fierceness and potential de-
structiveness with a definite admiration for them. Both his and
Saavedra Fajardo's descriptions of the Arab and Berber invaders participate in what will be characterized in the twentieth
century as a typical orientalist gesture. As explained by Rana
Kabbani, lasciviousness and violence are the two pillars by
which the West views the East as irremediably other:

In the European narration of the Orient, there was a deliber-
ate stress on those qualities that made the East different from
the West, exiled it into an irretrievable state of "otherness."
Among the many themes that emerge from the European
narration of the Other, two appear most strikingly. The first
is the insistent claim that the East was a place of lascivious
sensuality, and the second that it was a realm characterized
by inherent violence. (Kabbani 5–6)

Lust and violence, often combined as sexual violence, became the ultimate explanatory device for both the "loss" of
Spain and the AD 711 invasion. Israel Burshatin highlights the
combined importance of the two paradigmatic narrations about
Rodrigo's misdeeds: the two "(de)structuring violations—entering the House of Hercules, ravishing La Cava" (Burshatin,
"Narratives" 15).[13] The Moorish invasion, seen as divine
punishment, fits the crime, as it consists of similar violations.
The description of the nation's violation by military invasion is
embodied in the rapes of anonymous women. Saavedra Fajardo's text constructs a parallel between the two interconnected
aspects of Rodrigo's intrusion into sacred, prohibited space,

the public one in the House of Hercules and the private one in Cava's body, with the nation's violation at the hands of the Moors: "En todas partes sus sacrílegas manos han violado las aras y santuarios y abrasado los templos. Su bárbara lascivia no ha perdonado al honor de las mujeres ni a la pureza de las vírgenes y religiosas" ["Everywhere their sacrilegious hands have violated altars and shrines and burned the temples. Its barbarous lust has neither forgiven the honor of women nor the purity of virgins and nuns"] (Saavedra Fajardo 378). The paganism of Rodrigo's House of Hercules is replaced in this account by undoubtedly Christian symbols: altars, shrines, virginity, nuns. Alfonso el Sabio also mentions the violation of women in his account of the horrors Spain went through in AD 711: "A las mezquinas de las mugieres guardauan las pora desonrrar las, e la su fermosura dellas era guardada pora su denosto" (Alfonso 313); "They put the wretched women aside to dishonor them later, and their beauty was reserved to be their downfall" (Smith 21).

The violation of Spain and its women also finds a parallel in the private punishment of King Rodrigo, who undergoes castration as a penance for his sexual sins. The *Crónica del rey don Rodrigo (Crónica sarracina)* by Pedro del Corral describes this gory episode of the legend in the utmost detail. After abandoning the battle against the invaders, Rodrigo meets a hermit who tells him God's instructions for his penance. He must introduce himself, naked, into a grave, where there is a big, two-headed serpent. Del Corral tells us that, on the third day, "la culebra se levantó de par dél e subióle desuso del vientre e de los pechos. E començó de le comer por la natura con la una cabeça e con la otra en derecho del coraçón" ["the snake stood up on top of him and rose from under his abdomen and chest. And began to eat his genitals with one head and his heart with the other"] (del Corral 403). Rodrigo himself explains the reasons for the choice of these two places: "[e]l uno en derecho del coraçón con el qual él pensara quanto mal él avía fecho. E el otro por la natura, la qual fuera la causa de la grand destruición de España" ["one straight to the heart with which he had thought of the evils he had done. And the other for the genitals, which were the cause of the great destruction of Spain"] (del Corral 403–04).

One of the basic aspects of the story's "didactic appeal" (Burshatin, "The Moor" 125) was the Catholic vision of the severe punishment that awaits those who do not control their sexual passions. Consequently, the stories of the Reconquest emphasize "the obligatory princely virtue of sexual abstinence": the figure of Pelayo is emblematically chaste, since he must embody the opposite values from Rodrigo (Burshatin, "Narratives" 24). We also find here the traces of Américo Castro's observations of how Castile, as the region leading the Reconquest, positioned itself as an example of Christian chastity and purity, and characterized the Moors as the opposite (Castro 285). When Eulogius of Córdoba set out to write his exculpation of the Christian martyrs, he tried to explain to his fellow Christians that the two religions, contrary to their beliefs, are quite different, and that Islam is wrong. He was one of the first in a long tradition of polemicists that dedicated their lives to proving their own religion's superiority over the other. To do so, Eulogio emphasized the sexual, sinful nature of Islam: Mohammed, said Eulogio, was a lustful false prophet instigated by the devil, exercising his lust on the repudiated wife of one of his followers, and adapting the Christian's belief in an afterlife "to meet his own lusty needs until it resembled a brothel" (Wolf, "Christian" 97–100). The Moor as sexual threat will continue to be a constant presence in both literary and historical "invasion" texts throughout Spanish history.[14]

Ghostly Returns

The figure of the violent, lustful Moor, who invades Spain to kill and rape its inhabitants, has haunted the Spanish imagination, aided by what seemed to be "real" repetitions of the AD 711 invasion throughout Spanish history. Like Derrida's specter, which "comes by *coming back* [revenant] . . . a ghost whose expected return repeats itself, again and again" (Derrida, *Specters* 10), the Moor appears in Spanish history through repetition, through his feared and expected return: at the end of the eleventh century, in the invasion of the Almoravids, who consequently took control of al-Andalus; in the twelfth, by the subsequent Almohad invasion; in the sixteenth and seventeenth centuries, in the form of frequent naval attacks on the Spanish coast by Berber and Turkish corsairs. In more recent times, in the form of the mercenary Moroccan troops that fought on the

Nationalist side of the Spanish Civil War (1936–39), who had previously been used by Franco in 1934 to crush workers' uprisings in Catalonia and Asturias and were made wholly responsible for some of the worst atrocities committed in the war when their actions were obviously condoned and even encouraged, it seems, by their Spanish superiors (see Madariaga 296–99). As in the case of the naval attacks, these twentieth-century interventions were also perceived and interpreted as new "Moorish invasions," where much of the psychological terror caused by Moroccans was dependent upon this perception and "remembrance." The Republican side thus compared Franco with Julián and united the two historical events, utilizing each clichéd view of AD 711: Julián's treason, the rape of beautiful Spain and its women, and the bestiality of the Moors:

> Las cenizas del obispo don Opas y del conde don Julián se habrán estremecido de júbilo. No se ha extinguido su raza de traidores . . . abrieron las puertas de España al agareno, que ambicionaba poseer nuestras huertas feraces, nuestras ricas montañas, nuestra tierra incomparable, que deseaba gozar la belleza de nuestras mujeres . . . al cabo de varios siglos se repite su traición . . . sacan de lo hondo de las cabilas más feroces del Rif, los hombres de más bestiales instintos.
>
> [The ashes of Bishop don Opas and Count don Julián have probably shuddered from joy. Their race of traitors has not extinguished . . . they opened the gates of Spain to the Arab, who sought to possess our fertile gardens, our rich mountains, our incomparable land, who desired to get pleasure from the beauty of our women . . . after several centuries their treason is repeated . . . they take out from the depths of the most ferocious Rif tribes the men of most bestial instincts.] (Manifesto of the Central Committee of the Communist Party; qtd. in Martín 176)

Dolores Ibárruri repeated this idea of the sexual bestiality of the Moroccan mercenaries in a discourse from around the same time: "Morisma salvaje, borracha de sensualidad, que se vierte en horrendas violaciones de nuestras muchachas, de nuestras mujeres" ["Savage Moors, drunk with sensuality, that poured in horrible rapes of our girls, of our women"] (qtd. in Martín 181).

Several Republican romances also reproduce this sexual terror, comparing the Moors with savage animals, as Alfonso el Sabio had done seven centuries before. A romance by Al-cázar Fernández, published in 1937, warns: "¡No avances más, miliciana! / que el moro te está acechando / hambriento de carne blanca; / que hasta las bestias desean / morder rosas perfumadas" ["Don't press forward anymore, *miliciana*! / for the Moor is lying in wait for you / hungry for white meat; / for even beasts desire / to bite perfumed roses"] (qtd. in Madariaga 368). In the anonymous "Romance de Villafría" ["Romance from Villafría"], a boy warns his mother that the Moors are arriving, describing them through the same topics: cruelty, violence, lasciviousness. The romance mentions how "siegan niños y mozas / como si fueran espigas" ["they reap boys and young girls / as if they were spikes"]. "La Reconquista de Granada" ["Granada's Reconquest"] by Pascual Pla y Beltrán, whose title bears the play between past and present—using the term *Reconquest* to mean, this time, the Moorish re-Reconquest of Granada—also laments the Nationalist occupation of the city, emphasizing the Moors' attacks on women (Santonja 51–52).[15] The currency of this image was shown when Vicente Aranda, in his 1996 film *Libertarias*, reproduces it in a scene in which Moroccan mercenaries brutally rape and slit the throats of a group of *milicianas*.[16]

In the present, the arrival of large numbers of Moroccan immigrants, and their consequent new presence in Spanish territory, becomes the "recent real repetition of the event" that Freud indicates as characteristic of the awakening of the repressed. He contends that "[w]hat is forgotten is not extinguished but only 'repressed'; its memory-traces are present in all their freshness, but isolated . . . they are unconscious—inaccessible to consciousness" (Freud, *Moses* 94). Freud also explains that, under certain circumstances, the repressed material is able to "force its way to consciousness." This happens especially "if at any time in recent experience impressions or experiences occur which resemble the repressed so closely that they are able to awaken it" (Freud, *Moses* 95). We can thus interpret the special difficulty of welcoming Moroccan immigrants as a symptom. Freud's concept of latency explains how frequently traumatic symptoms appear long after the traumatic event that originated them (Freud, *Moses* 67).[17] A trauma, then, can be "forgotten" for a period of time, and later re-experienced through the compulsion to repeat; a "fixation" on the trauma (Freud, *Moses* 72–76). These elements constitute the condition known today as "post-traumatic stress disorder," explained by Cathy Caruth as

> a response, sometimes delayed, to an overwhelming event or events, which takes the form of repeated, intrusive hallucinations, dreams, thoughts or behaviors stemming from the event, along with numbing that may have begun during or after the experience, and possibly also increased arousal to (and avoidance of) stimuli recalling the event. (4)

The relationship of past and present becomes essential to comprehend the nature of the traumatized condition, marking it as a particularly *historical* experience, "a symptom of history" (Caruth 5), by which traumatic symptoms appear in "another place, and in another time" (Caruth 8).[18]

This generalized difficulty of welcoming Moroccan immigrants is not, however, a symptom of an individual's trauma. In *Moses and Monotheism*, Freud introduces the possibility of historical trauma alongside that of the individual; the possibility that "[c]ultures too can split off what cannot be dealt with at a specific historical moment" (Kaplan and Wang 7).[19] These memory-traces of the past would include both individual material and "elements with a phylogenetic origin—an *archaic heritage*." In this way, "[traumas] are not strictly limited to what the subject himself has really experienced . . . [certain] reactions only become intelligible phylogenetically—by their connection with the experience of earlier generations" (Freud, *Moses* 98–99). In order for a memory to enter this "archaic heritage," the event needs to be "important enough, or repeated often enough, or both . . . What is certainly of decisive importance . . . is the awakening of the forgotten memory-trace by a recent real repetition of the event" (Freud, *Moses* 101). As already suggested, the arrival of large numbers of Moroccan immigrants, and their consequent new presence in Spanish territory, becomes this Freudian "recent real repetition of the event."

Moroccan immigrants, in the Spanish collective imaginary, thus become the embodiment of everything there is to fear from their history, the ghosts of a past that has not stopped haunting them, the return of the repressed. Both literary representations of the arrival of Moroccan immigrants in Spain and social confrontations between them and Spaniards are structured and determined by the perception of their common past as trauma, a perception that has transformed this past into a phantasmagoric presence in the present. Derrida states that "[h]egemony still organizes the repression and thus the confirmation of a haunting. Haunting belongs to the structure of every hegemony" (Derrida, *Specters* 37). In the Spanish / North African context, the hegemonic discourse haunted by ghosts is that which assumes Spain's separation from the "Moors." Ever since the first negative reactions of Eulogius and Alvarus of Córdoba to the high level of intermarriage and cultural, religious, and social comingling of Christians with Muslims in the mid-ninth century, there has been a part of Spain that took as its mission to try to expurgate the "Moorish" mark from the national body. This was done through compulsory conversions to Catholicism, torture and burning of heretics, book burnings, cultural prohibitions, and physical expulsions from the Peninsula. A parallel expulsion was the discursive one, by which official historiography constructed an image of Spain in which the Muslim presence left no traces in the "Christians" that remained, so that those Muslims who arrived in AD 711 would have stayed separated from Christians and then left completely in the expulsion of 1609. Thus, given that the modern Spanish state was constructed upon the silencing and physical expulsion of this part of itself, and the contemporary rejection of migrants who are seen as descendants of those Spaniards of the past, it is not surprising that the repressed history of closeness between Christians and Muslims, Hispano-Romans, Visigoths, Arabs, and Berbers continues to haunt the official, hegemonic history of Spanish national identity.

This repressed Spanish history of closeness, constitutive of Spanish identity, returns in the figure of the Moroccan immigrant. He bears characteristics that can be read as close enough to those of the imaginary invading Moor to be transformed into him. Moroccan immigrants are seen thus as materializations of that constructed image. This return of the repressed becomes a return of part of the forgotten self. The recurrence, the repetition of its return, and its familiar/unfamiliar nature render it into an uncanny phenomenon. Freud begins his essay on "The Uncanny" by explaining the familiar/unfamiliar binary through an analysis of the German word *unheimlich*, which literally means "unhomely." *Unheimlich* relates to that which is frightening, "to what arouses dread and horror" precisely because it is *not* known and familiar (219–20; emphasis in the original). Its opposite, *heimlich*, means both "familiar, intimate, friendly" and "concealed, kept from sight, withheld, secretive." However, this second meaning of *heimlich* extends from something secret, private, to also include the notion of something obscure, inaccessible to knowledge, hidden and dangerous. This extension of its meaning thus is further developed, so that "*heimlich* comes to have the meaning usually ascribed to *unheimlich*" (Freud, "The Uncanny" 222–26). *Heimlich*, then, "is a word the meaning of which develops in the direction of ambivalence, until it finally coincides with its opposite, *unheimlich*" (226). This linguistic excursion serves Freud to explain that the uncanny is, precisely, frightening, not because it is unfamiliar, but because it is something very much familiar *made strange*: "this uncanny is in reality nothing new or alien, but something which is familiar and old-established in the mind and which has become alienated from it through the process of repression" (Freud, "The Uncanny" 241). Schelling's definition of the uncanny, quoted by Freud, points in this same direction: "*Unheimlich* is the name for everything that ought to have remained . . . secret and hidden but has come to light" (224). A factor that undoubtedly produces uncanny feeling, he explains, is that of the recurrence of the same thing. Repetition gives us the idea of something fateful and inescapable, out of our control, and thus it becomes a special category of the frightening: something repressed which *recurs* (234–41; emphasis in the original), "something secretly familiar . . . which has undergone repression and then returned from it" (Freud, "The Uncanny" 245).

As with Caruth's explanation about the status of truth in post-traumatic-stress-disorder, in which she explains that what characterizes an event as traumatic is not the experience itself but its reception, Freud adds to his explanation of the uncanny that it does not matter if what is uncanny and thus frightening today was itself originally frightening in the past (Freud, "The Uncanny" 241). So it doesn't matter if the invading Arabs and Berbers were "truly" the most violent, horrifying sight, as the later Christian chroniclers wanted us to believe (as we have seen, they were probably not regarded as such at the time): in many contemporary texts that describe Moroccan immigration their presence becomes uncanny because the distinction between the imaginary invading Moor of those Christian chronicles and the real-life Moroccan dissolves. As Freud suggests in his essay, the uncanny is easily produced by repetitions but also "when the distinction between imagination and reality is effaced, as when something that we have hitherto regarded as imaginary appears before us in reality, or when a symbol takes over the full functions of the thing it symbolizes" (Freud, "The Uncanny" 244). In contemporary Spain, Moroccan immigration is pervasively imagined through the anachronistic and deforming lens of a confrontation with medieval Moors. This is precisely what happens with time around ghosts, says Derrida: "*time itself* gets 'out of joint,' dis-jointed, disadjusted . . . *Anachronique*" (Derrida, *Specters* 22; emphasis in the original). We are presented with the "non-contemporaneity of present time with itself" (Derrida, *Specters* 25). This "untimeliness," as we will see in the following examples, occurs in the media coverage of the illegal crossings of the Strait of Gibraltar by boat as an unstoppable "invasion," in the episodes of violence that reproduce a language that belongs to medieval confrontations in the Peninsula, and in direct references to medieval invading Moors in fictional and non-fictional texts that are supposedly talking about contemporary Moroccans.[20] When the rhetoric of "invasion" is used to describe the incoming flux of migrants, it not only echoes the discourse that has permeated European views on immigration since the late 1970s. It also awakens and materializes the image that has been carefully constructed throughout centuries and confirmed in its historical repetition of a traumatic, violent originary exchange, when Spain was "destroyed" and "lost" to the Moors. As in Freud's description, the imaginary and the real collapse, transforming the Moroccan immigrant into a centuries-old ghost. His presence becomes that of the specter, "the tangible intangibility of a proper body without flesh, but still the body of some*one* as *someone other*" (Derrida, *Specters* 7). Derrida explains that transformation, such as this one, is one of the characteristics of an apparition (9): a ghost never returns as the same; it changes, returns as other. The 711

Moor becomes the Almohad, the corsair, the Moroccan soldier, the Moroccan immigrant, in a return as other that is, at the same time, the same.

The worst collective attack against Moroccans in Spain, that of 2000 in El Ejido, Almería, can be read, together with the explosive economic and social circumstances that surrounded it, as an instance when the imaginary Moor—that threatening and violent being who comes to Spain to rape and kill its inhabitants—was blurred with the real immigrant. The events of El Ejido started on January 22, 2000, when a Moroccan man was held responsible for the deaths of two Spanish men. On February 5, a young woman, Encarnación López Valverde, died from a knife wound inflicted by a mentally disturbed Moroccan man, who was later detained. Following her death, neighbors in El Ejido began protesting against the "lack of security" in the town. Soon these protests became increasingly violent, with attacks against immigrants and institutions dedicated to giving services to them, like Almería Acoge, Federación de Mujeres Progresistas, and several NGOs. For three days, immigrants were harassed and persecuted, and their houses, shops, and mosques were destroyed or burned (Checa 31–45). The confrontations were condoned by the town and the police, who, extremely passive, did not stop the attacks or detain anyone. The explanation of Juan Enciso, the Partido Popular's mayor of the town, as to the nature of the problem was, "We are Africa's door, and it is impossible to control all these people who illegally enter" (Constenla and Torregrosa 4). With these words the mayor justified the attacks against the immigrants as a "defense" of a town against foreigners' "illegal entry" when, ironically, the region's economic boom is due to the exploitation of the cheap labor available because of migrants' "illegal" status.[21]

The language of physical and verbal violence with which dozens of vigilantes from the town and the surrounding areas engaged the Moroccans was that of violent confrontations of the past, of "la caza del moro" ["Moor hunting"], echoed in the slogans "¡fuera moros!" ["Moors Out!"] and "¡muerte al moro!" ["Death to the Moor!"]. It is through this language of identification, when Moroccan immigrants (and anyone who is Muslim or Arab) are named "moros" ["Moors"], that we can most explicitly see the Moroccans' transformation into ghosts of the past. The inherent violence contained in this naming, and the rejection it implies, is explained in *Dormir al raso*. Published in 1994, several years before the events at El Ejido, it announces the type of violent rhetoric that was used there in February 2000. Describing disturbances that occurred in several towns of Valencia, Alicante, and Huesca (Foios, Puzol, Fraga, Monforte del Cid, etc.), it presents us with the common, anachronistic language by which Moroccan agricultural workers, hired for jobs that Spaniards no longer want to do, are collectively blamed and accused of any incident in which one of them is suspected to have been involved. The language, like that which was reproduced in El Ejido, is that of organized "Moor hunting" (140); accompanied by graffiti of "Moros al África" ["Moors to Africa"] (141). In the section "Me llamo Mohamed" ["I am called Mohamed"], we are presented with the inherent violence of that naming in a dialogue where Mohamed, called "moro" by Salvador, his supervisor, claims his name. Narrated by Mohamed, the dialogue goes:

> —Oye, Salvador, yo no me llamo moro, me llamo Mohamed.
> —Hombre, eso es igual —balbuceó.
> —Tú te llamas Salvador, ¿cómo te sentaría si te llamasen por ejemplo "baboso"?
> Se lo dije sonriendo. Se quedó cortado y se puso rojo.
>
> [—Listen, Salvador, I am not called Moor, my name is Mohamed.
> —Man, that is the same —he stammered.
> —You are called Salvador, how would you react if they called you, for example, "slimy"?
> I said this smiling. He was taken aback and blushed.]
> (Moreno Torregrosa and El Gheryb 124)

Nevertheless, in other moments of the text, the narrator becomes complicit with the Moroccan/Moor equation. This occurs in the case of the rhetoric of "invasion" for the translation of the crossing of the Strait in *pateras* (small, precarious open boats). Under the title of "Los ataúdes flotantes del Estrecho" ["The floating coffins of the Strait"] we are presented with information on some of the repeated drowning tragedies on the southern coast. In order to qualify the importance of one of these events for Spain, the narrator thinks of the Middle Ages, equating current migration with military invasion:

> El 7 de febrero de ese año [1992] desembarcan 300 personas de dos barcas en una misma noche en las costas de Almería. ¡Hacía aproximadamente ocho siglos, desde las últimas invasiones de almohades y benimerines, que no desembarcaban tantos árabes juntos en las costas españolas!
>
> [On February 7 of that year [1992] 300 people disembarked from two boats on the same night on the coasts of Almería. It had been approximately eight centuries, since the last Almohad and Benimerin invasions, that so many Arabs disembarked together on the Spanish coasts!] (Moreno Torregrosa and El Gheryb 57)

In a similar way, when talking about Tarifa and its attractiveness both for windsurfers and migrants' boats, the narrator reminds us of another, much older arrival: "Allí acudió también en el año 710 Tarif Ibn Malluk, lugarteniente de Tariq, que por encargo de Musa exploraba las costas de la península ibérica como avanzadilla de la invasión musulmana. Él fue quien dio nombre a la ciudad" ["There also arrived Tarif Ibn Malluk, Tarik's deputy, who was exploring for Musa the coasts of the Iberian Peninsula as an advance party for the Muslim invasion in the year 710 A.D."] (Moreno Torregrosa and El Gheryb 75).

The novel *Las voces del Estrecho* by Andrés Sorel struggles with similar issues. If in *Dormir al raso* what we have is the inevitable intertext of the medieval Moor as a haunting that will not let the contemporary migrant just *be*, but transforms him into a returning ghost, in *Las voces del Estrecho* the migrants are, literally, ghosts. They say "no podemos morir, sólo penamos" ["we can't die, we are in torment"] (Sorel 26). Through a complex structure of several narrative levels, the novel lets us hear the voices and life histories of those who have drowned crossing the Strait of Gibraltar, and who are now ghosts that tell their stories to Ismael, the town's gravedigger. Ismael lets Abraham, a painter, hear them, and Abraham, in his turn, "translates" them into paintings, letting us, as readers, hear them through him. Ismael explains the situation to Abraham as follows:

—¿Tú los escuchas?

—A mí me dejan, como si fuera uno de los suyos. Soy quien los recoge, cuida, su guardián, como si dijéramos.

—¿Y de qué hablan?

—De sus cosas: de cuando eran pequeños, de su tierra, del miedo que pasaron en la travesía, de lo que ahora penan. Y de su otra vida, de la de antes.

—Antes, ¿qué es antes?

—Antes de que desaparecieran bajo las aguas, antes de que yo recogiera sus cuerpos o lo que de ellos quedara. Me están agradecidos, al único. Yo les salvé, les devolví a la tierra; no a todos, claro, pero a muchos de ellos; cuido sus almas. Es otra vida, pero la tienen.

—Y qué son entonces . . .

—Ya te lo dije, sombras. Fantasmas que vagan por el cielo impulsados por los vientos, sombras que buscan sus cuerpos. Hasta que los encuentren no pueden descansar.

[—You hear them?

—They let me, as if I was one of them. I am the one who takes them in, who takes care of them, their guardian, let's say.

—And what do they talk about?

—About their stuff: about when they were little, about their land, about the fear they had in the crossing, about how they are now in torment. And about their other life, from before.

—Before, what is before?

—Before they disappeared under the waters, before I took their bodies or what remained of them in. They thank me, they only thank me. I saved them, I returned them to the earth; not all of them, of course, but a lot of them; I take care of their souls. It is another life, but it is one.

—And what are they then . . .

—I've told you, shadows. Ghosts that wander in the sky pushed by the winds, shadows that look for their bodies. They can't rest till they find them.] (Sorel 14)

The world of these specters is further explained in an opening epigraph by Ibn Arabi: "Cuando los espíritus vuelan al mundo *al-bazzah*, continúan en posesión de sus cuerpos y éstos adoptan la forma sutil en la que uno se ve a sí mismo en sueños" ["When spirits fly to the *al-bazzah* world, they continue having their bodies and they adopt the subtle form in which one sees oneself in dreams"]. At the end of that page, we find a definition of *al-bazzah*, the world of the text, presumably written by the author himself: "*Al-bazzah*: el 'istmo.' El universo observado entre los mundos de entidades sin forma y el mundo de los cuerpos" ["*Al-bazzah*: the 'isthmus.' The observed universe between the world of entities without form and the world of bodies"] (Sorel 7).

As in *Dormir al raso*, this text also has a clear denunciatory purpose, a purpose that is itself haunted by the ghost of the "Moor." The nostalgia for the past permeates both. After traveling through Tánger and Ceuta, the unnamed narrator of *Dormir* arrives in Tetuán, a space he can clearly identify through its medieval Spanishness:

> Cuando se ve desde lejos la ciudad no sabes bien si te encuentras en Andalucía o en Marruecos . . . Tetuán se pobló con judíos y musulmanes tras la pérdida de Granada, y a ella acudieron posteriormente moriscos expulsados de diversas regiones de España. En la arquitectura de las calles de su Medina, se ve la influencia de los musulmanes españoles.

> [When you see the city from afar you don't know whether you are in Andalusia or in Morocco . . . Tetuán was settled by Jews and Muslims after the loss of Granada, and later the *Moriscos* who had been expelled from several of Spain's regions arrived. In the architecture along the streets of Medina you can see the influence of Spanish Muslims.] (Moreno Torregrosa and El Gheryb 45)

The Moroccan city seems particularly visible through this Spanish connection, existing narratively because such a connection can be traced. If the description of Tetuán as a Spanish city in Morocco in *Dormir* seemed to contain a quasi-nostalgic tone, the voices of the ghosts in *Las voces* have an unequivocal one. The nostalgia for the past permeates their voices, nostalgia for their lives before drowning, but, especially, a deeper historical nostalgia of present Andalucia as past al-Andalus.[22] The leader of these ghosts, named "El Viejo de la Montaña" ["The Elder of the Mountain"], tells the others: "nuestros pueblos, Arabia, Iraq, el Magreb, eran el centro del mundo . . . Y en al-Andalus, donde ahora nos encontramos, construíamos las mayores y más hermosas mezquitas, y los más altivos y elegantes minaretes jamás contemplados" ["our nations, Arabia, Iraq, the Maghreb, were the center of the world . . . And in al-Andalus, where we are now, we used to build the greatest and most beautiful mosques, and the loftiest and most elegant minarets ever contemplated"] (Sorel 84).

This remembrance of al-Andalus by the ghosts of drowned immigrants, which seems innocent enough, embodies, however, one of the most contentious issues in the present relationship between Spaniards and Moroccans. As mentioned in the introduction, this contentious issue is based on the Spaniards' fear and perception of Moroccans, not so much as guests who have arrived in a territory that is foreign to them, but as hosts who have come to reclaim what was once theirs. This fear and fantasy about Moors re-conquering the Iberian Peninsula, so common during the sixteenth century, when the *Moriscos'* unrest was added to North African corsair attacks and tensions with the Turks, is voiced in various literary and cultural texts throughout Spanish history. One illustrating example occurs in Pedro de Alarcón's *Diario de un testigo de la Guerra de África*. After the fall of Tetuán into Spanish hands, Alarcón describes a conversation he has had with Abraham, a Jew from this city who has witnessed the war, like him, but from the Moroccan side. Abraham tells him that the "Moors" thought not only that they were going to win the war in their territory but also that they would continue it across the Strait. According to Abraham, the "Moors" said:

La hora se aproxima en que les echemos de nuestra tierra para siempre. Después nos meteremos en naves inglesas e iremos a desembarcar en el reino de Granada, que ha sido nuestro, y conquistaremos otra vez la Alhambra, y tomaremos a Córdoba, a Sevilla y Toledo, donde duermen nuestros padres, y acabaremos con Isabel II y con los españoles.

[The time has come when we will drive [the Spaniards] out of our land forever. After that we will get into English ships and disembark in the Kingdom of Granada, which was ours, and we will re-conquer the Alhambra, and we will take Córdoba, Seville and Toledo, where our forebears rest, and we will finish with Isabel II and the Spaniards.] (Alarcón 440)

A similar vision is placed upon the drowned characters of *Las voces del Estrecho*, whose prophets promise them that, with patience and hope, they will again become the owners of al-Andalus: "[a]hora lo atravesarían [the Strait of Gibraltar] con sus simples brazos, se establecerían en sus campos y ciudades, soportarían penalidades sin cuento, pero con su piedad y con la ayuda del Todopoderoso un día no muy lejano los vencerían [a los españoles]" ["Now they would cross [the Strait of Gibraltar] with their simple arms, they would establish themselves in their countryside and cities, they would endure unspeakable tribulations, but with their piety and the help of the Almighty, on a day not far off they would defeat [the Spaniards]" (Sorel 107).

This fantasy could be seen very clearly again when, in January of 2002, José Chamizo, who holds the position of Andalusian *defensor del pueblo* ["People's defender"], and is very much respected by immigrants as an ally in their economic, social, and political struggles, gave an interview to the newspaper *El País*, in which he talked about immigration issues in Spain. Answering a journalist's question as to why he thought there was more racism against immigrants from the Maghreb than against Sub-Saharan ones, he stated:

> Es verdad. Es porque el negro sabe que es negro, sabe que llama la atención y utiliza una estrategia de no ser visto; van a su historia, están muy agrupados, tienen sus locales y no molestan a nadie. *Son conscientes de estar en territorio ajeno. El magrebí, no. Por la distancia que nos separa, por los ocho siglos que estuvieron aquí, por la mezquita de Córdoba . . . Digamos que se creen que esto es de ellos.*

> [It is true. It is because the black knows he is black, he knows he attracts attention and utilizes a strategy of not being seen; they have their lives, their groups, their places, and don't bother anybody. *Not the Maghrebians. Because of the distance separating us, because of the eight centuries that they were here, because of Córdoba's mosque . . . Let's say that they think this is theirs.*] (Alameda; my emphasis)

They think this is theirs: this phrase probably contains the most explicit utterance of Spaniards' greatest fear regarding Moroccans. They don't occupy their proper role as guests, they don't have "their lives, their groups, their places." There is not enough distance, there are the eight centuries of closeness, there is the mosque of Córdoba. They behave like hosts. "They think this is theirs." This declaration by Chamizo, which he had to retract after ATIME, the Moroccan Immigrant Workers Association, issued a formal complaint, voices and justifies the Moroccan/Moor slippage that partakes so powerfully of anti-Moroccan feelings in Spain.

Like *Dormir al raso*, *Las voces del Estrecho* equates the crossing of the Strait by migrants with that of past military invasions. In this case, El Viejo de la Montaña identifies so completely with his ancestors, the Turks, that he narrates their 1612 attack on Zahara de los Atunes, where the present-day novel takes place, as if he were one of the invaders: "Qalat al-Sajra llamamos nosotros a este lugar . . . [n]os asomábamos a él con gritos de guerra y venganza desde nuestras costas. Corría la sangre, se elevaban por doquier las columnas de humo y luego regresaba el silencio" ["We called this place Qalat al-Sajra . . . we looked out on it with war and revenge cries from our coasts. The blood flooded, the smoke columns stood up everywhere and then silence returned"] (Sorel 84). Later on, the connection is explicitly stated: "las pateras de hoy no eran sino un pálido remedo del pueblo vencido frente al orgullo con el que El Viejo de la Montaña hablaba de las naves turcas del ayer" ["today's boats are only a defeated people's poor imitation of the pride with which The Elder of the Mountain talked about yesterday's Turkish ships"] (Sorel 89). The immigrants' ghosts are presented as rejoicing in these stories, especially those that highlight [Christian] Spaniards' suffering at the hands of their ancestors:

> le exigían a él . . . que les hablase de ello, eso, eso, las penalidades que sufrieron los infieles cuando ellos eran fuertes, poderosos, y con sus grandes naves dominaban las aguas del Estrecho, y los apresaban, los llevaban prisioneros, y los martirizaban y daban muerte a muchos y solamente liberaban a quienes les proporcionaban suculentos rescates

> [they demanded that he . . . talk about it, that, that, the hardships that the infidels suffered when they were strong, powerful, and dominated the waters of the Strait with their big ships, and captured them, made them prisoners, and martyred them and killed many and only liberated those who gave them succulent ransoms.] (Sorel 89)

El Viejo de la Montaña proudly tells them of the attacks, with all the details of the atrocities committed against the Christians and a gory emphasis on sexual violence against Christian women (Sorel 100).

The ghostly return of the medieval Moor does not occur solely on one side of the border. In July 2000, *El País* published "Cartas de la desesperanza" ["Letters of Desperation"], which included the autobiographical account of a young Moroccan woman who had immigrated to Spain. Her account inhabits, as do those problematic moments in *Dormir al raso* and *Las voces del Estrecho*, the imaginary space of al-Andalus in present Spain. She explains how her circumstances made her abandon Morocco and come to Spain, where she had to turn to prostitution. In order to explain this, she utilizes a peculiar language: "He querido a mi país con una pasión sin límite y he golpeado todas las puertas para llevar una vida decente. Pero la única puerta que se me ha abierto es la que me lleva a abrirme de piernas para acoger las flechas podridas de Castilla" ["I have loved my country with a limitless passion, and I have knocked on all doors trying to have a decent life. But the only door that has opened is that which made me open my legs to receive the rotten arrows of Castile"] (Cembrero 8). Through the references to arrows and to the sexual violence of Castile, the narrator evokes the same discourse of confrontation through sexual violence that filtered through *Las voces*, where the (un)encounter of Spain and Morocco is explained as having originated in and been reenacted through rape: that of La Cava by King Rodrigo, that of Christian women by the AD 711 invaders, that of Rodrigo by the serpent, that of Republican women by Moroccan mercenaries, that, also, of Encarnación López in El Ejido, violated by a Moroccan with a knife. The choice of "rotten arrows" to describe the sexual penetration by her Spanish clients takes us through its linguistic archaism again to the Middle Ages, with Castile also appearing as an allusion to the Christian Reconquest.

As happens with the Moroccan ghosts imagined by *Las voces*, the narrator of "Cartas de la desesperanza" also sets up a contrast between the pride of a glorious past and the degradation of the present. Talking about her boyfriend, she says:

Él, que era inflexible con el respeto de la virginidad, se conforma ahora, tras conocer mi suerte, con suplicarme que no le olvide. Imagínense a un descendiente de Tarik Ibn Zyad, el conquistador, pronunciando palabras tan humillantes.

[He, who was so inflexible about the respect of virginity, is satisfied now, after knowing my fate, with asking me to forget him. Imagine a descendant of Tarik Ibn Zyad, the conqueror, pronouncing such humiliating words.] (Cembrero 8)

In a similar manner, the Moroccan narrator of *Diario de un ilegal* [*Diary of an Illegal*] bitterly reflects upon the current "return of the Moors":

Dijo que España era maravillosa. Le dije que sí, que maravillosa, y que por eso mismo los árabes no soportaron su belleza y se marcharon todos. ¡Y mira tú por dónde ahora se han arrepentido y regresan! Uno a uno. Ahogados, la mayoría de las veces.

[She said that Spain was wonderful. I told her yes, wonderful, and that is why the Arabs could not stand its beauty and they all left. And look at that, now they have regretted it and they are coming back! One by one. Drowned, most of the time.] (Nini 9–10)

This narrator also uses the rhetoric of medieval confrontations in which Christians were humiliated and defeated to establish a contrast to the present situation. Looking at the Andalusian countryside with his Spanish friend Merche, he explains to her what they see as the remains of a triumphant al-Andalus:

En las cimas de algunas colinas se ven antiguas fortalezas. Señalándolas le digo a Merche: mira, ahí vivíamos antiguamente. Merche no comprende por qué teníamos que subir a la cima de la montaña para encontrar un lugar donde vivir. Construíamos esas fortalezas en lo más alto para poder vigilaros, porque vosotros vivíais en los llanos, le dije.

[On the mountaintops you can see old fortifications. Look, I tell Merche, pointing at them: in the old days, we used to live over there. Merche does not understand why we had to go all the way up the mountain to find a place to live. We built

those fortifications on the mountaintops to be able to watch
you, because you lived on the plains, I told her.] (Nini 11)

The troubling aspect of this kind of slippage of the medieval
past in social and fictional texts written both by Moroccans
and Spaniards is that, from the perspective of the reception of
Moroccan immigrants in Spain today, it creates the belief that
those who migrate do so, following Chamizo's words, "to claim
what is theirs," to re-reconquer lost al-Andalus. Obviously,
nothing could be further from the reality of their daily struggles
for economic survival and social integration. As pointed out
in *Diario de un ilegal,* "los conquistadores no invaden un país
sólo para doblar la espalda cogiendo tomates" ["conquerors
do not invade a country just so as to break their backs picking
tomatoes"] (Nini 98).

The equation of past and present, of the invading "Moor" and
the Moroccan migrant, goes much farther than any literary representation, and it has very real consequences in the lives of real
people. Rey Chow, in her analysis of the function of stereotypes
as representational devices (53–54), argues that the "dangerous potential of stereotypes is not, as is usually assumed, their
conventionality and formulaicness but rather their capacity for
creativity and originality" (Chow 58). So stereotypes are not
only clichéd, mechanical repetitions but also—and this is what
Chow stresses—"capable of engendering realities that do not
exist . . . Contrary to the charge that they are misrepresentations, therefore, stereotypes have demonstrated themselves to
be effective, realistic political weapons capable of generating
belief, commitment, and action" (Chow 59). This is the case
with the stereotype of the invading Moor, where the identification of Moroccan immigrants' crossing to Spain as the return of
the Moors produces a centuries-old rejection that can quickly
turn into a reality of irrational hatred and violence. Even in texts
like *Dormir al raso* and *Las voces del Estrecho* that otherwise
denounce abuses and misrepresentations, the ghost of the invading Moor seems an inescapable one. These apparitions serve,
paradoxically, a double purpose. Their invocation by Spaniards
attempts to dilute the most troubling ramifications of the past
regarding the Arab identity of Spain, positing "Moors" not as
an intrinsic aspect of this identity but in a definable space of
otherness, as strangers, invaders, and military enemies.[23] At the

same time, as I have already noted, these ghosts symptomatically alert us to the openness of the past.

This fixation on ghosts might suggest that what we have today in Spain is an unproductive melancholic attachment to the past. However, there is another possible dimension of these spectral returns. Having explained that trauma is caused by an absence of anxiety in the moment when the external stimulus breaches the protective shield, Freud concludes that the repetitive dream (or our discursive "return of the Moor") has a specific function:

> [The reason] dreams of patients suffering from traumatic neuroses lead them back with such regularity to the situation in which the trauma occurred . . . [is that they are] helping to carry out another task, which must be accomplished before the dominance of the pleasure principle can even begin. These dreams are endeavoring to master the stimulus retrospectively, by developing the anxiety whose omission was the cause of the traumatic neurosis. (Freud, *Beyond* 32)

Here Freud points out the psychological usefulness of these repetitions, so that they not only serve the function of indicating that a trauma exists but can also participate in its "cure." Along similar lines, both Derrida and Avery Gordon underline that besides frightening and unsettling the present, ghosts, as materializations of the repressed or the excluded from history, present us with the opportunity of welcoming the previously unwelcomed, of finally giving ghosts a home. Derrida talks of granting them "the right . . . to . . . a hospitable memory . . . out of a concern for justice" (Derrida, *Specters* 175). Gordon ponders the possible transformative power of the encounter with the ghost: "a future possibility, a hope" (Gordon 63–64).

In his recent study about trauma and its historical representation, Dominick La Capra analyzes Freud's conceptualization of mourning versus melancholia and proposes that these two processes, understood as working through and acting out, need not be seen in binary terms, but as interrelated processes (65), analytically distinguishable but intimately linked (71):

> In acting out, the past is performatively regenerated or relived as if it were fully present rather than represented in memory and inscription, and it hauntingly returns as the repressed.

> Mourning involves a different inflection of performativity: a
> relation to the past which involves recognizing its difference
> from the present . . . Still, with respect to traumatic losses,
> acting out may be a necessary condition of working through.
> (La Capra 70)

La Capra explains that there are, thus, problematic intermediary
or transitional processes between the two categories of melancholia and mourning, acting out and working through—conditions necessarily in the middle of these two (La Capra 71).
Contemporary Spanish responses to Moroccan immigration can
be read as precisely that: as elements in a transitional working
through process, where we can see symptomatic traces not only
of an unsolved trauma but also of a nation's effort at trying to
come to terms with its ghosts; attempting, not always successfully, to differentiate past and present, to get past its past in
order to inhabit its present.

Playing Guest and Host

Moors and Christians, Moroccans and Spaniards
in Historical Novels and Festive Reenactments

Era un verdadero moro, esto es, un moro de novela.

[He was a real Moor, that is, a literary Moor.]
Pedro Antonio de Alarcón
Diario de un testigo de la Guerra de África

This chapter examines the relationship between Moroccan immigration and the current popularity of the figure of the medieval Moor in the culture and tourist industry, focusing on the "boom" of historical novels and the multitudinous festivals of Moors and Christians. In both of these cases, the preoccupation with current changes in the racial and ethnic composition of Spanish society is displaced into a distant and safer past, the imaginary and idealized space of medieval Spain's "multiculturalism *avant la lettre*." Both the novels and the festivals are plagued by the anxiety of delimiting, in that past, the concrete space occupied by each group, to ensure that the limits appear well-established. The novels *Moras y cristianas* by Ángeles de Irisarri and Magdalena Lasala (1998) and *El viaje de la reina* by Ángeles de Irisarri (1991) attempt to reconstruct a past in which the domains of thought, activity, and residence of Moorish and Christian women can be clearly delineated. In the same way, the *Fiestas de moros y cristianos*, in which Spaniards reenact Christian triumphs over Muslims in medieval wars and sea attacks, constitute an example of the effort at performatively constructing a clear boundary between the two groups. In both of these cases, the efforts to delimit two clear spaces of separation fail. Moors and Christians become simultaneously guests and hosts in what Homi Bhabha calls a "third space" that is neither one of complete separation nor one of homogenization. These attempts to fix a Moorish other reveal the essential ambivalence of the stereotype in a relationship where the boundaries of belonging are never definitely traced. Encounters, as Sarah Ahmed reminds us, "involve both fixation, and the impossibility of fixation" (8).

In the texts analyzed in the previous chapter, the Moor was distanced through its transformation into a threatening, invading ghost that constantly returns to haunt the Spanish imaginary. The texts analyzed in this chapter perform a complementary distancing by trying to assure that the Moor stays in the safe space of (an imaginary) medieval Spain. At the same time, as is to be expected, these imaginary Moors cannot stay there, and they were never actually in medieval Spain to begin with. These historical novels and festivals acquire their current popularity and circulation because, precisely, the "Moors" have a physical presence in contemporary Spain. The current material presence of Moroccan immigrants inevitably changes the structure of reception for both novels and festivals and produces new meanings for these cultural and social productions.

The Festivals of Moors and Christians

Since the 1960s the traditional festivals of Moors and Christians of the Spanish Levant have experienced continuous growth in their size, showiness, and popularity, together with a gradual increase in the number of towns celebrating them. This double expansion is directly related to the continuous development of the tourism industry in Spain throughout the last forty years.[1] Each year in dozens of villages in Valencia, Andalusia, and Castile-La Mancha, the extreme fantasy of the festive parades of Moors and Christians reifies the fascination for the exotic Moor and for Spain's Arab past. This analysis concentrates on examples drawn from ethnographic research carried out on the Alicante festivals, mostly from Alcoy and Villajoyosa, during the year 2002, as well as from official publications of the organizers and publicity brochures.[2] In spite of local variations, these celebrations basically consist of a symbolic battle for the local territory that results systematically in victory for the Christian side.[3] Like all popular festivals, those of Moors and Christians become a "semiotic battlefield" (Guss 10), where conflictive interests and meanings confront each other. As David M. Guss mentions, "[t]he expanded audiences created by such forces as urbanization, tourism, and new technology . . . may multiply . . . the range of meanings suggested by these events" (4).

The imaginary Moors of the festivals, like those of the novels, contain the two aspects of a typical orientalist portrayal: they are treacherous and violent, as were the imaginary Moors analyzed in the previous chapter, but also sensual and creative. The symbols connoting their violence and cruelty, such as costumes covered with designs resembling scorpions or skulls, and their powerful scimitars and other weapons, are paraded side-by-side with the symbols of their past learning, artistry, and glamour, such as musical and scientific instruments and costly jewels. The festivals serve the purpose of both defeating the Moors militarily, thus conquering their violence, and appropriating them in terms of their creativity and past accomplishments as part of Spain's heritage. There exists a tension between the festive visibility of this imaginary Moor and the invisibility of contemporary Moroccans in the conflicts connected to their reception as immigrants. The popularity and success of the image of the medieval Moor in the festivals and the literary industry stands in sharp contrast to the repeated collective acts of rejection of Moroccan immigrants.[4] These two manifestations have more points of connection than it would appear at first sight. Current episodes of confrontation between Spaniards and Moroccans reproduce a discourse of physical and verbal violence that is also present, albeit in a ritualized and aestheticized form, in the festivals of Moors and Christians.

As we have seen in the previous chapter, when the xenophobic episode of El Ejido took place, the discourse utilized by the attackers was that of "la caza del moro," shouting slogans like "¡fuera moros!" and "¡muerte al moro!" Not far from this rhetoric, in the festivals, the Moors are defeated in combat and then converted to Christianity, or, in the case of some villages on the Alicante coast, they are "symbolically" thrown back into the sea. The possibility of Moroccan immigrants' participation today in the festivals further opens up the meanings of these performances. In an article about the relationships between Morocco and Spain, the Moroccan journalist and writer Mohamed Chakor describes his participation in the festivals of

Crevillent, Alicante, in 1998, in which "ante tres mil personas pedí misericordia para los vencidos; 'Tantomonta, montatanto / el moro como el cristiano'" ["before three thousand people I asked mercy for the defeated; 'It is as important / the Moor as the Christian'"] (Chakor 125). Interestingly enough, he says he is associated, not with one of the "Moorish" parades, but with the Almogávares one, which represents the famously fierce mercenaries who fought on the Christian side of the Reconquest.

The feelings of other Moroccan immigrants are revealed in *Dormir al raso,* where the narrator expresses an unfulfilled desire to participate in the festivals. He says: "Recuerdo el grupo de música árabe que queríamos formar en Valencia . . . surgió la idea de constituir un grupo musical . . . que nos permitiese disfrutar de nuestra música y por qué no, que tuviese su pequeña rentabilidad comercial. Actuando en las fiestas de Moros y Cristianos por los pueblos de Alicante, amenizando y dando autenticidad a una fila de moros" ["I remember the Arab music group we wanted to form in Valencia . . . we had the idea of forming a musical group . . . that would allow us to enjoy our music and, why not, that would have some commercial profitability. Performing in the festivals of Moors and Christians in the towns of Alicante, providing entertainment and authenticity to a Moorish parade"] (Moreno Torregrosa and El Gheryb 105).

Another case in which "real Moors" (not Moroccans, interestingly, but Algerians) participated in the festivals occurred in 1910 when, according to the text *Nostra Festa,* two people from Alcoy were commissioned to go to Orán and hire camels, donkeys, horses, and animal keepers to march in one of the parades of the Alcoy Festival. *El Heraldo de Alcoy* described their arrival, saying that the animals were accompanied by "tres arrogantes moros" ["three arrogant Moors"]. One of them "protagonizó el espectacular acto de la estafeta, montado en un caballo negro, y fue aclamado por el público" ["was the protagonist in the drama of the messenger, riding a black horse, and was acclaimed by the audience"] (Asociación de San Jorge 2: 48–49).

The question of Moroccan immigrants forming part of the audience is addressed in the text *Diario de un ilegal,* which reflects upon this issue when the Moroccan narrator, in Benidorm, witnesses part of a festival. He points to its historical inaccuracy and its one-sidedness, while recognizing, at the same time, its status as constructed spectacle for tourist purposes:

> Esta manera de contar la historia a los extranjeros me pareció simpática. No se pretende recordar a las nuevas generaciones lo que ocurrió realmente cuando los árabes fueron expulsados de Alándalus. La Inquisición. Las matanzas. La expulsión colectiva. Todas estas cosas no sirven para atraer a los turistas. Todo lo contrario. Le imprimirían al festejo un tono dramático inapropiado.

> [I found this way of telling the story to foreigners to be nice. They do not expect to remind the new generations about what truly happened when the Arabs were expelled from al-Andalus. The Inquisition. The massacres. The collective expulsion. All these things are not useful in attracting tourists. On the contrary. They would give the festivity an inappropriately dramatic tone.] (Nini 37–38)

Very soon, however, the narrator feels this spectacle is not meant *for him*. He is, after all, not a tourist: "De repente sentí que mi presencia en esa escena era una extravagancia aún mayor que el torneo imaginario en la playa . . . Volví a casa destrozado" ["Suddenly I felt that my presence in that scene was an even greater extravagance than the mock battle on the beach . . . I went back home destroyed"] (Nini 39).

Perhaps the true protagonist of these celebrations is the excess that permeates all the festive rituals at both the discursive and the performative levels. Analyzing the case of Alcoy, José Luis Bernabeu Rico interprets the extreme pomp and ostentation present in all elements of the festivals as a direct effect of their appropriation by the emergent industrial bourgeoisie, who use the parades as showcases of their wealth, economic success, and the craftsmanship of their industries (Bernabeu Rico 20). But the pervasive presence of this excess, coupled with the widespread affective investment of participants from all social classes, points toward something deeper than commercial opportunity, as we will see. The lavishness of costumes and parades is accompanied by an equally extravagant display of powder and fireworks, and by the participation of an unusually high percentage of the local population and dozens of musicians from the town and the surrounding area. There is also the rhetorical excess of the so-called *Embajadas* [*Embassies*], in which local amateur actors recite a grandiloquent, ornate Romantic text filled with praise of Christian courage and descriptions of the Moors loaded with orientalist commonplaces (Carrasco Urgoiti, *El moro retador* 32). Lastly, brochures and other publicity produced by the organizers of the festivals (to which I will return later) articulate the facts surrounding their origin through extremely complex narratives that aim at justifying an essential, Christian right to the land, while explaining away the presence of the Moors as something temporary and inconsequential. Each and every one of these excesses in every aspect of the celebrations attempts to reinforce a division between Moors and Christians into mutually exclusive categories. However, the overwhelming presence of this excess becomes an index of an underlying doubt, and, by its mere presence, it deconstructs the presumed clarity of the divisions between Moors and Christians that are insistently articulated in every element of the festivities.

In his 1999 work on Emmanuel Levinas, Jacques Derrida uses the ambiguity of the French word *hôte*, which simultaneously refers to both "guest" and "host," to deconstruct the opposition between these two social roles. Derrida explains:

> the *hôte* who receives (the host), the one who welcomes the invited or received *hôte* (the guest), the welcoming *hôte* who considers himself the owner of the place, is in truth a *hôte* received in his own home. He receives the hospitality that he offers *in* his own home, he receives it *from* his own home—which in the end does not belong to him. The *hôte* as host is a guest. (Derrida, *Adieu* 41)

Sarah Ahmed proposes that Derrida's deconstruction of the term *hôte* explains as well the relationship between "native" and "foreigner," reminding us that the "natives" are also "foreigners," aliens to the very place they inhabit. This does not imply, however, that there are no unequal power relations among the groups that occupy the positions of "guest" and "host" in one territory (Sarah Ahmed 190). The festivals of Moors and Christians have been explained as a carnivalesque instance of release from strict everyday behavior (Bernabeu Rico 99) and a space of resistance to ecclesiastical hegemony, where the profane meets the sacred (Harris 48, 59). Reading the festivals through Derrida's and Ahmed's conceptualizations of the categories of "host" and "guest," they can also be understood as a mechanism deployed to clarify, year after year, that the Christian side is the true "owner" of the territory of the Peninsula, the "natives" opposing the "invading" Moors. This semantic ambiguity of the word *hôte* is not only present but also further exposed in the Spanish word *huésped*. In his *Tesoro de la lengua*, Covarrubias collects the two meanings studied by Derrida but, in addition, tells us, along the lines of Sarah Ahmed's argument, that it also means "foreigner": [under *Espitalero*] "Huésped, el que recibe y el que es recebido; y este nombre tiene el forastero que posa en mesón o casa de posadas" ["Host, the one who receives and the one who is received, and this name applies to the foreigner who stays in an inn or a boarding house"] (Covarrubias 557). Furthermore, through the Italian *hostis*, Covarrubias connects the notion of *huésped* with that of an enemy of war: [under *Hospital*] "El italiano llama al huésped y al forastero *hoste*, del nombre *hostis*, que no embargante signifique el enemigo de la nación con la qual traemos guerra" ["The Italian calls the host and the foreigner *hoste*, from the name *hostis*, that signifies the enemy of the nation with which we make war"] (Covarrubias 702). Within the many rituals of separation between the two sides that make up the festivals, there are traces that reveal how the official discourse marking the Christians as hosts is only intelligible if one notes their position as guests in that same territory. During the celebrations, each one of the two groups takes turns at occupying the position of host, with an awareness of the transitory nature of this role, aware that both in the festival and in the history of the area, both Moors and Christians are guests.

Throughout the most visible events of the festivals, Moors and Christians take turns in parading their troops through the city and acting as owners of the castle, defending it from the attacks of the invading other, in pairs of ceremonies that contain exactly the same elements. Each group, Moors and Christians, succeeds the other as conqueror of the approaches to the village and the sword combats, defeating the interim owners of the castle and replacing their identifying flag on the highest tower of the castle. Especially in towns where the structure of the festivals is very rigorously followed, as in Alcoy, there is a striking parallelism between the different roles assumed by the two sides at different stages of the celebration. There is a Christian parade and a Moorish parade, a Christian *Embajada* and a Moorish one, and each group has its exclusive time to shoot their harquebuses around town. In this act of taking turns, both sides perform their double role of invaders and invaded, of hosts and guests. That which stays the same, the territory and its symbol, the castle, contains signs of its prior ownership by the other side. These signs also announce the possibility of changing hands again. In this way, the *mudéjar* castle of Alcoy, or the transformation of the territory in landscape through agricultural utilization and urban design, speaks of the results of a palimpsestic relationship between the two cultures. This aspect of the exchange between the two factions can also be seen in the organization that precedes the festivities. The inhabitants of Villajoyosa and Alcoy say that they become Moors or Christians for no apparent reason, without predetermination, and without the need of thinking of an affinity with the role. Furthermore, there also exists the possibility of changing roles through the years. The important part, say the *festeros*, is to participate in the celebration, no matter on which side. This apparent lack of concern and delegitimization of the possible connections between the characters impersonated in the festivals and their "real" homonyms shows us how the festivals of Moors and Christians present an instance of the vulnerability of the "host" and "guest" positions exposed by Derrida. Moreover, the process of ritualizing these positions in the festivals' context also acts as a strategic antidote that allows a transcendence of the inevitability of being a "guest" in one's "own" place. The festivals try to legitimize the presence of the local residents in their territory, regardless of the subject positions they choose to assume.

Every town that celebrates the festivals of Moors and Christians supposes they are celebrating the "Reconquest," understood as a definitive Christian victory over Islam, a victory that supposedly guarantees the legitimacy of their possession of the territory they inhabit. However, the narratives that explain the historical origin of the festivals town by town vary significantly. In Alcoy, where the largest and most publicized festivals take place yearly during the month of April, their origin is related to a specific battle between Muslims and Christians that occurred in April 1276. This battle has been explained as an essential event in the history of the region, in which the Christians, aided by San Jorge (Saint George), defeat the Muslims. The festivals thus commemorate the anniversary of this date, dedicating it to honor San Jorge. This battle, however, far from being a decisive moment in the fight between Moors and Christians for the territory of Alcoy, seems to have been an isolated, inter-Christian event, engineered by Castile to harass the king of Aragon (Baumann 236). The festivals seem to have originated in the late sixteenth century, related to the local militias in charge of defending the coast against the Turkish navy and Barbary pirates. These militias would engage in *soldadescas* (mock skirmishes) in which some soldiers began to dress as Moors or Turks and others as Christians (Harris 46; Baumann 266). In Villajoyosa, local tradition places the origin of the festivals in a Barbary naval attack on the village that took place in July 1538. Once again, the intervention of the local saint, Santa Marta (Saint Martha), proved decisive for the Christian victory. The festivals are thus celebrated annually in the last week of July to commemorate this event. In other towns, like Ontinyent (Valencia), they originated in 1860 to celebrate the capture of Tetuán by Spanish colonial troops. The festivals have proven so attractive for tourists that, since the 1970s, a number of coastal towns without a tradition of festivals of Moors and Christians have begun to celebrate their own during the summer (Orihuela, Benidorm, Guardamar del Segura, etc.). There are also several indications of a link between the origins of the festivals and the *comedias de moros y cristianos*, a very popular theatrical genre during the Golden Age (see Driessen; Carrasco Urgoiti, *El moro retador*).

The visual closeness between several elements of the festivals and events that usually surround the itineraries of undocumented immigrants further complicates the meaning of the mechanisms that are utilized in the festivals to solve the ambiguity of the relationship between guest and host. In Villajoyosa, as in other towns on the coast of Alicante and Valencia, the military confrontation between the two sides is solved in a spectacular simulacrum of a naval battle that ends in the

Christians' defeat as the triumphant "invaders" land on the shores and proceed to take the castle. This spectacle, known as the *"Desembarco"* ["Landing"], lasts about three hours, beginning in the early morning hours and ending at sunrise. In it, about a dozen ships carrying crescent banners approach the coast, as blustering sounds of exploding powder are fired from the shore, simulating the Christian counterattack. The nocturnal atmosphere of the *"Desembarco,"* the precariousness of the approaching boats, and the military presence of the troops waiting to seize the "invaders" as they land on the coast connect indexically to those other *"desembarcos"* that are taking place currently on the southern Spanish shores. These other *"desembarcos"* are those of the rickety *pateras* loaded with undocumented immigrants that approach the coast, frequently under the cover of night, while the Spanish police attempt to prevent their landing. Observing the special zeal with which the Spanish media reports on the wrecks of these fragile boats, Juan Goytisolo and Sami Naïr have labeled this coverage "el culebrón de las pateras" ["the soap opera of the *pateras*"] (Goytisolo and Naïr 57). News of the frequent wrecks of these boats as they attempt to cross the Strait of Gibraltar and the resulting deaths of their occupants by drowning appear almost daily on TV and in the print media during the summer months. These reports are frequently accompanied by images of drowned human bodies, which have become icons of illegal immigration. The central place occupied by both of these *"desembarcos"* in their respective contexts visually reinforces the concept of the non-belonging of the Moors in Spanish territory. The immigrant "Moors," like the Moors of the festivals, are rendered visible as foreign invaders in the act of their transit from another land and in their arrival as an "other" on the coast of a territory that does not belong to them.

The official publications produced by the organizers of the festivals show this same tendency: their historical narratives render invisible the Moor as an inhabitant fully settled in the territory for centuries, while highlighting the warlike episodes of Moorish arrival or attempted invasion. Because of the work of the Asociación de San Jorge, Alcoy has become the historical epicenter of the festivals and the guardian of the festive tradition. In 1982 this Association published *Nostra Festa*, a seven-volume text in large format organized as an encyclopedic compendium of all aspects of the festivals. The first volume, devoted to the historical evolution of the festivals, begins with a description of the demographic make-up of Alcoy during the Middle Ages. Its narrative contains many moments of remarkable ambiguity and contradictory arguments. It begins by disregarding the possibility of Muslim presence in medieval Alcoy. According to the text, Alcoy was founded in the thirteenth century while Jaume I of Aragón was king of Valencia. The text insists that during the period of Muslim rule over the area, Alcoy was not fully formed as a town: "En época musulmana Alcoy debió de tener ya una configuración no como pueblo formado sino como un conjunto de casas, alquerías, habitáculos desparramados cerca de sus ríos" ["In Muslim times Alcoy probably still had a configuration not as an established town but as a group of houses, granges, and dwellings scattered close to its rivers"]; "Alcoy en los años musulmanes tenía que ser únicamente una amplia red no demasiado tupida de alquerías y rahales" ["In the Muslim years Alcoy must have been only an ample web, not very dense, of granges and farmhouses"] (Asociación de San Jorge 1: 9).

The text also explains the Reconquest as a definite and conclusive moment in time where the demography of the place changed irreversibly: "Fecha clave, perfectamente determinada y documentada, es la de 1245, realmente cuando comienza para Alcoy la empresa de la reconquista, y a partir de cuyo momento el ya importante asentamiento musulmán va a debilitarse y a disminuir considerablemente" ["A key date, perfectly determined and documented, is that of 1245, when the process of Reconquest really begins for Alcoy, and when the already important Muslim settlement will weaken and considerably shrink"] (Asociación de San Jorge 1: 9). A contradiction arises when trying to give definitive meaning to 1245: in an attempt to explain how crucial the Reconquest was, and how it diminished the Muslim population of the area, it is necessary to explain that the area actually was densely populated by Muslims, thus contradicting the previous assertion that Alcoy was not "formed" before the Reconquest. Trying to establish the formation of the town as a post-Reconquest event, the narrative again stumbles upon itself:

Una vez, pues, tomadas estas tierras [lugares y castillos desde el río Júcar hasta la frontera con el reino de Murcia] por
los ejércitos de Jaime I de Aragón y de Valencia, es cuando
los cristianos crean, al igual que lo ocurrido con Gandía o
Pego, un centro urbano aglutinador de todo el término rural.
La fecha exacta es discutible. El historiador Diago, en sus
noticias, parece aducir a la Carta-puebla de Alcoy, documen-
to que aún no ha sido hallado y que, indiscutiblemente, se
convertiría en la auténtica partida de nacimiento del pueblo
alcoyano.

[Once these lands [dwellings and castles from the River Júcar
to the frontier with the kingdom of Murcia] were taken by the
armies of Jaime I of Aragón and Valencia, the Christians created, in the same way as in Gandía or Pego, an urban center
that held together the surrounding rural area. The exact date
is arguable. The historian Diago, in his narrative, seems to
point to the foundational Letter of Alcoy, a document that
has not yet been found and which, undoubtedly, would be the
authentic birth certificate of the town of Alcoy.] (Asociación
de San Jorge 1: 10)

The one document, then, that would undoubtedly establish the
Christian birth of Alcoy cannot be located.

The intention is, of course, to try to give Alcoy a Christian
origin, establishing the right of its Christian inhabitants as the
prevailing one. Because of this, the possibility of the name
"Alcoy" having an Arabic origin is emphatically denied. The
fact that in Spanish nouns the prefix "*Al-*" usually indicates the
presence of an Arabic-derived word makes this task even more
critically important for the authors. The explanation we receive
as to why the name is not an Arabic one does not clarify this issue at all, but rather, it seems to point in the opposite direction:

La cuestión del topónimo es otro problema. Desechada ya,
por inexacta, la probable explicación de que Alcoy es de origen árabe, remedo del Alcoll que Zurita en sus *Anales* sitúa
en el puerto de la ciudad de Constantina, al pie de una eleva-
da montaña en la costa septentrional de África. Mármol, en
su *Historia de África*, y al hablar de Túnez menciona a una
ciudad antigua denominada Coll al pie de una inmensa sie-
rra. Alcoll, el Coll, y Alcoyll son grafías que responden a la
realidad de Alcoy, el Alcoy medieval que se forma al doblar
su primera mitad el siglo XIII.

[The issue of the toponym is another problem. Cast aside, because of its inexactitude, is the probable explanation that Alcoy is of Arabic origin, an imitation of the Alcoll that Zurita in his *Annals* locates in the harbor of the city of Constantine, at the base of a high mountain in the Septentrional coast of Africa. Mármol, in his *History of Africa*, talking about Tunisia, mentions an antique city at the base of an enormous hill called Coll. Alcoll, the Coll, and Alcoyll are words that respond to the reality of Alcoy, the medieval Alcoy that forms after the middle of the XIIIth century.] (Asociación de San Jorge 1: 10)

Even though the text starts by stating that the name "Alcoy" is not of Arabic origin, the rest of the argument provides an explanation that it actually is. The name seems to be similar to those given in Arabic to cities located at the base of big mountains, which exactly describes the location of Alcoy. The need to establish the Christian origin of Alcoy can be read as a symptom of an anxiety about who has the right to the land. The text tries to convey the idea that, even if this was the case in other parts of Valencia, the town of Alcoy itself never had a Muslim quarter:

Çaval o Zaval, Colom, Ontoneda se reparten las heredades del término y el rey lo confirma el 29 de diciembre de 1256, empeñando su real palabra en no dejar establecer a partir de ahora otros moros en estos lugares, ni en el castillo de Alcoy, lo que explica perfectamente el hecho y la circunstancia de que Alcoy no conociera barrio moro o morería, tal y como ocurriera en la mayor parte de las poblaciones del reino valenciano.

[Çaval or Zaval, Colom, Ontoneda share the properties of the area and the king confirms it on 29 December 1256, promising from that point on to not allow the establishment of other Moors in this area, nor in the castle of Alcoy, which perfectly explains the fact that Alcoy was not going to have a Moorish quarter, as occurred in most of the towns of the Valencian Kingdom.] (Asociación de San Jorge 1: 11)

This text suggests a big contrast between, on one hand, the scattered, unorganized, and inconsequential presence of Muslims in the area, and, on the other, the seed of organization in an urban setting, and, therefore, a community with an identity and a will to permanence brought by the Christians. Subsequently, the text itself casts doubt over the clarity of this dichotomy when it presents Al-Azraq, the local Muslim warlord, who challenges the Christian dominance of the area, as a commander of a large and highly organized force. The text speaks of an army of 60,000 soldiers that was recruited in the vicinity of Alcoy, but again showing reluctance to any data suggesting an important and organized Muslim presence, disqualifies the number as "probably an exaggeration of historians" (Asociación de San Jorge 1: 11). Al-Azraq himself appears as a perfect figure on which to project all these ambiguities given his mixed Christian-Arab origin, an identity that the text finds deserving of legendary admiration: "tan importante militar moro nace en los confines del reino de Murcia, siendo hijo de padre musulmán y de madre cristiana . . . su físico era de muy agradable disposición, muy diestro en las armas, de tez morena y de ojos azules" ["such an important Moorish military man was born within the boundaries of the Kingdom of Murcia, of a Muslim father and a Christian mother . . . his physical appearance was very agreeable, very able with weapons, with dark skin and blue eyes"] (Asociación de San Jorge 1: 12).

The contradictory and highly ambiguous content of this text can be explained as an effort to erase all possible traces of Muslim residence in Alcoy. This paradoxical way of writing, that both denies Muslim presence and the history of the place, while leaving enough clues to recompose it, parallels the symbolic structure of the festivals, with their interplay between the visibility and invisibility of the Muslim past. This interplay relates to anxieties about demography and land rights, an essential subtext of *Nostra Festa*, and a pervading factor in the relationship between "Moors and Christians" in the area. Interestingly enough, Valencia, the Autonomous Community with the strongest presence of festivals of Moors and Christians, was the area with the greatest *Morisco* population in the Peninsula:

> On the eve of the expulsion . . . more than 60 per cent of the *moriscos* were concentrated in the south-east quarter of the country. In Valencia, where the concentration was greatest, they amounted to 135,000, or about 33 per cent of the population, one *morisco* for every two Christians . . . In the eyes of the government . . . the problem was aggravated by the fact that the *morisco* population was growing more rapidly than

the Christian. In Valencia, between 1565 and 1609, population growth among the *moriscos* was in the order of 69.7 per cent, compared with 44.7 per cent in the non-*morisco* sector. (Lynch 59–60; see also Lezra 9)

Today Valencia is also one of the communities with the highest percentage of Moroccan immigrants. As Bernabé López García points out in *Inmigración magrebí en España: el retorno de los moriscos* [*Magrebian Immigration in Spain: The Return of the Moriscos*], current Moroccan economic migrants have moved into the same geographic areas where sixteenth-century *Moriscos* lived before their expulsion. There they work mainly in agriculture and services, as *Moriscos* once did (López García et al. 17–20). However, while in the sixteenth century Valencia had 135,000 *Moriscos*, in 2001 the number of registered Moroccan residents was 18,655 (8,545 in Alicante, 4,739 in Castellón, and 5,371 in Valencia), constituting only 0.4 percent of the total population (España, *Censo*).[5]

As with the *Moriscos*, the differences between Moorish and Christian identities in the festivals lie not in elements of race, culture, or religion, but rather in dress, in disguise. As Barbara Fuchs puts it, "to mime [an encounter with the other] is . . . to set the self adrift in a space where identity becomes nothing but props and costume" (Fuchs, *Mimesis* 1). Manifestations of "passing" and disguise abound in historical events concerning exchanges between Moors and Christians in the Peninsula. The preeminence of disguise in the festivals contains elements that either connect or allude to that history. In Villajoyosa the ceremony of the "*Desembarco*," in which local Spanish men and women take the role of invaders by disguising themselves as Moors, resembles closely some episodes of the war against the *Moriscos* in the sixteenth century, in which disguise was used as a military strategy. Pérez de Hita describes how in 1569, for example, a Christian fleet of galleys with sailors and boats dressed *a la morisca* simulated a Muslim naval attack on the coast of Almería. They had the secret intention of seizing those among the local *Moriscos* who would come to the beach to be rescued by their apparent fellow Muslims (Pérez de Hita 260–62; qtd. in Baumann 241).[6] Today, in the context of current North African immigration, "passing" has become more complex. The lightness with which "ethnic" disguises are used in the festivals contrasts sharply with the rigidity of the reception of aspects of dress of Moroccan immigrants, especially when these articles of clothing identify them as Islamic. A good example of this would be the controversy amply reported by the media in February 2002 surrounding the refusal of a school in El Escorial to accept a 13-year-old girl who wanted to attend classes wearing the traditional Moroccan headscarf (which will be analyzed in more detail in the following chapter). For real "Moors" in the present, what could be read as the festive celebration of "Moorish dress" acquires a totally different meaning when worn by Moroccan immigrants, and it is re-semantized as part of the perceived threat that immigrants pose for Spanish "cultural integrity."

In Alcoy there has been a recent change in a central element of the festivals. A large arrangement of flowers now covers the base of the processional sculpture of San Jorge that is paraded throughout the main streets of the city on the last day of the celebrations. The sculpted figure shows the Saint in the act of throwing his spear at a cluster of men who lie with frightened expressions under the hoofs of his horse. Turbans, beards, and complexions much darker than the rosy-white figure of the saint visually identify these fallen men as Moors. The Asociación de San Jorge, stern protector of the tradition of the festivals in Alcoy, has allowed these flower arrangements at the base of San Jorge's sculpture to expand to the point where they cover the fallen figures of the Moors. Small as it might seem, the consent to this change in the tradition of the festivals is very significant if we take into account that the Association has denied the implementation of other changes that could directly benefit the festivals, claiming that tradition was more important than any other concern. For example, it has refused to change the rule that prevents women from performing most central roles in the festivals, and it has also kept in place the traditional street circuit for the parades even though a proposed change would make these acts accessible to a growing public. As flowers are allowed to cover the dying Moors, the violence of the image and therefore of the saint becomes less visible. Even though the festivals of Moors and Christians present themselves as the result of the evolution of a popular tradition that has grown naturally through history, the heavy regulation of changes by the Asociación de San Jorge reveals their constructed nature. As Guss points out, "authenticity and tradition are coconspirators in ensuring that the socially constructed and contingent nature of festive practice will continue to be misrecognized" (Guss 14–15). As has been argued by both Raymond Williams and Eric Hobsbawm, all traditions are "invented," highly selective, and dependent on power relations (Williams 115–20; Hobsbawm and Ranger 1–14; Guss 15).

Apparently, according to some people in Alcoy, the reason for the addition of the flowers is related to the desire to prevent criticism about the lack of sensibility for the victimized Moors. This change also points toward a tacit acknowledgment of a connection between the representations directed toward the Moors of the past, and the present reality of Spain as a country to which many workers from Morocco immigrate. We must wonder whether other towns throughout Spain might decide to modify or remove their iconic symbols of the Reconquest. A highly significant step has already been taken by the Cathedral of Santiago de Compostela. In May 2004, as the city prepared for the Xacobean Year, the Cathedral authorities announced the removal of an eighteenth-century sculpture of Santiago "Matamoros" [St. James "Killer of Moors"] located in its interior. In the context of the Madrid train bombings by Al-Queda two months earlier, the removal was explained as a gesture in order to "no herir a otras etnias" ["not hurt other ethnicities"] and "no herir sensibilidades" ["not hurt sensibilities"] (Hermida). This gesture, similar to the one of covering the fallen Moors in Alcoy's sculpture of Saint James, actually has a precedent at Santiago de Compostela. María Rosa de Madariaga describes the peculiar situation of Mohamed ben Mizzian, the highest-ranking Moroccan officer of the nationalist army. A very close friend of Franco's—he had, in 1924, saved Franco's life—he was appointed Commanding General of Galicia in the 1950s. As such, he had to present, in Franco's name, the annual offering to the Apostle. It seems that in order to lessen the embarrassment of a "Moor" presenting the offering to the mythological "Killer of Moors," the severed heads of Moors at the feet of Santiago's horse were covered by flowers or a blanket (Madariaga 276).

The unavoidable connection between the past and the present became painfully clear in Alcoy when in April 2004 the artist in charge of designing the posters decided to include, for the first time, a translation in Arabic of the posters' text. His intention was "to express the closeness of two cultures that coexisted and coexist in Spain." However, once translated into Arabic, the 15,000 posters read, instead of "Festivals of Moors and Christians," "Festivals of Arabs and Sionists" (Gadea). Next day, a Professor of Arabic Studies from the University of Alicante, Mikel de Epalza, declared that the translation "error" was intentional, and that the translator, of Moroccan nationality, was making a "political interpretation" of the festivals, due to the "falta de conocimiento del traductor sobre las fiestas alcoyanas, en las que no existe ningún tipo de racismo ni enfrentamiento violento" ["translator's lack of knowledge of the Alcoy festivals, in which there is not any kind of racism or violent confrontation"] ("Un arabista"). The intention of keeping the festivals in the safe space of an imaginary, "peaceful," and apolitical past was here interrupted by the inevitability of the festivals' relationships with the "unsafe," "political" present. In a similar manner, in the midst of the crisis over the publication of the European cartoons of Mohammed at the beginning of 2006, another change was introduced in the festivals: in February, the traditional burning of a giant puppet representing Mohammed was canceled in Bocairent, Valencia (see Socolovsky).

The growing presence of Moroccan immigrants in Spain thus radically transforms the possible readings of the festivals of Moors and Christians, questioning the assumed chronological and geographic remoteness that provides the basis for the exotization of the Moor. The festivals also provide a window into the symbolic structures that lie under current conflicts over the presence of Moroccan immigrants in Spain. Like the overabundant bouquets of flowers piled at the feet of San Jorge's statue in Alcoy, the logic of the excessive visibility of the exotic Moor on which the festivals are predicated betrays the desire to relegate Moorish presence to a remote past and to distant lands, thus predetermining the invisibility of the real Moroccan immigrant of today. But the immigrants exist, and their mere presence dismantles this carefully constructed complex of rituals woven over centuries in order to erase all possible doubts about the Christian Spaniards' status as owners of their national territory.[7] The festivals provide the symbolic structure through which contemporary Moroccan immigration is perceived simultaneously as a return to the period of conflict predating the origin of the festivals, and as an announcement of a threatening future. Both are periods in which identities could not be regarded as mere disguises and in which both Moors and Christians were or will be guests in their "own" territory.

Moras y cristianas and *El viaje de la reina*

Irisarri and Lasala's *Moras y cristianas* (1998) and Irisarri's *El viaje de la reina* (1991), both representatives of the Spanish "boom" in historical novels, have had significant commercial success in the years since their first editions.[8] Both texts attempt to represent medieval Spain through the stories of women, who are their narrators and protagonists. While *Moras* consists of the stories of several women organized by their occupation—prostitutes, bartenders, peasants, intellectuals, and noble Moorish and Christian women, *El viaje* describes the journey of Toda Aznar, the Christian Queen of Navarre, to Córdoba, the capital of the Muslim Caliphat, in the year 1000. Through the life stories of these women, the novels construct a negotiation between difference and its impossibility, between the desire for fixity and its impossibility, between the assumption of the cultural separateness of Christians and Moors and the recognition of their interconnectedness, creating a space of ambiguity that tests the limits between the two groups. In the context of an immigration that is perceived as "the return of the Moor," these historical novels attempt to rethink the relationships of "Moors and Christians" in a historical period far enough removed from the present so as not to constitute a direct comment about it. Like the festivals, both texts avoid and engage with the present of Moroccan immigration through the construction of an exoticized, imaginary past.[9] We can thus explain the success of these types of narratives as a displacement of the anxiety—cultural, racial, religious—produced by "the return of the Moor."

Moras y cristianas makes its intention of separating Moorish and Christian women very explicit in its paratextual elements. The title alludes to two ethnic and religious groups that are clearly differentiated: Moors, on one side, and Christians, on the other. The text's structure supports this differentiation: the

115

novel is divided into several sections, each representing a different type of woman: slaves, prostitutes, peasants, etc. Among each of these divisions we find one chapter dedicated to a Moorish woman and one to a Christian one. These divisions speak of the continuity of difference and sameness: although the experience of each Christian woman appears to be separated from the experience of a Moorish one, both are grouped under the same occupational umbrella. The biographical presentations of the two authors at the back of the book underline this separation once more, at the same time that they offer the opportunity to question it: Ángeles de Irisarri is presented as "*the Christian one*, born in Zaragoza in 1947" and Magdalena Lasala as "*the Moorish one*, born in Zaragoza in 1958" (emphasis in the original). As Edward Said notes about orientalist stereotypes, these phrases "are all declarative and self-evident, the tense they employ is the timeless eternal" (Said 72). Irisarri *is* Christian, and Lasala *is* Moorish. Inevitably, some problems arise from these affirmations. Is it possible to identify clearly the identities presented as self-evident for each author? Can Lasala be both "Moorish" and "Spanish"? How does the cultural norm that prevents us from wondering how Irisarri can be both "Christian" and "Spanish" work?

The photographs of each author appear as visual support for the stereotypes constructed around each group of women. "Christian" Ángeles de Irisarri has pale skin, short hair, and we only see her serious facial expression, without makeup, and her hands covering part of her face and neck. Her image seems to coincide with the Christian stereotype of asceticism and sobriety. "Moorish" Magdalena Lasala, to the contrary, appears smiling, wearing makeup, earrings, with long, loose hair, and a low-necked dress. We have thus a typical orientalist portrait of sensuality and exoticism. These paratextual elements, based on the stereotypes of Christian austerity and Moorish voluptuousness, which demarcate separation and difference, are explicitly reproduced in the introduction to *Moras* by Rosa Regás. Identifying Irisarri with supposedly "pure" Christian characteristics and Lasala with Moorish ones, she says:

> Ángeles de Irisarri representa el conocimiento científico, la sensatez, la inconmovible fe y tesón de las mujeres de los reinos cristianos, mientras que Magdalena Lasala aporta el

conocimiento poético . . . apasionados y envolventes los [conocimientos] de una, como los jardines y la voluptuosidad de los ambientes de la morería, sofisticados y exquisitos, que describe; parcos, escuetos y certeros los de la otra, con humor soterrado y sentimientos inamovibles, igual que imaginamos el temple de las cristianas.

[Ángeles de Irisarri represents scientific knowledge, good sense, the unshakeable faith and constancy of women in the Christian kingdoms, while Magdalena Lasala contributes poetic knowledge . . . passionate and enveloping, like the gardens and the voluptuosity of the sophisticated and exquisite Moorish settings that she describes; while Irisarri's knowledge is spare, bare and certain, with hidden humor and unmovable emotions, in the same way that we imagine Christian women's temper to have been.] (Regás 11)

This simplification by Regás coincides with the vision of Spanish culture as pure and homogeneous, with two sides perfectly separated and each intrinsically different from the other. But this vision in the prologue to *Moras* is questioned by the text itself, which, although apparently supporting this view, constructs the relationship between the two groups as a much more ambiguous space.

The first "Moorish woman" we encounter seems to fit this stereotype of unlimited sensuality: Báhar, the slave bought in Córdoba to entertain a Berber prince, "hacía hervir la sangre y los deseos más escondidos" ["made blood and the most hidden desires boil"] and had "la más hechizante mirada" ["the most bewitching look"] (Irisarri and Lasala 26). In contrast, the Christian slave is described through the stereotypes of Christian obedience and sacrifice. Albina, slave of Queen doña Mayor de Nájera, "apenas salía del aposento de su señora" ["hardly left the room of her lady"] (36), and "andaba con la cabeza baja, sin mostrar su buen aire, sin enseñar su rostro perfecto" ["went everywhere with her head bowed, without showing her nice disposition, without exhibiting her perfect face"] (37). The stereotypes of both cultures are reproduced again in the case of the prostitutes. Sihr, the Moorish prostitute, uses her sexual powers to deceive: "finge el más loco placer en el fragor de la relación carnal, para dejar contento a su cliente y cobrar más alto precio" ["she pretends the most crazy pleasure in the carnal act, to make the client happy and charge a higher price"] (47). Lupa, the Christian prostitute, tells us through confession of her harsh life, in which prostitution is justified as her last resource to survive hunger (63), and emphasizes her benefic activities, such as helping Christian penitents in need (67).

Bhabha proposes that the stereotype is "a complex, ambivalent, contradictory mode of representation, as anxious as it is assertive" (70). One of its basic contradictions is that it portrays its object as "at once an 'other' and yet entirely knowable and visible" (70–71), recognizing cultural and racial difference and, at the same time, disavowing it, oscillating "between delight and fear" (73). The stereotype's ambivalence, its contained difference and sameness, is played out in the fantasy of "reforming" the other: "the colonial fantasy . . . proposes a teleology—under certain conditions of colonial domination and control the native is progressively reformable" (Bhabha 83). In our specific context, the stereotypical characterization of the Moors and their "reformability" depends on the possibility of and the desire for their conversion to Christianity. Under that circumstance, they can "change" and become part of the desired cultural norm.[10] It is this mechanism of the stereotype that the novel subsequently reveals, as we find out that Báhar, the Moorish slave, probably has a Frankish or Galician origin, that she has "white and fine skin" and "light eyes and hair" (Irisarri and Lasala 24), as does the Christian slave, Albina, who is of Northern European descent (36). This common ethnic origin for the two women who are initially presented as corresponding to the stereotypically Moorish or Christian "character" reveals the constructed nature of ethnic belonging to one group or the other and, consequently, shows the learned nature of the cultural norms they adhere to when acting as "Moorish" and "Christian" slaves. The narrative both speaks of their difference, and disavows it, fixing it as part of a stereotypically "Moorish" or "Christian" identity in a corresponding section of the book.

In *El viaje de la reina*, Queen Toda herself, a woman occupied with earthly political matters, does not fit the stereotype of Christian piety and religiosity in the way Regás suggests in her introduction. On the way to Córdoba, the retinue runs into the bishop of Oviedo, who offers to celebrate a mass in honor of Sancho. The Queen does not disguise her disinterest: "Toda tuvo que consentir. . . . Tuvo que ceder a los deseos de Su Eminencia porque era malo negarse a un obispo y porque Elvira le recordó que no habían oído misa. Accedió, pues, sin ganas" ["Toda had to consent. . . . She had to yield to His Eminence's wishes because it was bad to say no to a bishop, and because Elvira reminded her that they had not heard mass. She accepted, then, without enthusiasm"] (Irisarri 156). Throughout the novel, she often gets upset with the representatives of the Church, who follow an orthodoxy she does not agree with (255, 288, 316).

Another aspect of the utilization of the stereotype is its explicit and intentional construction of a *separation* that justifies the mission of the colonial power by showing the lack of capacity of the colonized (Bhabha 83). In this aspect *El viaje de la reina* presents one of its constant ambivalences, one that becomes representative of the particular cross-cultural relationship in which Muslims and Christians were engaged in medieval Spain. Although certain Muslim practices are scrutinized and criticized, Córdoba, a quintessentially Muslim city, and the cultural practices and artifacts they encounter there, become a constant source of admiration for the Christians. Cordoban architecture, art, and markets leave them in awe, as do the medical techniques and medicines available (Irisarri 258, 275–76, 321–22).

El viaje begins with the same assumption as *Moras* about the intrinsic separation of Moors and Christians: the novel narrates the long and harsh trip, the risky and difficult displacement that Queen Toda decides to undertake from Christian to Moorish territory. The novel seems to initially suggest that this displacement underlines the existence of two territories that are clearly separated, with a clear frontier that must be trespassed between the two. Said comments that it is precisely this separation that imaginary geography attempts to produce, when a culture decides "[to] intensify its own sense of itself by dramatizing the distance and difference of what is close to it and what is far away" (Said 55). It is this imaginary clear frontier between Christian and Muslim territory that the novel attempts to reinforce through a careful walk-through of their "differences." Toda Aznar's first reaction toward Moorish territory is one of profound admiration, marked by the certainty of difference:

> La reina notó enseguida que estaban en tierra de moros. A
> ambos lados del camino se veían ricos campos, recorridos
> por canales y otras técnicas de riego ... Y en las cercanías
> de aldeas y lugares se veía a las gentes aplicadas a las labores
> agrícolas. No era como en Pamplona, donde sólo se aprove-
> chaba la vega del Arga, y donde los campesinos se limitaban
> a sacar las vacas a los pastos.

> [The Queen realized right away that they were in Moorish
> lands. On both sides of the road you could see rich fields,
> covered by canals and other irrigation techniques ... and
> in the proximity of the villages and hamlets you could see
> people dedicated to agricultural activities. It was not as in
> Pamplona, where only the Arga's fertile lowland was ex-
> ploited, and where peasants limited themselves to grazing
> cows.] (Irisarri 138)

The comparison constantly expressed by Queen Toda between wealthy Muslim lands and poor Christian ones as a sharp
divide between the two territories is always accompanied by
admiration for the work and techniques that have produced
this wealth, seen in a non-essentialist manner (Irisarri 93, 138,
183). The clear frontier between the two territories is also delineated through fear, in the characterization of Moors as military
enemies: although the travelers encounter a friendly reception
by the inhabitants of Medinaceli, the first Muslim city they
come to, they cannot avoid feeling terrified (140). Their fears
are confirmed when, on the way to Sigüenza, they find along
the road skulls and bells from Christian churches belonging to
Abd-ar-Rahmán III's first military campaign against Christian
territory (Irisarri 140). These two reactions, admiration and
fear, mark the Christian point of view throughout the novel,[11]
an ambivalence between disdain and admiration that characterizes Spanish orientalism. The crossing of the Christian/Muslim
frontier is not only a geographical one, but it initiates a questioning of the ideas Christians have about Moors. Although they
continue to be seen as enemies, as the novel and the trip advance,
each people is also viewed in a much more ambivalent manner.

Lisa Lowe and Susan Morgan show how some female
French and British writers defy the received male representations of the Orient to construct a series of comparisons that
link Eastern and Western women by emphasizing their com-

mon experience as women (Lowe 31–32; Morgan 12–16). In a similar way, both *Moras* and *El viaje* narrate this possibility of commonality in the female experience. *El viaje* insists on a description of Moorish difference, but it also reveals the difficulties entailed. On several occasions the Christian women are confronted by cultural practices they cannot understand, and their reactions vary from surprise to horror. One of these is polygamy (Irisarri 169). Bhabha explains how a culture's limits should be thought of as a problem related to the enunciation of cultural difference. This enunciation, in the moment of its appearance, reveals the ambivalence of cultural authority, since it is constructed as superior precisely in the moment of its enunciation, and, consequently, depends on the other for its existence: "The concept of cultural difference focuses on the problem of the ambivalence of cultural authority: the attempt to dominate in the *name* of a cultural supremacy which is itself produced only in the moment of differentiation" (Bhabha 34). In *El viaje*, it is only through their contact with polygamy and their perception of this practice as "cultural difference" that the Christian women think about their own institution of marriage, and explain it as superior, even when this silences the aspects of their own practices that could be easily compared with polygamy, such as the habitual infidelity of their spouses. At the same time that certain cultural stereotypes are reinforced, as in this case, other "cultural discoveries" reveal unsuspected closeness between the two groups of women.

On the road to Córdoba, Queen Toda's retinue finds "un puchero humeante, depositado en medio del camino" ["a smoking (covered) cauldron, deposited in the middle of the road"] (Irisarri 179), a circumstance that contrasts the perceptions of Muslims and Christians: to the Muslims, it seems a danger that should be avoided, while to the Christians, it is a harmless cauldron (179). Ironically, even though the narrative always follows the Christian point of view, the cauldron does end up causing harm: don Aamar de Quiberón, the boy from Bretaña who accompanies Queen Toda's retinue, opens the pot and laughs, making fun of the Moors while saying that there is only incense in it, when, suddenly, the pot falls and produces a big explosion, burning him terribly (Irisarri 180). In this way, an episode that begins by marking the distance between the perceptions of the two groups ends up in a negotiation of meaning in which both were correct: it was just a pot, but the Moors were right to keep their distance from it, since it did indeed cause a misfortune. This episode further unites the two initially contrasted points of view. Aamar dies, in the opinion of the doctor Hasday, as a consequence of his wound's infection. However, both Moors and Christians share the opinion that Aamar has died as a result of a curse by which he was punished, and they agree that the best solution is to burn the body in order to dispel the curse (Irisarri 184). While the idea of the curse was initially explained as a Moorish superstition, at this point in the novel everyone believes it, even King García, Queen Toda's son, who tells them of a dream he has had in which his sister told him that Aamar, "conjurado por el habitante del pucherico, vagaba por el firmamento por los siglos de los siglos" ["bewitched by the cauldron's inhabitant, wandered the firmament for ever and ever"] and that "era un escapado del infierno que estuvo durante doscientos años encarnado en sapo y luego en don Aamar" ["he was a Hell's runaway who had been incarnated in a frog for 200 years and now in don Aamar"] (187). His death textually bridges the gap between the two groups, and the novel speaks now of both "Moors and Christians" reacting in the same way (Irisarri 184–88).

A similar negotiation takes place after the visit to a mental hospital in Córdoba by Queen Toda and her *damas* [ladies in waiting]. During the visit, the ladies are harassed by the inmates, who become considerably agitated (Irisarri 293–96). Wanting to compensate for this disagreeable experience, the Muslim princesses Wallada and Zulema arrest the hospital's director and, after her confession about the lack of care given to the patients, Wallada orders her to be beheaded (298). Next day, the Christian women receive the "gift" of the severed head, which horrifies most of them and makes Elvira, the abbess, faint (297). Once again, the narration initially seems to follow the horror felt by Elvira, who condemns the cruelty and savagery of the act. However, the next thing we read is Queen Toda's explanation to Wallada: "Mi nieta sufre horror a la sangre. Cuando lo supe también me extrañó que no hubiera visto ahorcados, empalados, apaleados o muertos a espada, *como cualquiera de nosotras*, y que se impresionara tanto" ["My granddaughter dreads blood. When I found out I was also surprised that she had not seen people hanged, impaled, beaten to death, or killed by the sword, *like any of us*, and that she would be so affected"] (Irisarri 298; my emphasis). "Like any of us," says Toda: in her clarification about the conduct of Elvira, the Christian Queen reveals that the cultural shock over this Muslim practice is not really general: it is unique to Elvira's fragile nature. The beheading, Toda tells Wallada, is in fact similar to Christian cultural practices.

As a representative of Christian orthodoxy, Elvira insists on seeing, or creating, the separation or distance commented on by both Said and Bhabha. In this way, when the Christian ladies appear happy after an enjoyable bath, Elvira reprimands them, saying that bathing is sinful when done for pleasure and not for the need of washing the body, and that "los baños de solaz eran lujos de infieles . . . . lujos que alejaban a los cristianos de la Salvación" ["bathing was a luxury of the infidel . . . a luxury that prevented Christians from salvation"] (Irisarri 197). The ladies then engage in an argument with Elvira, arguing that they had actually done exactly the same thing in the public bath in Pamplona (197). Once again, as in the case of the punishment of the mental hospital's director, Elvira insists on the strangeness of a Muslim cultural practice, but the rest of the Christian retinue explain that it is one shared in the Christian kingdoms.[12]

As in Bhabha's concept of "Third Space," these texts test the possibilities of clearly delimiting where one cultural space ends and the other begins, constructing a representation of medieval Spain that becomes much more complex than it initially seemed. Bhabha questions our perspective about cultural identity through a critique of the positive value, both aesthetic and political, that we ascribe to unity or totality (35). Cultures, he says, "are never unitary in themselves, nor simply dualistic in the relation of Self to Other" (Bhabha 36). Utilizing Jacques Derrida's concept of *différance*, in which a trace, at the time it is traced, is simultaneously erased, producing a difference to itself (Derrida, "Différance" 23–24), Bhabha proposes that a text's interpretation pact is never simply an act of communication. The production of meaning depends on the interrelation of these two places, production and reception, in a "third space." This space represents the conditions of language—the impossibility of reproducing meaning in a mimetic way—and the implications of enunciation at a moment in particular, implications that the enunciation itself is not aware of. This produces ambivalence in the act of interpretation, introduces ambiguity into the message, and impedes its transparency, questioning our assumptions about the historic identity of a culture as a homogeneous and unifying force. Since a culture's texts are constructed in this contradictory and ambivalent space of enunciation, it is impossible to think of an inherent purity that would be represented there, beyond the possible historical demonstration about the specific culture's hybridity (Bhabha 36–37). The separation of two clear Moorish and Christian spaces that the two novels seem at first to perform—similar to the separation that the performance of the festivals attempts to accomplish—not only lacks correspondence with the historical reality of medieval Spain but also appears to be textually and performatively impossible.

In *Moras y cristianas,* cultural identity is never a contained category, but one whose borders are highly porous. Christian and Moorish women are never inscribed solely as one or the other, be it because of explicit cultural hybridity, or as a result of mixed marriages. In the section about Aysûna, the Moorish peasant, there is the description of two women who are daughters of a Muslim man and a Christian woman and live in between both cultures. They are accused of practicing Christianity by a relative who wants to keep their land, but they respond that they live according to Muslim law. At the same time, they declare that they do not want to do what their relative says and only follow their father's religion (Irisarri and Lasala 77–79). Proud of their mixed education and religion, they want to maintain their own convictions (81). The case of Jammara, the Moorish tavern keeper, shows the instability of the margins of Islam and Christianity through the common practice of conversion. Jammara, who belongs to a family that converted to Islam after the Arab occupation of Granada, points out how the conversion allowed her family to hold onto their possessions and continue their normal lives (95). This affirmation speaks of the practical nature of conversions, the fluidity of the limits between the two religions, and the simultaneous existence of a Muslim identity that keeps Christian practices and vice versa. In this sense, both

Moras and *El viaje* emphasize *convivencia* as coexistence, or living together. In *Moras*, in Jammara's section, we read about how both Christians and Arabs drink together in the tavern, and how "en poco se diferenciaban unos y otros" ["there was little difference between them"] (101). Sîbawayh, the Moorish healer from Toledo, has Moorish, Jewish, and Christian clients (149). In Aysûna's story, we read about the festivals in which women danced together, and Moorish and Christian women shared that common experience (Irisarri and Lasala 76).

In *El viaje,* the initial assumption that the Moors are an enemy easily distinguishable from the Christians is gradually replaced by a vision of greater closeness, in which that threatening "other" is difficult to distinguish from the "us." The retinue from Pamplona finds out that there are three ways of cooking in Cordoba: Andalusian, Christian, and Jewish (204), and that these three ways of life not only coexist, but there is a high degree of hybridization between them. When meeting the Christian community in Cordoba, Toda Aznar reflects upon their way of life and their proximity to Muslims:

> los cristianos de Al-Andalus no tenían otra cosa en común con los del Norte que la adoración al mismo Dios, pero que en sus vestiduras, nombres de pila, modo de enlazar sus palabras con otras y en costumbres eran totalmente musulmanes.

> [the Christians of al-Andalus only had in common with those of the North the adoration of the same God, since in their clothing, names, way of putting words together and customs they were totally Muslim.] (Irisarri 234)

As with the conversions in *Moras*, the Mozarabs of Córdoba from *El viaje* provide an example of the combination of both cultures. Toda discovers through her encounter with the Mozarabs that the one thing that seemed the most important, the belief in a Christian God, is not the only characteristic that constitutes a Christian person, and that these Christians—the Mozarabs—of Córdoba are actually Christian and Moors at the same time.

The Christian visit to Córdoba produces such a heightening of affection on both sides that Queen Toda openly expresses her newly found motherly affection for the Muslim princesses (Irisarri 228, 235). When the Christian visitors are ready to return to Pamplona, and the farewell ceremony is organized, "[l]os mozárabes comentaban entre ellos que a las embajadas de los emperadores de Germania y Constantinopla no se las había tratado así. Nunca imaginaron a tantos reyes cristianos y al moro unidos en la amistad" ["the Mozarabs commented among themselves that the representatives of the Emperors of Germania and Constantinople had not been treated so well. They had never imagined so many Christian kings and the Moors united in friendship"] (Irisarri 325). Even Toda's grandson, Sancho, following the success of his cure, seems to be infected by the climate of tolerance in Córdoba, and "se interesaba por las costumbres moras y judías e, además, ha comenzado a estudiar la lengua árabe y ha gustado de vestir como un musulmán" ["he became interested in Moorish and Jewish customs, had begun to study Arabic, and liked to dress as a Muslim"] (303). The Pamplonese ladies are surprised by the change produced by Córdoba in Sancho, who is now thin, healthy, and good-spirited, and, after his cure, seems to embody the good virtues of both peoples (Irisarri 304). These good relationships appear to be exemplified once more in the trip of Oviedo's bishop to Toledo, still a Muslim city, where he goes "a secarse de la humedad y a tratar con la próspera comunidad mozárabe de la ciudad del Tajo . . . . [quienes] le habían regalado y honrado y dado aceite, joyas y dineros para iniciar la construcción de una catedral" ["to rest from the humidity and to deal with the prosperous Mozarab community of the city . . . who honored him and gave him gifts such as oil, jewelry and money to begin the construction of a Cathedral"] (155). Both Mozarab communities, in Toledo and Córdoba, enjoy a high standard of living, as is remarked by the bishop of Córdoba, who comments to Queeen Toda that, thanks to the tolerance of the Caliph, "tanto mozárabes como judíos tenían la vida mejor acomodada" ["both Mozarabs and Jews had the most comfortable life"] (Irisarri 233).

This familiarity touches a turning point when it surpasses the limit of friendship: Andregoto, the brave lady of Nájera who had always disdained men and was never interested in them, falls in love with the Caliph and provokes the anger of Toda Aznar. Andregoto tries to explain to her aunt that she has spent the last few days re-creating in her mind "la imagen de don Abd-ar-Rahmán, magnífico en su trono del salón de Audiencias" ["the image of don Abd-ar-Rahmán, magnificent in his Audience Room throne"], and that "no podría maridar con otro hombre después de conocer a éste" ["she could not marry any other man after meeting this one"] (261). If her aunt allowed it, and the Caliph wished it so, says Andregoto, she would like to follow in the steps of Queen Iñiga, who married a Muslim emir (262). But Queen Toda rejects the idea vehemently. In the face of this threat of a closeness that ventures too far, she feels compelled to demarcate distances and does so through an enumeration of stereotypes about Muslim sexual practices: the Caliph is a man "que tiene todos los vicios" ["that has all the vices"], "un pervertido" ["a pervert"], "[que] elige él sus esposas legítimas y sus concubinas, según le place, y cuando se cansa dellas las abandona o, sencillamente, si le contrarían las manda matar" ["who chooses himself his wives and concubines, according to his whim, and when he gets tired of them he abandons them or, simply, if they annoy him, he orders them killed"] (262–63). Queen Toda orders her niece to rectify the image she has constructed of the Caliph as an admirable man and replace it with that of a malicious enemy:

> En adelante, te ordeno que retires de tu mente el retrato que has hecho de mi sobrino, que destierres todas las bondades de carácter que le hayas añadido, pues es un malvado y el mayor enemigo de Dios y de nuestro pueblo, aunque ahora moremos bajo su techo por razones muy principales.

> [From now on, I order you to remove from your mind the portrait you have constructed of my nephew, I order you to banish all the goodness of character that you have added onto him, because he is a wicked man and the biggest enemy of God and of our people, even though now we are staying under his roof for important reasons.] (Irisarri 263)

This interesting order encapsulates the ambivalence of the Christian perception of the Moors. The need to remember that they are in enemy territory arises from their fascination and infatuation with them. The representational nature of the stereotype is explicitly stated when Toda orders her niece to modify and replace her constructed image of the Caliph with a different, negative, one. The Caliph must constantly be viewed as an enemy and a stranger in order for Toda to assure herself of her own Christian identity ("he is . . . the biggest enemy of God and of our people"). As Sarah Ahmed reminds us, "identity does not simply happen in the privatized realm of the subject's relation to itself. Rather, in daily meetings with others, subjects are perpetually reconstituted: the work of identity formation is never over, but can be understood as the sliding across of subjects in their meetings with others" (7).

The difficulty of maintaining this necessary distance, however, is also made explicit when we are reminded that Al Nasir, the powerful Caliph, is the nephew of Queen Toda, a relationship that the text remarks upon once and again: "voy a reconocer a mi sobrino, don Abd-ar-Rahmán, como mi soberano" ["I will recognize my nephew, don Abd-ar-Rahmán, as my sovereign"] (101); "todo había sido empeño de su sobrino, el emir, ahora califa" ["everything was the effort of her nephew, the Emir, now Caliph"] (123); "Toda encontró a su sobrino muy avejentado" ["Toda found her nephew very mature"] (198–99). Toda Aznar remembers other family links between the Caliph's family and hers, such as the case of Queen Iñiga, widow of her father, who was given as wife to Al Nasir's grandfather (150). The text vacillates, together with Queen Toda, between the thought of Al Nasir and the Moors as strangers or as part of her family, as enemies or friends. When she presents herself to render homage to the Caliph, she tells him "te deseo muchos días de dicha, que seas feliz hasta la muerte, sobrino" ["I wish you many days of joy, and to be happy until the end, my nephew"], but soon she realizes she is speaking to her enemy and regrets her kind words (201). When her nieces argue about which is the true religion in front of the Moorish princesses, Toda gets upset and clarifies for them that "Dios y Alá pueden ser enemigos o no, que no lo sabe ningún nacido, pero los reyes que lo representan y sirven en esta tierra, son amigos" ["God and Allah can be enemies or not, that nobody knows, but the kings that represent them and serve them on this earth are friends"] (Irisarri 230–31). Once again, this pronouncement by Toda reveals the intrinsic ambivalence of trying to name that "other" that is both friend and enemy at the same time. In order to explain their relationship, Toda uses the Christian notion of God and Allah as two separate (and perhaps confronted) entities, a notion that the Muslims would not agree with. This seems to reinforce the distance of Christians and Moors and the impossibility of *convivencia*, since the other cannot be named without being also negated. However, at the same time, Queen Toda's phrase affirming their friendship contains the performative power of her authority: if the Queen says it is so, it means the two groups *are* friends.

We cannot forget that this notion of pacific *convivencia* and friendship between Moors and Christians—even taking into account the constant ambivalence of its representation—contains a high degree of idealization and fantasy projection. Spanish national identity has been constituted for so long through the rejection of its non-Christian elements that we are not surprised to read in *Moras y cristianas* that Irisarri is "Spanish" and "Christian" at the same time, but we wonder how it is possible that Lasala can be "Spanish" and "Moorish" at the same time. Moorish and Christian identities coexist in these texts in that "third space" theorized by Bhabha, an "in-betweenness" which consists of neither the simple separation of the two groups as strangers and opposites, nor of their homogenization. In the same way Queen Toda is unsure whether she should see the Caliph as nephew, ally, enemy, or monster, and she cannot truly decide what this man means to her. These texts expose the mixed relationships between Moors and Christians by separating and connecting them at the same time, needing the "others" to speak of the "ones." Sarah Ahmed explains how "the stranger is an effect of processes of inclusion and exclusion, or incorporation and expulsion, that constitute the boundaries of bodies and communities" (6). The imagined medieval Moors of these novels, like those of the festivals, are produced as a new negotiation of belonging takes place in contemporary Spain, once again testing the boundaries of what it means to be a Spaniard. The enormous popularity of both historical novels and festive reenactments speaks to us about the enormous appeal of an apparently simplified vision of history, in which these boundaries are clearly traced.

Chapter Four

Impossible Love

The Presumed Incompatibility of
Islam and (European) Spain

The European (mostly retirees) and Latin American (mostly political) immigrants of the 1970s and early 1980s were seen as generally belonging to the same "cultural traditions" as Spaniards. In contrast, the arrival of African and North African immigrants in the late 1980s and 1990s were received with increasing concern, as they were seen as a "foreign" population, without close cultural, religious, or linguistic ties to Spain. This chapter analyzes the love stories between Spanish women and immigrant men in current Spanish film and fiction as a symptom of Spain's "locational uneasiness" between Europe and North Africa. Even though these texts strive to show positive images of immigrants, they reveal, through failed romance plots, a profound anxiety about racial/cultural contagion and miscegenation.

One of the synthesizing focuses of the "Moroccan problem" is the increasingly popular argument that these immigrants belong to a very different cultural tradition and therefore cannot be easily integrated into Spanish society. This belief partakes of the phenomenon that several critics have called European "new racism." Analyzing the discourses of British right-wing politicians, Martin Barker argued in the 1980s that they displayed a new racism that was based not on notions of biological superiority but on what he called a "pseudo-biological culturalism" (Barker 23). This meant that it was "in our biology, our instincts, to defend our way of life, traditions and customs against outsiders—not because they are inferior, but because they are part of different cultures" (Barker 23–24). Outsiders were the main targets of this "new racism" because, as explained by Étienne Balibar some years later in analyzing the French case, "the category of *immigration* [is used] as a substitute for the notion of race" (20). New racism

> is a racism whose dominant theme is not biological heredity
> but the insurmountability of cultural differences, a racism
> which, at first sight, does not postulate the superiority of
> certain groups or peoples in relation to others but "only" the
> harmfulness of abolishing frontiers, the incompatibility of
> life-styles and traditions. (Balibar 21)[1]

This new or *differentialist* racism, which justifies racist conduct, propagates the notion that cultures exist as isolated capsules whose wellbeing depends on the maintenance of limits with other, "foreign" cultures, and, consequently, that the best way to avoid racism is to maintain "cultural distances" (Balibar 22). Through this form of cultural nationalism, national barriers become naturalized, as if it were "human nature" to form bounded communities who feel threatened by outsiders (Barker 2, 21; Gilroy 2).[2]

This culturalist racism is especially pertinent in the case of Muslim immigrants, whose cultural traditions are seen as "Islamic," and therefore as incompatible with the supposedly democratic, modern, secular values of Western Europe (see Balibar 23–24; Asad 11–17; Ballard 36–40), a view that is shared, in its different national contexts, not only by the right, but by the whole political spectrum (Asad 11–12; see also Nederveen Pieterse 6). Jan Nederveen Pieterse has argued that "[t]he keynote in the self-assessments of Europe remains that of modernity . . . the common European interpretation of 'fundamentalist Islam' is as a revolt against modernity (that is, against Europe)" (8).[3] This particular understanding of modernity, as that which differentiates Europe from Islam, then, becomes the evaluating parameter of choice to show Spain's allegiance to Europe and its distance from those encompassed under the broad heading of "Moors."

Since 1990, Spanish cinema has produced a variety of stories centering on African and North African immigrants' lives.[4] Most of these films—*Las cartas de Alou* [*Letters from Alou*] (Montxo Armendáriz, 1990), *Bwana* (Imanol Uribe, 1996), *Saïd* (Llorenç Soler, 1998)—show their difficult arrival in Spain and the racism they encounter and try to denounce, with differing results, and the abuses immigrants face. In later films, such as *En construcción* [*Under Construction*] (José Luis Guerín, 2001), *Poniente* [*West*] (Chus Gutiérrez, 2002), *Tomándote* [*Two for Tea*] (Isabel Gardela, 2000), and *Susanna* (Antonio Chavarrías, 1996), the focus shifts from the dramas of arrival and the threat of police persecution and deportation to the depiction of immigrants' daily lives and work in Spain as their home. In order to explain the difficulties Spaniards and immigrants face when confronted with each other, these films (with the exception of *En construcción*, where the Moroccan workers are not the center of the narrative) resort to the convention of intercultural romance. The pattern they follow is that of the impossible romance between an immigrant man and a Spanish woman: in *Las cartas de Alou*, its protagonist, an immigrant from Senegal, falls in love with Carmen, the daughter of a bar owner in the Catalan *maresme*. In *Bwana*, the film makes allusions to the sexual fantasies that the African immigrant, Ombasi, awakens in Dori, the unsatisfied mother and housewife. In *Saïd* a Moroccan immigrant struggling to make a living in Barcelona falls in love with Ana, a Spanish journalism student who is writing an article about immigrants' lives in Barcelona. The romance in *Poniente* develops between two Spaniards, Lucía and Curro, but the close friendship between Curro and Adbendi, a Moroccan immigrant who has lived in Almería for several years, follows the same pattern. In *Tomándote* the focus of the film is the romance between Gabi, a liberated young writer, and Jalil, a conservative Indian immigrant who works in a flower shop, whereas in *Susanna* a love triangle develops between Susanna, a rehabilitated drug addict, Álex, her married lover, and Saïd, a Moroccan immigrant who works in a butcher shop.

The conventional narrative of heterosexual romance has been the object of many critiques. First and early second wave feminists (Kollontai, Beauvoir, Comer, Firestone, Greer) were extremely critical of romance narratives, which they saw as helping to justify women's subordination to men, rendering them complicit in that subordination, and diverting their energy from more productive endeavors (Jackson 50). Romance, however, has successfully survived these critiques and remains immensely popular: "the trappings of 'classic romance' . . . remain as commercially viable as ever" (Pearce and Stacey 11).[5] The intercultural or interracial romance adds extra "excitement" to this commercial formula, since "[i]nterracial love has a complex relationship with romance, being in a sense still forbidden love, even if it is no longer prohibited" (Perry 173).[6] This "extra-excitement" becomes probably the main reason why in the filmic version of Josep Lorman's novel *La aventura de Saïd* there is a conspicuous additional emphasis on the topic of interracial love. In the novel, the Spanish female protagonist, Ana, is presented as a journalist writing a piece on Moroccan immigrants' lives in Barcelona. She wants to know about their reasons for having left Morocco, and the difficulties they experienced after their arrival. In the film, after interviewing Saïd and Ahmed, Ana tells them she would also be interested in "meeting Moroccans who have gotten married to Spanish girls, or the other way around" ["También me gustaría conocer a marroquíes que se hayan casado con chicas de aquí, y al revés"]. An added dialogue between Saïd and his friend Taïb, who lives with a Spanish woman, highlights the film's interest in interracial romance: Saïd asks Taïb whether his Spanish girlfriend and he have a difficult time understanding each other, since she is "European" and he is Moroccan, and therefore, they are "different."

The romantic relationships between North African, African, or Asian immigrants and Spaniards portrayed in contemporary Spanish films, however, consistently end in failure. Even in films like *Las cartas de Alou* or *Saïd*, where the reason for this failure is the immigrants' illegal status, and the consequent deportation that ensues when the police catch them without papers, there are glimpses of other, stronger obstacles in these relationships. In all the films, Spanish males intervene as protectors of a hegemonic sexual order in which Spanish women should not attempt to choose any other but a Spanish male as a sexual or romantic partner. This intervention often functions as a complement or as a substitute for the Spanish state's policing of its immigration laws. Unfortunately, all the films sanction this policing, allowing one obstacle or another to precipitate the end of the romance, and in so doing, they unwittingly endorse the belief in the relationship's impossibility.

In *Las cartas de Alou*, Alou and Carmen's relationship develops in secret, since Carmen's father strongly disapproves of the romance. One Sunday, as Alou is saying good-bye to Carmen in the Barcelona train station, he is arrested by the police and subsequently deported. Their relationship presumably ends at this point (although this is the only film where we cannot be completely sure, since Alou will try, at the end of the film, to come back to Spain and to Carmen). The arrest occurs right after Carmen has promised him she will talk with her father about their relationship. As observed by Molina Gavilán and Di Salvo, "[a]lthough Alou is presumably arrested for not having an approved work contract, the film points to another reason why he must be deported. His arrest comes at the very point that his relationship with Carmen threatens to become visibly real." The romance, then, stops before becoming public and being put to the test. The film and audience have an investment in its success, but the film substitutes the circularity of the migration plot for the more linear happy ending.

In *Bwana* the romance occurs at the level of Dori's erotic fantasies with Ombassi. The film prevents this imaginary transgression from becoming anything close to a reality precisely at the moment when Dori decides to act upon her fantasies, in a way similar to the moment when Carmen decides to confront her father in *Las cartas de Alou*. The brief encounter between Ombassi, who at sunrise jumps in the water to swim naked, and Dori, who joins him, is immediately interrupted by the skinheads' policing of Spanish racial/sexual frontiers (see Molina Gavilán and Di Salvo; Santaolalla, "Close Encounters"). Ombassi is hunted down and presumably brutally castrated.[7] The obstacles in *Saïd* also involve an attack by a group of skinheads who cannot stand the sight of a Spanish woman with a "Moor." Having survived this attack, Saïd is later detained by the police when they find him without papers. Like Alou's relationship with Carmen, Saïd and Ana's romance is interrupted and presumably ends with his deportation back to Morocco. This time, however, Saïd has no intention of returning to Spain. Even on the level of its secondary characters, *Saïd* is more pessimistic than *Las cartas de Alou* about the future of intercultural romance. In *Las cartas de Alou* at least the interracial secondary couple, Mulai and Rosa, do stay together; they even have a child together, a possibility that does not recur in any immigration film to the present day. In *Saïd*, however, the romance between Taïb, a Moroccan man, and Sonia, a Spanish woman, also falls apart (this breakup also constitutes an addition to the plotline of the novel, where this relationship is left in suspense). The impossibility of these relationships is also emphasized in *Poniente*. When the conflict over the immigrants' demands for better working conditions begins and racial tensions rise, the friendship between Curro and Adbendi ends in a scene that underlines their differences and seeming incompatibility of interests. In trying to explain to Curro his involvement in the immigrants' protest, Adbendi tells him, "no puedo cruzarme de brazos y mirar lo que pasa . . . ¿Tú sí?" ["I can't cross my arms and pretend nothing is happening . . . Can you?"]. When Curro answers, "Sí" ["Yes"], Adbendi's summarizing conclusion is, "Tenemos las mismas raíces pero estamos hechos de diferente manera" ["We have the same roots but we are made in a different way"]. These recurring failures, especially when the films' intent is a denunciation of racism and discrimination, cannot be separated from a fundamental belief in the incompatibility of immigrant and Spaniard. This incompatibility, only hinted at in these films, is explicitly developed in two more recent features, the comedy *Tomándote* and the thriller *Susanna*.

Tomándote and *Susanna*

What makes *Tomándote* and *Susanna* especially interesting is how the two films use the convention of romance to explore Barker's and Balibar's notion of a new racism based on the belief in the insurmountability of cultural differences and the need to preserve "one's own" identity from all forms of mixing. In both films, the male character (both Muslim, though one is Indian, and the other Moroccan) falls in love with a young Spanish woman. In each case, their romantic relationship is rendered impossible because of "cultural differences." The crucial difference, not surprisingly, is that the men are "Muslim" (i.e., conservative, oppressive to women) and the women "Spanish" (i.e., liberated, modern, secular). Both films also give us an opportunity to measure Spanish anxiety in relation to, precisely, its status as a liberated, modern, secular, "European" nation.

In *Tomándote*, the female character, Gabi, is a young Catalan writer whose first novel has just won the top prize for erotic literature, the *Premio "La Sonrisa Vertical."* Created in real life in 1977 by Luis García Berlanga, as director of a collection by the same name,[8] the prize was seen by many as an icon of the newly found sexual liberation of women in Post-Franco Spain. Played by Nuria Prims, the same actress who plays Ana in *Saïd*, Gabi falls in love with Jalil, who is Indian, Muslim, and works at a flower shop in Barcelona. In his visits to the apartment where Gabi is staying, they engage in a series of what seem like intercultural interviews, each stating his and her opinion on love, sex, and relationships. Very soon the two seemingly incompatible lifestyles become obvious: Jalil has only had sex twice, believes in having sex only when one is in love, and wants to settle down with a "nice" girl, get married, and have children. Gabi has had sex more times than she can remember, in threesomes and with both men and women, and she wants to keep experimenting, in search of material for her second novel. This obvious contrast between the two was intentionally sought by director Isabel Gardela, who stated in an interview that she was primarily interested in the opposite views on life of the two main characters. She says: "Lo que me interesaba, sobre todo, era la oposición entre las miradas sobre la vida de cada uno de ellos. Por eso son tan diferentes. Y eso era lo que me apetecía narrar" ["What interested me most was the opposition between the views on life of each of them. That is why they are so different. This is what I wanted to show"]. Furthermore, Gardela finds this "opposition" between the two to be of real-life quality: "Es la vida misma, es la relación entre dos personas: una que es cristiana (entre comillas, porque no es practicante) y él que es musulmán (y practicante)" ["It is life itself, it is the relationship between two people: one who is Christian (between quotation marks, because she is not a practicing Christian) and him, who is Muslim (and a practicing Muslim)"] (Páez).

In the meetings between the two, Jalil seems to be the one interviewing Gabi, since it is he who starts questioning her about every aspect of her life. But in reality it is Jalil who is truly being interviewed, since *his* beliefs are the ones being judged. Partly because the film takes Gabi's perspective, showing her surprise and disbelief at Jalil's opinions, she occupies the subject position and becomes the narrative source of rationality and common sense. In contrast, Jalil's behavior is constantly rendered strange; it is hard to understand the motivations for his actions and to agree with his views. The editing of these interviews shows a curious play of the shot-reverse-shot technique in which long close-ups of Jalil explaining his points of view are frequently interrupted by reaction shots of Gabi showing her playful disbelief and amazement at the ideas he expresses. In these encounters, Jalil gets "othered" as a conservative Muslim on the basis of their contrasting views offered on a variety of topics: sex, relationships, short hair, dress, smoking, drugs, alcohol. Predictably, Jalil becomes jealous and warns Gabi he will not see her again if she sees another man. He announces very early on that he does not like pornography, prostitutes, or short hair, prohibits her from saying certain words, and admonishes her for smoking and drinking.

Through the connection of conservatism, sexism, and Islam, Jalil is further typified as "*moro.*" In a scene with her new friend and hashish provider, Mai, Gabi complains about Jalil's austerity when it comes to smoking and alcohol. Mai's response is that she is not surprised, since he is, after all, a "*moro,*" meaning, basically, that he is controlling and oppressive, a connotation that is picked up in the English subtitles, where "*moro*" is directly translated as "sexist." It is in this scene that Jalil's nationality as an Indian is explicitly subsumed under the category of "Moor," the main category at play in the Spanish imaginary about otherness.[9] The uneasy conflation of the categories of "Indian" and "Moor" remains, however, at the core of Jalil's character and explains the otherwise confusing contradictions he embodies. Although, on one hand, he reveals to Gabi his very conservative views about sex and women, as any "Moor" would, on the other hand, the relationship they develop is a highly sexual one. Most of his appeal for Gabi resides in what she sees as a highly sophisticated, Oriental, non-Christian, and specifically Indian practice of physical pleasure, "Kama Sutra style" (to which the title alludes in an orientalist way, *Tomándote* meaning both taking or drinking tea and sexually "taking" you). The simultaneous attraction and rejection Jalil inspires in Gabi—and presumably in the audience—because of this contradiction is reflected in the unconsciously revealing story director Gardela tells relating to the casting of Jalil's character. She says:

En Barcelona hay una zona, en La Rambla, en donde está lleno de pakistaníes e indios musulmanes . . . colgamos carteles buscando "actor musulmán para protagonizar una película," pero no vino nadie . . . pusimos nuevos carteles buscando "musulmán para protagonizar una película" y empezaron a venir. *Yo quería un personaje atractivo y no había ninguno, no llegaban a cumplir las condiciones necesarias . . .*

Yo tengo una amiga que es actriz y trabaja en una agencia de *casting* y se me ocurrió pedirle que me ayudara . . . Resulta que por la misma calle donde está la agencia andaba Zack Qureshi, que luego hace el personaje de Jalil. Ella lo paró y le preguntó . . . Yo cuando lo vi al entrar en mi despacho me dije "joder, esto ya tiene buena pinta, éste está muy bien." Le hice la prueba, y *como él es un chico muy listo, muy natural, no me costó nada trabajar con él . . . Pero él es más inglés que indio, entonces es muy cool. Enseguida entendió lo que tenía que hacer, no me dio ningún problema. Se aprendió los diálogos, hacía los matices que yo le pedía, estuvo muy bien.*

[In Barcelona there is a neighborhood, in La Rambla, which is full of Pakistanis and Muslim Indians . . . We hung up flyers looking for "Muslim actor to star in a movie," but nobody came . . . We put up new flyers looking for "Muslim to star in a movie" and they began to come. *I wanted an attractive character, but there was nobody, they didn't fulfill the necessary conditions . . .*

I have a friend who is an actress and works for a casting agency so I thought of asking her for help . . . It ended up that Zack Qureshi, who plays Jalil, used to walk around the same street where the agency is located. She stopped him and asked him . . . When I saw him come into my office I thought, "Shit, this already looks good, this one looks really good." We had an audition, and *since he is a very smart, very natural guy, it wasn't an effort to work with him . . . But he is more English than Indian, so he is really cool* [in the original]. *He immediately understood what he had to do; he didn't give me any trouble. He learned the dialogues, he found the subtle differences that I asked him to, he was very good.*] (Páez; my emphasis)

If it was impossible to find a Muslim man that Gardela *liked* in immigrants' neighborhoods, the (attractive) answer was found in a very different type of immigrant, glamorous enough because, precisely, of his "un-Moorishness:" a "cool" *British* Indian, hence at least partly European and "modern," who knew perfectly well what to do because, we suppose, of his "cool-ness," presumably not shared by "Spanish" immigrants.

The relationship between Jalil and Gabi deteriorates and finally ends when Gabi announces to Jalil she has found the ma-terial she needs for her second novel in their relationship. Jalil becomes angry and reminds her that he wants a girl to marry, and if it is not Gabi, then she should find him someone else, let-ting her also know her sister could be a possibility. Gabi does write her second novel, with the help of a professor of Islamic Studies. The novel's presentation becomes a performance of the presumed exoticism of the book's content, with Gabi having "gone native," wearing an Indian sari and serving tea in a room decorated with Mudejar mosaics, designed to suggest a Spanish performance of the Orient. There Gabi meets the professor's wife, the presumed origin of his interest in Islamic culture, wearing a Muslim headscarf, a visual reminder of what Gabi—and the audience—are led to believe would have been Gabi's future if she had stayed with Jalil. At this point Gabi meets her next love interest, the Argentinean Guillermo Ríos. The cul-tural closeness between them is emphasized by the ending of the film, where we realize that a year after their first encounter, he has played on Gabi the same "trick" she played on Jalil, turning their love affair into the content of his novel, entitled *Más boluda que macanuda* ["More silly than great"]. Even as Guillermo and his title are presented in a highly stereotypical fashion (the title, not making much sense, contains typical Ar-gentinian slang, which Guillermo also uses more often than is contextually needed), this distance disappears once we find out he is able to play the same game she plays. This kind of cultural sex/relationship tourism can work both ways with an Argentine, but not with a "Moor." In contrast to the relationship with Jalil, there is no cultural incompatibility between them.

While *Tomándote* responds to the conventions of romantic comedy, in *Susanna* the cross-cultural romance is developed within the very different framework of a sexually explicit thriller. Susanna, the female protagonist, is a rehabilitated drug addict who is involved in an obsessive sexual relationship with a married man, Álex, who abuses both her and his pregnant

wife. With Álex temporarily absent from her life, since he has
been caught stealing from his manager and put in jail, Susanna
meets Saïd, a young Moroccan man who works in a butcher
shop and wants to get married and have a family life, just
what Susanna has repeatedly told Álex she wants. The conflict
arises when Álex and Susanna meet again, while she is with
Saïd at a party. Susanna becomes torn between her passionate
but abusive sexual relationship with Álex and her asexual but
otherwise appealing relationship with Saïd. As in *Tomándote*,
the presumed incompatibility between her lifestyle and Saïd's
is illustrated repeatedly during the film. Even at the phenotypical level, Susana's bleached blond hair sets her apart from Saïd
and his Moroccan family and friends. Their incompatibility
becomes very clear in a scene at the top of a hill where they talk
while looking at Barcelona. Saïd's hopeful comment, "[Our
children] would be from here," is answered by Susanna with,
"I don't want to have children." Saïd's wish will be unfulfilled,
in the same way that Hussein's wish to have children "who
would belong to this land [Spain]" in the film *Saïd* will also be
truncated. In case Susanna's position about the impossibility
of reconciling their differences was not clear enough, the film
offers very soon afterward a scene in Saïd's mother's house
so saturated with orientalist and differentialist stereotypes of
Moroccan life in Barcelona that it becomes almost comical.
The scene contains such stereotypical elements as the rigid and
authoritarian mother-in-law, the women in exoticized, colorful
garments sitting on the floor around a circular tin-top tea table,
untranslated Arabic, and sexist views about women's behavior.
Although Susanna is ostensibly the one being interrogated and
judged by the mother and grandmother to determine whether
she would be a fitting wife for Saïd, instead, in an inversion
similar to what occurs in the interviews of Gabi and Jalil in
Tomándote, the orientalist surroundings and sexist attitude of
the Moroccan women engage the spectators in a process of
judging *them*, not Susanna. When the scene begins, the two
women are crying, presumably because of Saïd's decision to
marry a "liberated" Spanish woman. While the grandmother
observes Susanna with evident distrust, the mother speaks
in untranslated Arabic to a neighbor, who communicates to
Susanna: "está diciendo que nosotros somos musulmanes, y si

quieres casarte con su hijo tienes que serlo tú también" ["She is saying that we are Muslim, so if you want to marry her son, you also have to become one"]. Later on, they ask with whom Susanna lives, if she has family, and if she has "known" any man before Saïd. Susanna's answers are not the ones they wish to hear: she lives alone and has no family. Susanna, however, lies in response to the last question, assuring the women she has "never" been with another man.

As with Jalil in *Tomándote*, although Saïd wants to belong to Spain and have a "Spanish" life, his being Moroccan, and the "traditions" he therefore carries—even if he does not want to follow them—are presented as an insurmountable obstacle in his relationship with Susanna. Like Isabel Gardela, *Susanna*'s director, Antonio Chavarrías, states that he sees "culture" as the obstacle between the two characters: "una cultura es una cosa maravillosa pero en un contexto difícil como es el de la inmigración se convertía en una barrera . . . que hacía un poco más complicada la relación entre ellos" ["Culture is a wonderful thing but in a difficult context like immigration it becomes a barrier . . . it makes the relationship between them a bit more complicated"] ("Entrevista"). In two different scenes of the film, Saïd makes very clear his intentions of going forward in his relationship with Susanna regardless of traditional Moroccan customs. Juxtaposed with Susanna's interview with his mother, and directly following the Arabic-translated statement "dice que nosotros somos musulmanes y si quieres casarte con su hijo debes serlo tú también" ["She is saying that we are Muslim, so if you want to marry her son, you also have to become one"], we see Saïd in a different bedroom of the house, nervously telling his brother, "esto son tonterías" ["This is ridiculous."] When his brother replies, "Son las tradiciones, nuestras costumbres" ["It is tradition, our customs"], Saïd answers back saying "a mí no me gustan las costumbres" ["I don't like tradition"]. Shortly afterward, in a conversation with a fellow worker at the butcher shop, Saïd tells him he is going to marry soon. When his workmate replies, "Si Dios quiere" ["God willing"], Saïd's desire to break away from what is shown in the film as Moroccan convention is evidenced again in his answer, "quiera [Dios] o no quiera, yo voy a casarme igual" ["God willing or not, I'm getting married anyway"]. However, Susanna cannot decide between Saïd and Álex. She keeps seeing both of them at the same time, and eventually she gets caught in a motel room with Álex by Saïd and his friends. The culminating scene occurs when Álex, having stolen money from his new manager, comes to take Susanna away from Saïd. Enraged by her affirmative answers to the questions of whether she has had sex with Saïd and whether she liked it, Álex shows her a knife while threatening to use it on Saïd. Susanna then agrees to go away with Álex, asking him not to harm Saïd. Realizing that she is probably in love with "el moro," Álex kisses and stabs her. Susanna is murdered because of her sexual transgression, especially when she sexually chooses a "Moor" over a Spaniard. At the end of the film, Saïd is framed and blamed for the crime, and Álex walks away with impunity, back to his wife who has just delivered their baby.

Both *Tomándote* and *Susanna* set up a contrast between the sexual liberation and progressiveness of Spanish women and the conservative, traditional sexual mores of Moroccan and Indian (Muslim) men. Even though they make it very clear that the two female protagonists are attracted to these men and to the faithfulness and commitment they demonstrate, the films insist on the idea that these relationships are not "natural" and are not "meant to be," that for the women, they would involve an abandonment of their "true" identity. What makes this notion very intriguing is that the films painstakingly strive to show how miserable these two women were when they were being "authentic" with supposedly "modern" Spanish men, who are portrayed as abusive, coarse, fixated on sex, and obsessed with proving their virility. One must wonder whether the attraction these young women characters feel toward the masculine type of the benignly sexist immigrant is set up so as to equate it with women's desire for a nostalgic return to more traditional gender roles. After all, what seduces Gabi and Susanna the most are Jalil's and Saïd's promises of an earlier model of heterosexual relationships: a traditional, monogamous marriage, in which women cede to male control in exchange for protection and security. But this kind of marriage will not take place, as we have seen, since the price of European modernity demands its rejection. These films thus convey two very different lessons: "Modern" Spanish women no longer have access to traditional gender roles (a debatable issue in Spain today, as can be seen in the many cases of domestic violence against women), but the male prerogative—exercised against a "primitive" male, as well as against the modern woman—still obtains. Films like *Bwana, Saïd,* and *Susanna* make very explicit their warning against the risks entailed in daring to challenge Spanish males' sexual access to Spanish women: the price to pay for this challenge is brutal physical punishment, near-death, or prison. In Susanna's case, as we have seen, it is death.

In emphasizing Muslim men's difference, the films clearly blame *them* and their alignment with their "cultural traditions" for the failure of the romance. When the two female protagonists help in precipitating the end of the relationship, it is because of their modernity and self-assurance. If these representations of intercultural relationships, like others of different nations and periods in history, articulate "the ideal of cultural harmony through romance" (Hulme 141; qtd. in Pratt 97), they state that social harmony and the success of the relationship depend on how much Muslim immigrants are willing to abandon "their culture" and assimilate into Spanish society; "culture" standing in this view as a static, isolated entity that separates them. Certain Muslim religious practices are thus highlighted in the films as collaborating in the buildup of the unbridgeable distance that differentiates immigrants from Spaniards. In *Las cartas de Alou,* we have a collective prayer by male Muslim immigrants; in *Saïd,* a Muslim funeral procession is observed with suspicion by Spanish neighbors; in *Tomándote,* Ramadan is portrayed as a series of senseless prohibitions; and, in *Susanna,* we see a gruesome close-up of the ritual slaughter of a lamb. The highlighting of these elements, clearly identifiable as "Muslim" practices, collaborates in the films' setup of this particular "cultural difference" as an insurmountable obstacle to the relationship between these immigrants and Spaniards.

These impossible-romance films about Africans, Asians, and "Moors" stand in contrast to other contemporary Spanish films that present, also through romance, the gradual but successful integration of some Latin American migrants. A case in point is the film *Flores de otro mundo* [*Flowers from Another World*] (Icíar Bollaín, 1999), which shows romantic encounters involving issues of migration and displacement in relation to

Latin American migrants.[10] The film shows the arrival of a group of women in Santa Eulalia, a small rural town that has been steadily losing population and has invited them to meet the town's bachelors in the hope that some of them would want to stay and help save the town from disappearance. Two of the three female protagonists of the film are from the Caribbean: Patricia is Dominican, and Milady is Cuban (the third female protagonist is a Basque urban woman, also portrayed as an outsider to the small town in Teruel where the film takes place). Among the three relationships that they develop with the men of Santa Eulalia, the one that succeeds is that between Patricia and Damián: she becomes his wife, her children his children. Even though Patricia is criticized "because of the way she cooks, the music she listens to, and the way she dresses" (Martín-Cabrera 49), she is also presented, through her acceptance of certain cultural norms, as a model for the assimilation of migrants. The film's next-to-last scene, depicting Patricia's daughter's first Communion, inscribes integration alongside Christianity, the common cultural denominator (together with language) that makes Latin Americans good candidates for integration into Spain; the existence of non-Christian Latin Americans is totally absent in these discourses. As José Manuel del Pino has indicated, this scene, with Janai dressed completely in white, presents the Communion as the "normal" step to be taken toward social integration, with a disturbing closeness to past Spanish colonial projects of religious conversion and evangelization in Africa and the Americas. The film's selection and privileging of this event to show Patricia's family's definitive integration naturalizes certain cultural practices supposedly dominant in the community (del Pino). In a film that has been acclaimed as constructing a powerful social critique of racism and xenophobia, where one would expect the questioning of the "naturalness" of these practices, they come out instead highly reinforced. As Yeon-Soo Kim argues, this film shows the shortcomings of good intentions, disregarding the ideological debates inherent in the issues it tackles (174), and only being able to show a new national community in terms of a homogeneous way of life (185), in which the "ultimate rationale remains unity and cohesion, founded on similarities of religion, language, and traditional gender roles" (Kim 188–89). The integration of the immigrant in *Flores* is thus defined in terms of assimilation (del Pino). The "happy ending" of this film tells us that the desired immigrant subject is a female, Catholic, Latin American who wants to marry a rural Spanish man and thus saves a disappearing way of life for Spain, since, as Susan Martin-Márquez argues, "it is the immigrant woman who facilitates the revival of the traditional Spanish household" ("A World" 268). In contrast to the impossible romances of the previous films, *Flores* shows that it is with a female Latin American immigrant who fulfills a traditional gender role that a successful romantic relationship can be imagined and represented today in contemporary Spanish cinema.

If "[i]t is . . . characteristic of sentimental fiction to cast the political as erotic and to seek to resolve political uncertainties in the sphere of family and reproduction" (Pratt 101), the outcome that the "impossible romance" films present about the current relationships between Spaniards and (African, North African, Asian) Muslim immigrants is a rather bleak one. These films discourage Muslim involvement, showing how it brings about—in *Susanna*'s case—tragedy and death and—in *Tomándote*—disappointment and betrayal. As critics have pointed out in relation to colonial love stories, interracial love always turns bad:

> Such is the lesson to be learned from the colonial love stories, in whose dénouements the "cultural harmony through romance" always breaks down. Whether love turns out to be requited or not, whether the colonized lover is female or male, outcomes seem to be roughly the same: the lovers are separated, the European is reabsorbed by Europe, and the non-European dies an early death. (Pratt 97)

Sherzer, analyzing colonial and postcolonial French films, finds the same results: "the interracial relationships are not represented as viable. Transracial physical pleasure and attraction can exist, but the meetings have to occur clandestinely and in a marginal place where reality is suspended, and they do not lead to a durable relationship" (Sherzer 239).

We must ask, however, what is specific about the particular failed romances of these contemporary Spanish films. These particular breakups, which strive to show how different and incompatible Spaniards and "Moors" are, stand in sharp contrast to earlier Spanish films that present "successful" heterosexual romances between Spaniards and others. Films made under early Francoism present positively the scenario of mixing with the other: as analyzed by Labanyi—in missionary films such as *Misión Blanca* [*White Mission*] (Juan de Orduña, 1946), *La manigua sin Dios* [*The Godless Swamp*] (Arturo Díaz Castillo, 1948), *La mies es mucha* [*Great is the Harvest*] (José Luis Sáenz de Heredia, 1949), and *Cerca de la ciudad* [*On the City's Edge*] (Luis Lucía, 1952)—"otherness" is assimilated and incorporated through miscegenation: "territorial and sexual conquest were thus seen as two sides of the same process" (Labanyi, "Internalisations" 28–30). In these films, however (as in *Flores de otro mundo*), the male incorporates the female: in every one of the "successful" miscegenation scenarios, the incorporated alien is figured as feminine (Labanyi, "Internalisations" 29, 32). The desirability of assimilating the other disappears when the gender dynamic changes and the other is figured as male, both in these missionary films of the 1940s and 1950s and in contemporary films about immigration.

Another case in point is *La canción de Aixa* [*Aixa's Song*] (Florián Rey, 1939), the first of the Francoist film genre known as the "Africanist Cinema."[11] Aixa, its mixed race protagonist (born of a Spanish father and a Moroccan mother) must choose which of her two Moroccan cousins to marry. One is Westernized and fond of modern technology, while the other is traditional and conservative. As analyzed by Susan Martin-Márquez, this film emphasizes the closeness and friendship of Morocco and Spain in order to justify the latter's economic and military interests in North Africa, valorizing tradition over modernity (Aixa chooses her traditional cousin and not her Europeanized one) as a statement about Spain's colonialist policy compared to France's: "By insisting that Moroccan traditions function better in Morocco than do modern technological advances—as in the scenes in which literal horsepower is shown to be more effective than automobiles—the film works to justify Spain's presumably more 'hands-off' policy, which contrasts with France's imposition of Western education, technology, and industrial development within its portion of the protectorate" (Martin-Márquez, *Disorientations*). Aixa's rejection of her Europeanized cousin also serves to defend Franco's internal policy in Spain: "while in this film Morocco signifies, logically, Morocco, it also symbolizes Spain, a nation set to embark upon a period of autarky characterized by the Francoist regime's rejection of a modernity now deemed 'foreign,' and its exaltation of time-worn national traditions" (Martin-Márquez, *Disorientations*). In this way, *La canción de Aixa* erases Moroccan/Spanish differences, emphasizing their commonality.

In contrast, by the time *Tomándote* and *Susanna* were produced at the end of the 1990s, Spain had undergone a transformation from dictatorship and relative backwardness to democracy and modernization, and it had officially achieved a much-desired "European" location. These immigration films, through the allegory of romance, strive to show Spain's difference and distance from "the Moors" and painstakingly try to reassure Spaniards of their unquestionably modern status, choosing to completely silence those old ties that made Aixa a hybridized Moroccan/Spanish subject, and aligning themselves with a concept of Europe and modernity as absolute opposites of Islam.

La cazadora and *La aventura de Saïd*

La cazadora, published in 1995 by Encarna Cabello, is a text where racism very explicitly manifests itself as the "false or boomerang compliment" (Shohat and Stam 21). Stereotypes of primitivism and bestiality are attached in this novel to Moroccan characters and recoded as the positive libidinal freedom that Spaniards lack, thereby constructing a solipsistic erotic fantasy quite useless to the very real economic and social struggles of Moroccan immigrants. This fantasy, however, does give us an interesting and highly self-conscious perspective on the gendered and racialized dynamics of the romance between the narrator, an unnamed Spanish woman, and a male Moroccan immigrant, Nur. *La aventura de Saïd* (Josep Lorman, 1996), the novel on which the film *Saïd* is based, also falls into the trap of reproducing new racism at the same time that it explicitly attempts to combat "traditional" racism. (The cover of the book, for example, contains on its right-hand side the phrase "¡Echa abajo los prejuicios racistas!" ["Down with racist prejudices!"]. Like *Tomándote* and *Susanna*, Lorman's novel builds up a sharp contrast between the character of the Spanish woman and that of the immigrant (Moroccan) man, so much so that the novel puts these words in the mouth of a Moroccan immigrant, Ahmed: "La hospitalidad no es precisamente la virtud que caracteriza a la gente de aquí . . . cuanto más dinero, más egoísmo. Se tiene más que perder y se desconfía más de los extraños. Y *nosotros somos los más extraños de todos: otro color de piel, otra lengua, otra religion, otra cultura*" ["Hospitality is not precisely the virtue that characterizes people from here . . . more money, more selfishness. You have more to lose so you distrust strangers more. *And we are the strangest of all: another skin color, another language, another religion, another culture*"] (Lorman 53; my emphasis). While Ahmed begins his statement by criticizing Spaniards' lack of solidarity, he ends by justifying it through differentialist racism in a rhetorical movement that makes us doubt whether this statement could plausibly have been said by his character.

As in *Susanna*, where the female protagonist appears as a bleached blonde, these novels construct racial difference at the phenotypical level. In *La cazadora* we find an essentialist physical presentation of Moroccan immigrants when the female Spanish narrator, bored of hearing "Spaniards' voices" in the street of her apartment building in downtown Madrid, goes out to Atocha Street to find "una muchedumbre de cabezas morenas, de pelo negro, ensortijado: marroquíes" ["a crowd of dark heads, of black hair, curly: Moroccans"] (Cabello 19). Her "ecstatic eyes" when she sees them anticipates what will be further developed in the novel as her exoticizing physical attraction to them (Cabello 19–20). She becomes a spectator of what she sees as an exotic, primitive energy centered in physicality. Seeing Nur and his brother do physical work, she thinks "la vida era de ellos, la poseían esos cuerpos trabajados en la adversidad . . . a mí me era regalado el espectáculo de su vitalidad" ["Life was theirs, it was possessed by those bodies worked in adversity . . . I was blessed with the spectacle of their vitality"] (Cabello 31). After a visit to Nur's home town in Morocco, she concludes that he has been brought up "primitive style, tied to the earth" (32). This primitivism is decoded as a source of eroticism associated by the narrator with everything Moroccan, so that Nur's body becomes an object of erotic pulsion much like other ethnically marked elements of Moroccan culture, such as food (Cabello 30, 56, 81).

In *La aventura de Saïd*, *Saïd*'s lead actor (Naoufal Lhafi) is shown on the front cover of the book as having a dark complexion, while Ana, quite uncharacteristically for a Spanish woman, is later discursively presented as having blonde hair and blue eyes (Lorman 58–59). In a text that attempts to combat traditional (biological) racism, the emphasis on physical traits is highly suspicious. The importance of Ana's blondeness is made very clear throughout the novel, emphasized as if it were the materialization of a profound difference that would show the impossibility of her relationship with Saïd. The cultural capital of being blonde, moreover, makes Ana especially desirable for Spanish men and, therefore, turns her relationship with Saïd into an offense to their masculinity. It is this physical trait of Ana's that seems to be the cause, once and again, for Spanish men's assaults on their relationship. The more explicit attacks happen at the hands of a group of skinheads—like those in *Bwana*, where the skinheads also embody the policing of intercultural sexual relationships—and at the hands of the police, as in *Las cartas de Alou*, where the possibility of a public display of affection between a Spanish woman and an immigrant man is cut off when the police arrest him. The skins' dialogue before attacking Saïd, Ahmed, and Ana explicitly reveals the dynamics of Spanish men's relationship with "the Moor" when seen as a sexual competitor:

> —¿Y qué hacen dos moros de mierda a estas horas de la noche en la calle *con una rubia*? . . .
> —A lo mejor han ligado.
> —Imposible. Los moros son todos maricones . . . .
> —¿Y si han raptado a la chica y se la llevan para violarla?
> —¡No jodas!
> —Los moros son capaces de eso y de mucho más.
> —Pues si es eso, no podemos permitirlo. ¿No os parece?
> Ya habían encontrado la excusa para atacarlos.

> [—What do two shitty Moors do at this time of night in the street *with a blonde*? . . .
> —Maybe they got lucky.
> —Impossible. All Moors are fags.

—And if they have kidnapped the girl and are about to
rape her?
—Don't fuck with me!
—The Moors are capable of that and a lot more.
—Well, if it is that, we can't allow it, can we?
They had already found the excuse to attack them.]
(Lorman 77; my emphasis)

The police's interruption of Ana and Saïd's display of affection
happens as they exit a Pakistani restaurant where they have had
dinner and talked about their relationship. As they hold hands
and enjoy each other's silence, two policemen stop them and
ask to see Saïd's papers. When Saïd protests and asks to see
their identification, one of them replies: "Te pido los papeles
porque me da la gana y porque me toca los huevos verte pasear
por mitad de la Rambla cogido de la mano de una rubia" ["I ask
you for your papers because I feel like it, and because it gets
me in my balls to see you walking in the middle of the Rambla
hand in hand with a blonde"] (Lorman 101). Spanish men, then,
whether policemen or skinheads, serve the function of extending the policing work of the Spanish state. In *La aventura de
Saïd* they actually bring about the end of a possible love affair
between Ana and Saïd, as also happens in *Las cartas de Alou*
and *Bwana*.

In *La cazadora* Spanish men also intervene, momentarily
disturbing the relationship, although in this case they are not
able to destroy it. Like the police detention in *La aventura de
Saïd*, three policemen stop Nur (the female Spanish narrator's
Moroccan boyfriend), his brother, Muhassan, and the narrator
as they stroll kissing and laughing in downtown Madrid. Immediately, the three of them believe the policemen's anger is
related to Nur and the narrator's romance; Muhassan is sure the
policemen had followed and spied on them, and the narrator
regrets having dressed provocatively (Cabello 45). The next
day at the police station, when the narrator notices a reaction
of repulsion on the policeman's face when she kisses Nur, she
thinks: "a saber cuáles eran sus verdaderos sentimientos: tal
vez frustración y hasta envidia de lo que un 'moro de mierda'
obtenía delante de sus narices y de una nacional" ["Who knows
which were his real feelings: perhaps frustration and envy at
what a 'shitty Moor' was getting in front of him and from a

native Spanish woman"] (Cabello 48). If in *Las cartas de Alou*, the pioneering immigration film, the policemen were shown enforcing the policies of the *Ley de Extranjería*, in these latter two novels policemen seem to be more concerned about policing sexual frontiers than legal ones.

Even though in *La aventura de Saïd*, as in *Susanna*, the ones who precipitate the ending of the relationship between Ana and Saïd are the Spanish state or other Spanish males, the text also makes sure we understand that even if these obstacles did not exist, the romance would not have been possible. These are clear moments where the novel engages in justifying the pervasive differentialist racism that exists against Moroccan immigrants. In several moments of the novel, Saïd compares the women he knows as potential romantic partners, and he explains the radical difference between Moroccan and Spanish women:

> ¡Ana era tan distinta de las chicas marroquíes! Decidida, independiente, con estudios . . . ¡Qué poco se parecía a la chica que hasta ahora tenía como modelo de esposa! A él le habían enseñado a valorar en una mujer la modestia y la sumisión. Había aprendido a mirar los ojos tras un rostro velado o inexpresivo . . . entre musulmanes . . . las esposas vivían encerradas en casa.

> [Ana was so different from Moroccan girls! Decided, independent, having studied . . . She had so little in common with the girl he had had as wife-model until now! He had been taught to value modesty and submission in a woman. He had learned to look at eyes behind a veiled and inexpressive face . . . among Muslims . . . wives lived locked at home.] (Lorman 97–98)

In a compilation of clichéd views of Moroccan and Spanish women, Saïd denies the possibility of Moroccan women being any other way than dependent, submissive, uneducated and veiled, with all the affective and political charges of this last affirmation. Conversely, he denies the possibility of Spanish women being any other way than independent, decided, and educated, thus repeating the same type of polarized discourse that surrounded the Fátima Elidrisi controversy (see below). In case these stereotyped descriptions were not clear enough,

Saïd clarifies for the readers that his biggest worry is the issue of who will dominate whom in the relationship: since he is "poor, uneducated and Muslim" and Ana is "rich, educated and Christian, . . . will he be able to dominate her? Will she accept being dominated?" (Lorman 97). Saïd realizes that since "they are in Spain and not in Morocco," he would probably be the one who will have to change and "accept Western customs," even though this would probably mean having to abandon Islam, his religion (Lorman 98). Saïd doubts whether he would be able to do this: "Él se había criado dentro de las estrictas reglas islámicas; su visión de las cosas y sus valores estaban fijados por la ley del Corán. ¿Podría dejarlos de lado y sustituirlos por otros más próximos a los de Ana? No lo sabía, pero algo muy íntimo y profundo le decía que no" ["He had been brought up with strict Islamic rules; his views and his values were mandated by the law of the Koran. Would he be able to abandon them and replace them with others closer to Ana's? He did not know, but something intimate and profound told him that he couldn't"] (Lorman 99).

The issues of domination and control raised by Saïd in this monologue are interestingly paralleled by the thoughts of Spanish women. In a dynamic that is only hinted at in other texts but never explicitly stated, the narrator of *La cazadora* presents us with a highly explicit and self-conscious reflection about the choice of an immigrant man as lover. She tells us that her object of desire is always someone "de un medio social inferior. No espero de él que sea joven . . . pero sí—parece ser—que sea casi analfabeto" ["of inferior social means. I don't expect him to be young . . . but I do expect—it seems—that he be almost illiterate"] (Cabello 58). Through a discourse organized around traditional gender positions, she tells us the story of how she came to realize this fact: "No sé si es porque yo iba para lesbiana . . . cierta primavera, adolescente aún, tuve la fantasía de dominar a una chica imaginaria de mi edad y de mi nivel cultural; y que al cruzarse, ese mismo verano, en mi camino jóvenes humildes de origen modesto, encontré en ellos *a mi dominado, a mi mujer*" ["I don't know if it happened because I could have been a lesbian . . . one spring, still an adolescent, I had the fantasy of dominating an imaginary girl of my age and my cultural level; and when, that same summer, I met some young guys who

were poor, I found in them *someone to dominate, my wife*"]
(Cabello 58; my emphasis). In this explanation, the narrator
naturalizes patriarchal values of male domination over women
and concludes that she wants that too; she wants to occupy the
male position of power (and desiring this power becomes, in
this mode of thinking, a lesbian desire, since it is equivalent
to desiring other women). The inherent violence of this desire
is picked up in the linguistically ambiguous title of the novel,
since "*cazadora*" means both "jacket" and "hunter."

In addition to his already-mentioned racialized erotic capital,
the immigrant lover becomes desirable because of his economic
marginalization (she says "es para mí un orgullo mantener al
amante" ["I am proud of supporting my lover"] (Cabello 58),
which makes him "female" in the power struggle of the relationship. We can assume that Nur's "illegal immigrant" status
probably becomes one more step in this direction of desiring
someone to subordinate and control. The narrator speculates
that this attraction might also be related to a desire to return to
her own impoverished childhood and to the figure of her illiterate father, but that this explanation is easier. The first one, she
says, is the hardest to confess: "vergonzoso por abominable
eso de tomar a un hombre por una mujer" ["It is shameful and
repulsive to take a man for a woman"] (Cabello 59). As Kathryn
Perry observes about all interracial romantic relationships, "In
a drama of control, the complex exchange of dominance and
submission, present to some degree in most sexual encounters
. . . is additionally charged with the weight of the racialized exchange" (Perry 175). Albeit far more timidly, Ana in *La aventura de Saïd* also lets us imagine that this play of domination and
control is an important component of her relationship with Saïd.
When stopped by the two policemen in the street, who comment
on the fact that Saïd is holding her hand, Ana quickly responds:
"—El no me ha cogido la mano. He cogido yo la suya" ["—He
has not taken my hand. I have taken his"] (Lorman 101).

Reciprocally, for Nur the relationship with a Spanish woman
has a psychological significance that goes further than any other
relationship: in their first sexual encounter, after they have just
met in the street, his thoughts are not exactly about her but
about his own power struggle with Spanish men. While caress-
ing and kissing her, he remembers how earlier that afternoon at

the construction site where they work some Spanish men began insulting his father and him, saying "—¡Moros de mierda! ¡Idos a casa!" ["—Shitty Moors, go home!"], while threatening them with bricks. Nur recalls his father's silence and his inner struggle:

> Los marroquíes callan. El viejo, en actitud amedrentada, mira hacia otra parte como si no hubiera oído bien. El joven muestra los brazos al descubierto, serpenteados de tatuajes. Los brazos, de músculos generosos, parece que quisieran hacer algo, pero no se lanzan. La mirada del joven es una amalgama de odio, impotencia, tristeza, hacia los agresores, pero también calla.

> [The Moroccans are silent. The old one, frightened, looks the other way as if he had not heard well. The young one shows his naked arms, covered by tattoos. The arms, with generous muscles, seem to want to do something, but they don't. The look of the young man is an amalgam of hate, impotence, sadness toward the aggressors, but he also is silent.] (Cabello 21–22)

Thus, Nur's relationship with the narrator is presented as also having a reparative function for him, partially compensating for the humiliation and subordination he has to endure from Spanish men.

La cazadora solves the "intercultural conflict" between the narrator and Nur in an unusual way. Rejecting her fellow Spaniards' enthusiasm for Spain's modernity, the narrator decides to "go native" and move with Nur to the shantytown: "Había elegido vivir modestamente, pero a su lado. Para no ser sólo la espectadora complaciente de la comparsa, del arte gratuito y subyugante de sus miserias" ["I had chosen to live in poverty, but next to him. So I wouldn't be only the spectator of the fascinating and free of charge art of their misery"] (Cabello 80). Even though this ending seems more optimistic than the breakups of the previous films, it coincides with them in showing that a relationship between a "Moor" and a Spaniard can never be fully possible in modern Spain. The narrator is the one capable of change, who is actually able to "go native" without bringing about tragedy, as happens in the films when migrants try to do the same. Spaniards, according to this novel, can fully share the stereotypical pre-modern world of migrants, but not vice versa.

Like the other immigration texts, this novel cannot imagine a Moroccan immigrant entering the European modernity of contemporary Spain.[12]

The Case of Fátima Elidrisi

The story of Fátima Elidrisi partakes of the same assumptions about the incompatibility of Islam and modern Europe as the impossible romance plots of immigration novels and films. The case of this 13-year-old Moroccan girl from El Escorial, Madrid, occupied the headlines of Spanish newspapers in mid-February 2002. For five months, Fátima had not attended classes because the school did not allow her to use the traditional Moroccan headscarf. The question of Muslim women's "submission" (of which the veil supposedly becomes the symbol) was the example used in a recent issue of *The Economist* dedicated to Muslims in Europe, which had a veiled Muslim woman's photograph on its front cover, to illustrate how "some aspects of Islam do reinforce the isolation of Muslims in Western Europe" ("Muslims" 22).

The pervading tone with which newspapers narrated the story was, from the very beginning, one of extreme alarm. The first article about it to appear in *El País* was entitled "Una niña marroquí está sin escolarizar porque su padre la obliga a llevar el chador" ["A Moroccan Girl without Schooling Because Her Father Makes Her Wear a Chador"] (Galaz). The title implied that the father was the one at fault for making the girl wear a garment that prevented her from attending classes. The reason she was not going to school, we find out later, was not really because the father was making her wear something, but because that "something" was perceived as "Islamic" in the school. Fátima had solicited a place in the public school of El Escorial after classes had already started, but, since the school was full, she was accepted by a religious (Catholic) one—what is called a *colegio concertado*. The condition was that she should not wear the headscarf, and that she should instead wear the school's uniform.

Mabel Galaz, the journalist who wrote this first article, also asserted that the piece of clothing was a *chador*, and that "esta prenda, que cubre totalmente el cuerpo de la niña y tapa parte de su cabeza, es preceptivo de la corriente islámica chií" ["This article of clothing, which totally covers the girl's body and part of her head, is mandatory within the Islamic Shiite faction"] (Galaz). The garment in question, however, was not a *chador*, or a veil, as was also stated, but a much less spectacular and less exotic Moroccan headscarf, not that different from those widely used until very recently by rural Spanish women. Indeed, as explained by Abdelhamid Beyuki, president of the Association of Moroccan Immigrant Workers in Spain (ATIME), in an online interview in *El País*, "el pañuelo que lleva Fátima no es el *hiyab*, ni mucho menos el *chador* o la *burka*, no es ni signo religioso, ni de sumisión, es una vestimenta más igual que la que lleva Rigoberta Menchú" ["Fátima's headscarf is not the *hiyab*, much less the *chador* or the *burka*, it is neither a religious sign, nor one of submission, it is a garment more like the one worn by Rigoberta Menchú"].[13] Through a mechanism similar to that of explicitly making the female protagonists in *Susanna* and *La aventura de Saïd* blonde, the alarm sparked by Fátima's garment reveals exactly what these texts expect their audiences to not see: Moroccan/Spanish closeness. In the same way that in most cases the phenotypical differences between Moroccans and Spaniards would not be as evident as the blonde/dark contrast sought in *Susanna* or *La aventura de Saïd*, a headscarf does not constitute in Spain a foreign, exotic garment associated with the threat of Islam, but it is a common garment widely used by women until very recently.

The other important collusion presented in this first article, in which the other narratives in this chapter also participate, is an all-too-familiar displacement of the discourse of women's rights. The mediator hired to intervene in Fátima's case was quoted as commenting that there had not been any prior cases of problems when trying to integrate Moroccan boys into school, but that girls were "more of a problem." She assured the journalist she was "prepared to fight till the end so that Fátima could have the same rights as other girls her age," and that she hoped this was not a case of a refusal of education due to "religious traditions." With these affirmations, the mediator was basically operating from the assumption that Fátima, being Moroccan, did not have the same rights as Spanish girls, and therefore she required the mediator's help to stop her father from denying her an education. Tacitly, it was understood that these "religious traditions" referred to Islam. Even Tomás Calvo, the director of the Center for the Study of Migration and Racism, added to this racist view, stating that this was "what generally happened in traditional Muslim culture"; families "preferred teenage girls to stay at home and learn to be housewives, the sublime ideal of womanhood" ("El número"). In any case, the mediator instructed the public school to admit Fátima, where, she said, "in theory" she should be able to wear a headscarf (still called *chador*).

The manipulation of the discourse of women's rights only intensified the following day, when the director of the public school, Delia Duró, said it was "unconstitutional" to wear the headscarf (which on this second day was called *hiyab*), that it conspired against women's rights, and that it should be prohibited (Sánchez and López Escudero). Several women's associations supported the statement, reported the Catalan newspaper *La Vanguardia* (Prats). The Education Minister, Pilar del Castillo, affirmed that Fátima was going to have to go to school "in the same manner as the other girls." The Minister of Labor and Social Issues, Juan Carlos Aparicio, again intensified the controversy when he stated that the headscarf was a sign of discrimination against women, and compared it with female genital mutilation. He assured the readers that he was not going to allow in Spain such unacceptable behavior which could not possibly be understood as a religious or cultural concept, a "salvajada" ["savagery"] ("El Ministro").

This appropriation of the discourse of women's rights participates in the much larger debates related to the integration of Muslim immigrants into Europe, the still very present scars of colonialism, and the relationships between first-world feminisms and third-world practices. As many Arab and non-Arab thinkers have explained, present uses of *hiyab* by Muslim women are overdetermined by the history and politics of colonial domination and nationalist movements. The very specific discourse of women's rights deployed by Spanish officials in the case of Fátima Elidrisi can be traced to colonialist discourses that characterized Arab societies as inferior because of their treatment of women. "Civilized" Europeans were, of course, exempted from sexism.[14] The fact that these "civilized"

Europeans did not include Spain in their picture of "civilization" did not prevent most of the Spanish protagonists of the Fátima Elidrisi case from engaging in this same discourse today.

As it relates to the veil, "[t]he colonial masquerade of giving women power by unveiling them was merely a ruse for achieving power over men" (McClintock 97). Frantz Fanon explains how the unveiling of the Algerian Woman was part of France's "civilizing mission," and how this position by the colonizers guaranteed the opposition of nationalists.[15] As Fátima Mernissi puts it in her preface to *Beyond the Veil*, "[t]he fact that Western colonizers took over the paternalistic defense of the Muslim woman's lot characterized any changes in her condition as concessions to the colonizer" (Mernissi, *Beyond* vii). Wearing the veil, then, became a sign of defiance against the West's invasion and destruction of Islam. Similarly, some years ago in France and Belgium, when veil use by female immigrants was identified with religious extremism and targeted with racist measures, its symbolic value as an object of cultural pride was reinforced (Blommaert and Verschueren 93). This happened once again in France when President Jacques Chirac decided in 2003 to prohibit all use of "religious symbols" in French schools.

This discourse used to prevent what was thought to be the "veiling" of a Moroccan girl in El Escorial also relates to larger issues of First- and Third-World feminisms. As Chandra Talpade Mohanty and others have argued, Western feminists have often been blind to their own position of power and authority toward other women. They have often produced in their texts the singular monolithic subject of the "Third World Woman" and sought ways to "rescue" her from her exploitative society. This move has often turned out badly, since it was easy to see it as ethnocentric and imperialistic. So Cynthia Enloe describes how Egyptian feminists in the early twentieth century "felt compelled to defend Islam against racist Orientalism" (Enloe 53). The West's understanding of the veil only in terms of repression and submissiveness has been an oversimplification of the matter, itself a construct of orientalist thought, and not necessarily an accurate description of the experiences of Muslim women (Yegenoglu; qtd. in Young 378).

This issue seems to have been present in the mind of at least one person in Spain at the time, the president of the Federació de Col·lectius d'Immigrants a Catalunya (FCIC, Federation of Immigrant Communities in Catalonia), Eva Cham. She declared to *La Vanguardia* that "the debate over whether the *chador* is discriminatory to women or not doesn't correspond to a European country but to the country of origin of the immigrants" (Prats). Kadiatu Kanneh, in her analysis of feminist responses to female circumcision, also mentions how "[t]he battle over the Black Third World woman's body is staged as a battle between First World feminists and Black Third World men" (Kanneh 348). Like the Muslim men's characters in the films and novels discussed, the Muslim man's role was essential in the journalistic portrayal of Fátima's story. Even though both the father and Fátima were quoted as saying that she was the one who wanted to wear the headscarf, the sensationalistic headlines insisted on *his* making her wear it, and on *his* refusal to let her attend school.

Fátima's case was resolved when Carlos Mayor Oreja, of the Education Council of Madrid, forced the school to let Fátima attend classes, arguing that her right to education was the highest priority in the case, and that the prohibition of the wearing of a headscarf was a discriminatory measure. By this time, the Partido Socialista Obrero Español (PSOE, the Spanish Socialist Party) had already declared that the prohibition by the public school's principal was a violation of Fátima's fundamental right to education and an assault against religious freedom ("Ministro"). The manner in which newspapers and government officials handled this story betrays the lack of attention paid to fundamental issues of cultural difference in regard to Muslim immigrants, and the increasingly hostile environment that has been created around them. The informal polls conducted by both *El País* and *La Vanguardia* following the controversy showed a secure majority of votes that didn't agree with the decision of allowing Fátima to attend school with the headscarf.[16]

Integration and Assimilation

The prevailing discourse about Moroccan immigrants' integration in Spain blames them for not making enough of an effort to assimilate, and thus threatening a presumably fixed and homogeneous "Spanish" (or "Catalan," as we saw in chapter 1) identity. The narratives of impossible romance (*Tomándote*, *Susanna*, *La aventura de Saïd*), or those of the impossibility of integrating "Moroccan" culture into modern Spain (*La cazadora*, the case of Fátima Elidrisi) participate in the differentialist vision of new racism, and thus they perpetuate a vision of cultural nationalism quite incompatible with the modern, democratic project of a diverse, multicultural Spain. Sami Naïr comments on how the integration issue has to be understood the other way around, since the ones who should be worried about losing their identity due to immigration are not Spaniards but the immigrants themselves, who do not have a choice but to adapt to the new circumstances in order to survive, as any minority culture has to do. Commenting on the arguments against religious Muslim practices in Spain, José María Ridao asks "¿por qué se le exige al Islam algo que el Cristianismo no hizo, y lo que es peor, algo que ninguna religión puede hacer, como es convertirse en una creencia laica?" ["Why do we ask Islam to do something Christianity didn't do, and, what is worse, something that no religion can do, which is to become a lay belief?"] (Ridao). As in the case of France analyzed by Balibar, in Spain there is also "[a] need to differentiate and rank individuals or groups in terms of their greater or lesser aptitude for—or resistance to—assimilation" (Balibar 24). Muslim immigrants (again, mostly Moroccans), in contrast to Latin Americans or Eastern Europeans, are widely perceived as resisting assimilation. Partly as a consequence of this differentialist racism, Moroccan seasonal workers who had picked the harvest in Huelva and Almería for years have been replaced in the last few years by Eastern Europeans. The reason for this change can be traced to the Popular Party government's idea of "cultural ties," which implies that (Christian) Eastern Europeans have culturally more in common with Spaniards than Moroccans do. Both Sami Naïr and Juan Goytisolo have noticed the hidden racist agenda of this statement: "cultural closeness" stands in this case for Christianity and light skin, since there is no doubt that Morocco has much closer historical and cultural ties to Spain than the countries of Eastern Europe. Blommaert and Verschueren note similar assumptions in the case of Belgium, where Poland is seen as a close peer and the Congo (like Morocco for Spain) as a foreign, exotic other:

> What then does this affection for Polish culture or the observ-
> able aversion to Central African culture stem from? How can
> it be that, despite three-quarters of a century of intense, deep
> contacts of which the impact is still visible, Belgians still ap-
> proach Congolese culture with the greatest exoticism, while
> unconditionally accepting our ties with groups that, certainly
> since World War II, have lived in a literally separate world?
> (Blommaert and Verschueren 95)

In the case of Spain with Morocco, there is a centuries-long
relationship of mutual exchange, in contrast to an almost non-
existent shared history with Eastern Europe. Although Blommaert and Verschueren do not provide a direct answer to their
rhetorical question, the answer lies, as indicated by Naïr and
Goytisolo, in issues of Christianity and Whiteness. These same
assumptions are at play in news reports on how Moroccan children are the worst students and the hardest to integrate among
immigrant children in schools. As portrayed in these fictional
and social narratives, the assumption behind these statements
and policies is that "Moors" in Spain are the ones furthest away
from the "Spanish" hegemonic norm, which is infused with
the positive values of Europeaness and modernity. As Balibar
argues for the British and French cases,

> for a "Black" in Britain or a "*Beur*" in France, the assimila-
> tion demanded of them before they can become "integrated"
> into the society in which they already live (and which will
> always be suspected of being superficial, imperfect or simu-
> lated) is presented as progress, as an emancipation, a conced-
> ing of rights. And behind this situation lie barely reworked
> variants of the idea that the historical cultures of humanity
> can be divided into two main groups, the one assumed to be
> universalistic and progressive, the other supposed irremedi-
> ably particularistic and primitive. (Balibar 25)

The irony, of course, is that if there is something that has always
characterized Spain it is its heterogeneity, its cultural, religious,
and racial contact with precisely those subjects that are now
represented as completely foreign. The painstaking nature of
the effort tells us that the belief in the European status of Spain
as radically opposed to everything African and Muslim still
needs psychological reinforcement. These immigration texts,
that take for granted Spain's European location seem to demonstrate that reassurance regarding this location is still needed.

Chapter Five

Testimonies of Immigrant Life

Fact, Fiction, and
the Ethnographic Performance

As it attempts to establish clear-cut differences with Moroccans, the narrative strategy explored in this chapter is what I call the ethnographic performance. Its formula constructs immigrants as subalterns to be interviewed, analyzed, and written about by Spaniards, in an attempt to represent an "accurate picture" of what their lives are like. Texts like *Dormir al raso* (Pasqual Moreno Torregrosa and Mohamed El Gheryb, 1994), *Yo, Mohamed: historias de inmigrantes en un país de emigrantes* (Rafael Torres, 1995), *Todo negro no igual* (Beatriz Díaz, 1997); documentary films like *Todos os llamáis Mohamed* (Maximiliano Lemcke, 1997); and novels like *Las voces del Estrecho* (Andrés Sorel, 2000) constitute less-than-successful efforts to "give voice" to the immigrants by using the testimonial genre, which often results in actually taking away their voices. A similar relationship between fact, fiction, and the construction of subalternity is also present in sociological studies of immigration that contain "personal testimonies" such as César Manzanos Bilbao's *El grito del otro: arqueología de la marginación racial* (1999) and Gema Martín Muñoz's *Marroquíes en España: estudio sobre su integración* (2003).[1] This chapter also analyzes the recurrent fictional character of the Spanish journalist who looks for information about immigrants' lives and, in doing so, reflects upon ethnographic constructions of otherness. This occurs in two short stories of the collection *Por la vía de Tarifa* (Nieves García Benito, 1999), in the novel *La aventura de Saïd* (Josep Lorman, 1996), and in the film *Ilegal* (Ignacio Vilar, 2002). Another focus is what happens when an immigrant refuses to speak, as in the short story "Fátima de los naufragios" (Lourdes Ortiz, 1998).

These texts, in their attempts to give voice to immigrants and let their stories be heard, have a close relationship to the genre of Latin American *testimonio*. Like *testimonio*, they are located at the intersection of the oral and the written, literature and non-literature, truth and fiction, and authored and edited discourse (Gugelberger, Introduction 10–11). They are the result of a more-or-less explicit collaboration between an informant—an immigrant whose native language is not Spanish—and a sociologist, journalist, or writer, who gives written form to the oral exchange and publishes it. The inherent imbalance of power of this relationship produces in the Spanish case the same kind of problems that exist in the Latin American *testimonio*. As Elzbieta Sklodowska has argued, there is an inescapable tension produced in the difference between living, surviving, or witnessing racism, injustice, or deprivation and transcribing it. One of the problems with *testimonio* is that the ethnologist or editor insists on creating "an illusion of seamless, mutually (re)created reality" through mechanisms destined to make us believe that what we are reading is the "authentic" voice of the informant, the "real" author of the book (Sklodowska 87–89).[2] The reality of the exchange between informant and interlocutor, however, is not one of mutuality but one determined by an unequal, extra-discursive power relationship between, in the Spanish case, an immigrant, often in a precarious economic, social, and legal situation, and a Spaniard, situated in a position of safety and relative privilege. Control of the text production inevitably resides in the latter, who decides "what to reveal, how and when" (Sklodowska 90). As James Clifford reminds us, the representation of the Other always entails relations of domination. Ethnography—and the production of *testimonio*—"is always caught up in the invention, not the representation, of cultures" (Clifford 2). Furthermore, it becomes a "strategy of containment," by which the Other "is forever the exegetical horizon of difference, never the active agent of articulation" (Bhabha 31).

The Traps of *Testimonio*

Like the collaboration of Elizabeth Burgos Debray and Rigoberta Menchú in *I, Rigoberta Menchú*, or Moema Viezzer and Domitila Barrios de Chungara in *Let Me Speak!*, the text

Dormir al raso is the result of the collaboration between Spaniard Pasqual Moreno Torregrosa, an agricultural engineer and writer, and Moroccan Mohamed El Gheryb, who emigrated to Spain some years ago. The project strives to be an equal collaboration; it gives parallel credit to both authors, contains parallel Spanish/Moroccan prologues (by Manuel Vásquez Montalbán and Mahdi Elmandjara, respectively), and its introduction is written in first-person plural, presumably by both authors, not solely by the "interlocutor," as is the case in Menchú or Barrios de Chungara. Nevertheless, this introduction describes the same type of uneven power relations and division of labor in the production of the text analyzed by Sklodowska in the Latin American context. Like other *testimonios*, it aspires to achieve the status of truth; the introduction explains that the objective of the project was "reflejar lo más fielmente posible la vida de los inmigrantes magrebíes en España" ["to reflect as faithfully as possible the life of Magrebian immigrants in Spain"] (Moreno Torregrosa and El Gheryb 7). In order to achieve this, the authors spent months gathering documentation, conducting interviews, and visiting immigrants at home and at work.[3]

Although as a result of this investigation they accumulated documents, reports, and testimonies, the introduction tells us, "vimos que era necesario pasar por la experiencia directa" ["we saw it was necessary to go through the direct experience"] (Moreno Torregrosa and El Gheryb 7). This "direct experience" had to be lived by El Gheryb, even though he had *already* lived it years before, when he migrated to Spain. Thus, instead of remembering his experience and narrating it for Moreno Torregrosa, as would be the case in a traditional *testimonio*, El Gheryb re-lives this experience for the purposes of the book. His role becomes then a highly ambivalent one, marked by the tension between "acting as an immigrant" for the purpose of the book, and having been, and still being, one. The introduction to *Dormir al raso* describes this process in the following way:

> Y es aquí cuando Mohamed El Gheryb *actuó de inmigrante, de lo que es.* Se fue a Marruecos y durante varias semanas *se hizo pasar* por alguien que deseaba a toda costa y como fuese entrar en España. Paseó por el Puerto de Tánger, durmió en las pensiones de Tetuán . . . entró en España, y continuó *interpretando su papel de inmigrante* . . . Partió en busca de

trabajo al Ejido y recolectó hortalizas en sus invernaderos, sin papeles, como tantos otros de sus compatriotas . . . Estuvo luego en Murcia viviendo en las chabolas de Fuente Álamo y más tarde en . . . el País Valenciano, *rehaciendo un camino que le es propio.*

[It was then that Mohamed El Gheryb *acted as an immigrant, as what he is.* He went to Morocco and, for several weeks, *acted like* someone who wanted to enter Spain more than anything and by any means. He walked through the port of Tangiers, slept in the pensions of Tetuan . . . He entered Spain, and continued *interpreting his role* of immigrant...He went to look for work in El Ejido and collected produce in its greenhouses, without legal documents, like so many of his countrymen . . . He then stayed in Murcia, living in the shanties of Fuente Álamo and later in . . . Valencia, *retracing his own steps.*] (Moreno Torregrosa and El Gheryb 7; my emphasis)

El Gheryb thus "acted" and "interpreted his role" but, at the same time, this narrative suggests, an immigrant is "what he is," and he was "retracing his own steps." So—is El Gheryb an immigrant "like so many of his countrymen"? The fact of his *performing* his role of immigrant undoubtedly set him apart from those undocumented countrymen who were working alongside him in the greenhouses of El Ejido or sleeping alongside him in the shanties of Fuente Álamo. While he was at some risk in this undertaking, El Gheryb was forearmed with a knowledge and familiarity not possessed by the others. At the same time, if he was privileged enough to be illegally working only as a performance, and solely for the purpose of the book, he was not privileged enough, or non-immigrant enough, to be able to *not* do it. In the logic of this "collaborative" project, the mutuality stops at the level of the division of labor. In a choice between Moreno Torregrosa and him, "passing" for an undocumented Moroccan immigrant corresponded only to El Gheryb.

As editor and material author of the writing itself, Moreno Torregrosa's clear main role, as stated, was "giving the book form through the final redaction" (8). He was, therefore, responsible for the organization of the material that we read as *Dormir al raso*: its chapter divisions and subdivisions with their respective titles, its appendices with information about Spanish agriculture, its notes with Spanish translations of Arabic phrases or words, its bibliography. Moreno Torregrosa's editing highly influences the way we read this text. The numerous titles of its subdivisions are texts in themselves that prompt us to make specific cultural connections and read what comes under them in specific ways. One of the subsections of the first chapter, for example, which talks about the corruption of the police in Tangiers, is entitled "Llega Colombo" ["Colombo Arrives"] (31). Another one, "Bienvenidos a la Costa del Sol" ["Welcome to the Costa del Sol"] (83), makes an ironic allusion to a Spanish tourist slogan while narrating the dreadful working conditions in Almería. At times, Moreno Torregrosa includes quotes from Spanish poets and writers in the text. For example, when the narrator visits Tarifa's cemetery and wonders why Spanish cemeteries are enclosed, in contrast to the openness of Moroccan ones, we find the quote "si los de fuera no quieren entrar y los de dentro no pueden salir" ["since those outside do not want to enter and those inside cannot get out"], by Galician poet Celso Emilio Ferreiro, as indicated in a corresponding footnote (178), completing the thoughts of the Moroccan narrator (77). A quote from Spanish poet Rafael Alberti, in turn, serves as one of the subtitles of the chapter "Bajo un mar de plásticos" ["Under a Sea of Plastic"]: "Mira que árbol como aquel . . . todos recelan" ["A tree such as that one . . . everybody suspects"] (Moreno Torregrosa and El Gheryb 101).

But before talking about the actual transcription and editing of the material, the introduction explains Moreno Torregrosa's contribution to the investigation itself:

> Por su parte Pasqual Moreno *en aras de la objetividad hacía paralelamente el mismo recorrido* visitando las ciudades del norte de Marruecos, las zonas agrícolas del Mediterráneo español, apoyando a Mohamed El Gheryb en las entrevistas, asegurando la infraestructura del libro, el trabajo de documentalista, aportando también sus experiencias y finalmente dándole forma al libro a través de la redacción final.

> [For his part, Pasqual Moreno *for the sake of objectivity took the same route in parallel*, visiting the cities of Morocco's north, the agricultural zones of the Spanish Mediterranean, supporting Mohamed El Gheryb in the interviews, insuring the book's infrastructure, the work of documentation,

167

collaborating also with his experiences and finally giving the
book form through the final redaction.] (Moreno Torregrosa
and El Gheryb 7–8; my emphasis)

For the sake of objectivity: this phrase (an explanation? a justification?) resonates at the core of the controversies over *testimonio* and its status of truth. This remark (Moreno Torregrosa's
voice, perhaps?) tells us that this account of Moroccan immigrant life is not a subjective one, only reflecting El Gheryb's
experience or information, and, perhaps, bias, but an "objective" one, representing a collective experience and guaranteed
in its status of truth by the presence of a Spaniard, Moreno
Torregrosa. His role was a "parallel" one to El Gheryb, since he
traveled the same route. We do not hear, however, of the differences between the two. It would probably be safe to assume that
they did not sleep in the same accommodations or have access
to the same commodities and conveniences. We can be sure, for
example, that Moreno Torregrosa did not stay in the same pensions in Tetuán, in the precarious housing designated for workers in the greenhouses of El Ejido, or in the shanties in Murcia.
It is altogether not clear what the phrase "collaborating also
with his experiences" means. As Sklodowska explains in relation to the Latin American *testimonio*, the problem with these
texts, as revealed in their explanatory introductions, is that they
intend "to create an illusion of a common front and give unity
and uniformity to a project which *ex definitione* should address
the issue of difference and not erase it" (Sklodowska 89). The
supposed equality of the two authors quickly vanishes when we
read the introduction. As Rey Chow reminds us, "all humans
and all discourses are created equal—but some are more equal
than others" (Chow 17).

The text *Yo, Mohamed: historias de inmigrantes en un país
de emigrantes*, by Rafael Torres begins with an "Advertencia"
["Warning"], in which the author denounces the basic hypocrisy
alluded to in his subtitle, that of Spain's difficulty in welcoming much-needed immigrants after having been itself a country
of emigrants. He explains that this book is not, however, an
explanation of immigration, racism, or xenophobia, but an attempt to rescue the individual and unique stories of twenty-five
immigrants:

[Éste es] un libro de vidas robadas por el autor a veinticinco trabajadores extranjeros, hombres y mujeres, inmigrantes y refugiados, que, no bien llegaron a España, perdieron el nombre, el pasado, la consideración social y los más elementales derechos, siendo el propósito de estas páginas individualizarlos de nuevo, cabalmente, rescatarles del marasmo de cifras, datos, estadísticas y lugares comunes más o menos sociológicos que les sepulta y que a todos señala con un mismo nombre, Mohamed.

[[This is] a book of lives stolen by the author from twenty-five foreign workers, men and women, immigrants and refugees, who, as soon as they entered Spain, lost their names, their pasts, social consideration, and their most basic rights, the purpose of these pages being to individualize them again completely, to rescue them from the stagnation of more or less sociological numbers, data, statistics, and stereotypes that bury them and point at them all by the same name—Mohamed.] (Torres 14)

And, in fact, as we will see, Torres does precisely what he describes: steals lives and immigrants' voices from them. He explains that "Mohamed" is the name by which they are rendered invisible, losing their identity to be subsumed under the category of being an "immigrant." As we have seen in the previous chapters, this identity is fixed in the figure of the "Moor," and Torres's "Mohamed," a Muslim male name, signifies precisely that: the conversion of any immigrant into a "Moor." In order to denounce this mechanism of anonymity and fixation, however, Torres problematically uses this same mechanism, presenting the stories as "the stories of twenty-five *Mohameds*" (Torres 29; my emphasis).

The tension between individualization and collectivization is rampant in the text. Trying paternalistically both to "rescue" the uniqueness of each immigrant story and to give each a uniform discursive structure within the context of his book, Torres finds himself in the middle of a riddle. The twenty-five testimonies belong, in fact, to Torres, who, after interviewing his informants, wrote their stories himself. Once again, as in the case of other *testimonios*, the problem here is the editor's, or author's, need to create the illusion of these voices as "the genuine voices of immigrants" instead of acknowledging the heavy mediation, even protagonism, of his own voice. Torres thus assures us, "será el propio Mohamed el que tome la guía del relato y el que hable" ["Mohamed himself is the one who will guide the narration and speak"] (Torres 29). At the same time, in a surprisingly arrogant gesture, Torres claims to actually know his informants' lives better than they themselves:

> Conocerán por [este libro] a veinticinco personas, y en algunos casos mejor de lo que esas personas se conocen a sí mismas, pues muchas de ellas transitan aturdidas y perplejas por su presente de desarraigo, de soledad y de ciudadanía de tercera.

> [Through this book you will get to know twenty-five people, and in some cases better than they know themselves, since many of them journey in a stunned and perplexed state through their present of uprooting, loneliness and third-class citizenship.] (Torres 20)

It is Torres's transcription, thus, that provides their lives with meaning and makes them intelligible. He also knows, better than they do, who they really are, so he explicitly acknowledges his manipulation of the collected material in order to make it fit "reality," even if this means, quite contrary to his initial intention, for example, depriving two of the interviewed people of their individuality: "son veinticuatro [historias] en vez de veinticinco porque a dos personas, un matrimonio marroquí, las he metido en la misma vida, pues así es en la realidad, a la que se somete, sin condiciones, este libro" ["These are twenty-four stories instead of twenty-five, because I have put two people, a Moroccan couple, into the same life, since it is this way in reality, to which this book submits, without conditions"] (Torres 21).

The homogenizing structure that Torres uses to tell the lives of his informants is one in which each of the twenty-four "testimonies" begins with a short first-person paragraph in italics: "Yo, Mohamed, me llamo . . ." ["I, Mohamed, my name is . . ."], followed by the "real" name of the immigrant, their country of origin, and, in most cases, how they arrived in Spain. This paragraph is followed by a third-person narration of the person's life centered on one particular topic or characteristic that distinguishes that immigrant. Accordingly, each story has a title that alludes to that characteristic or topic. The first story, for example, is entitled "Vicio de árboles" ["Vice of Trees"] and tells the story of Ahmed Belaud as someone whose life has been determined and guided by his love of trees. This highly arbitrary selection of "life material" is accompanied by the also highly arbitrary and capricious organization of the stories into chapters. Some of these chapters carry "ethnic" titles, such as "Moros" ["Moors"], "Negros" ["Blacks"], and "Sudacas" [literally "Southerners," a derogative word for "South Americans"]. Some, instead, are organized thematically, like "El Trabajo" ["Work"], "La Violencia" ["Violence"], "La Familia" ["Family"]. Some encompass categories that are obviously also represented in other titles, such as "La Identidad" ["Identity"] and "La mujer" ["Woman"].

Like Moreno Torregrosa in his explanatory introduction to *Dormir al raso*, Torres sees his role both at a level equal to that of his informants, and, at the same time, as a guarantor of truth whom the reader can trust more than the people whose stories are being told. As Moreno Torregrosa spoke of his "parallel journey" to that of El Gheryb, so Torres speaks of having shared his informants' lives so much that he was not just listening to them, but he was also living their lives with them, thus obliterating his obvious privileges and power. He says: "no es que me hayan contado sus vidas, que por supuesto me las han contado, sino que durante seis meses *las he vivido*, en parte, junto a ellos, con sus amigos, o con sus familias, o en sus chabolas" ["the point is not that they have told me their lives, of course they have, the point is that over the course of six months *I have lived them*, in part, with them, with their friends, or their families, or in their shanties"] (Torres 20; my emphasis). And, as Moreno Torregrosa spoke of his presence as a guarantor of "objectivity," Torres assures his readers that, although they might not believe his informants' words, he was there with them and can thus guarantee the stories' status as truth: "por eso me consta que lo que se cuenta aquí, si bien inverosímil muchas veces, es enteramente cierto" ["that is why I am certain that what is told here, although very often unbelievable, is completely true"] (Torres 20).

In her analysis of the foundational Latin American *testimonio The Autobiography of a Runaway Slave* by Miguel Barnet, in which Barnet edits and transcribes the life of Esteban Montejo, Elzbieta Sklodowska points out that, as a traditional anthropologist, Barnet "embarks on a search for his own identity through his encounters with Montejo" (Sklodowska 91). It is, indeed, a similar slippage between the quest for the other and the quest for the self that we can detect in Torres's explanation of the motives that prompted him to produce *Yo, Mohamed.*

> al objeto de saber de primera mano, en primera persona, quiénes son, qué buscan, de qué huyen, qué pasa, qué nos pasa, qué nuevo virus de impiedad y de violencia ha penetrado en nuestro tejido social enfermo.
>
> [with the objective of knowing first-hand, in first person, who they are, what they are looking for, what they are running from, what happens, what happens to us, what kind of virus of impiety and violence has entered our sick social fabric.] (Torres 15)

These immigrants' stories, reconstructed and retold by Torres, seem to be the therapeutic instrument through which to explore that "virus," which has everything to do with the "we" and little with the "they."

Todo negro no igual: voces de emigrantes en el barrio bilbaíno de San Francisco by Beatriz Díaz begins, like *Dormir al raso* and *Yo, Mohamed,* with an explanatory introduction by its author, who tells us how she came to know her informants and tell their stories. From the very beginning of this introduction, entitled "Mis vecinos" ["My Neighbors"], Díaz establishes a clear-cut difference between what is native and what is foreign. She explains that she moved to the San Francisco quarter of Bilbao, now home to many immigrants, after returning from "foreign lands," and that she enjoyed the pleasure of "sentirme una más entre *mi gente* . . . disfrutaba de cada bocado de comida local, de cada detalle cotidiano que me hacía identificarme con *mi cultura*. Volví, pues, a *mi tierra*" ["feeling like one more among *my people* . . . I enjoyed every bite of local food, every daily detail that made me identify with *my culture*. I returned, thus, to *my land*"] (Díaz 9; my emphasis). *My people, my culture, my land*: we are, no doubt, in the terrain of essentialist notions of belonging that are unavoidably linked to the assumptions of culturalist racism. The immigrants with whom Díaz establishes a dialogue serve her as a therapeutic mirror in which she sees "la imagen de foránea que yo trataba de olvidar" ["the image of foreignness I was trying to forget"] (Díaz 9), i.e., as a way to come to terms with her recent personal experience of having been "in foreign lands." There is, thus, no room for ambivalence or subtlety in this structure: there is foreign land, and there is native land, and one is happy and enjoys one's own land and not the foreign one.

Díaz's description of her relationship with her informants, like those of Moreno Torregrosa and Torres, silences the inequality of the exchange, claiming, in fact, that she has at moments experienced their lives with them, so close was their communication: "A veces, sin saberlo, me hice cómplice, me sumergí por segundos en su propio río" ["sometimes, without realizing it, I became an accomplice, I submerged myself in their own river"] (Díaz 10). She also obliterates the material conditions and "asymmetrical translations" (Sommer, "No Secrets" 134) of the exchange, claiming that her neighbors simply talked to her, and she simply listened: "¿Qué pasaría si no hay entrevista, si no hay preguntas . . . ? ¿qué pasaría si nos acercamos y, desde la misma altura, sencillamente escuchamos?" ["What would happen if there is no interview, if there are no questions . . . ? What would happen if we get close and, on the same level, we simply listen?"] (Díaz 14). Díaz's naïve assumption that "simply listening" is possible is coupled with the misleading suggestion that she has not done interviews or asked questions. As if to convince her readers of the veracity of these "natural" dialogues, the first "testimony" she includes in the text, entitled "A mí me gusta hablar" ["I like to talk"], presumably the words of "Jawad, from Algeria," begins with "Gracias . . . me ha gustado mucho hablar contigo, de verdad" ["Thank you . . . I have liked very much talking to you, really"] (Díaz 15). The book's origin, thus, is explained as something completely unplanned by Díaz, who happened to be the repository of all of her neighbors' stories, and could not help herself but transcribe them: "durante muchas noches no tuve más remedio que tomar el bolígrafo y escribir, desde ellos y desde adentro, lo que había escuchado" ["during many nights I had no other choice but to take the pen and write, from them and from inside, what I had heard"] (Díaz 10).

Like any other editor of a *testimonio*, Díaz also needs to justify her editing work, and, through this explanation, she unwittingly highlights her role as manipulator of the stories' content and form:

> recogí especialmente los testimonios que me ayudaban a desdibujar mitos y prejuicios . . . busqué una y otra vez un modo de agruparlos que facilitara su lectura . . . He intentado también dar claridad al contenido, y por eso a veces he adaptado el lenguaje mejorando levemente algunas expresiones, agrupando conversaciones, añadiendo contexto en el relato o traduciendo los testimonios que me fueron ofrecidos en portugués o francés.
>
> [I gathered especially the testimonies that helped me to undo myths and prejudices . . . I looked once and again for a way of organizing them that would facilitate their reading . . . I have also tried to give clarity to their content, and that is why I have sometimes adapted the language, lightly improving some expressions, joining conversations, adding context in the story or translating the testimonies offered in French or Portuguese.] (Díaz 10–11)

Ultimately, the most salient editing choice Díaz makes in her book is that of transcribing (inventing?) her neighbors' broken Spanish. The language of these testimonies is in fact so broken that it unavoidably distances the readers from their content. Díaz, it seems, only found testimonies that proved her essentialist assumptions of national belonging. As she puts it at the end of her introduction, "ésta es la voz de algunas personas de tierras y culturas diferentes a la mía" ["this is the voice of some people from lands and cultures different from mine"] (Díaz 11). We can certainly doubt that these are *their* voices, and whether these "lands and cultures" are mostly characterized by this essentialist difference, but there is no doubt that the voice we are hearing here is very much Díaz's own.

Maximiliano Lemcke's *Todos os llamáis Mohamed* originates with the same assumption as Rafael Torres's *Yo, Mohamed*: the centrality of the constructed image of a threatening "Moor," encapsulated in the name "Mohamed," all key elements of the Spanish imaginary about immigration. Mixing fictional and documentary techniques, this short film attempts,

like the previous texts, to show what immigrants' lives are like.
The narrative content is transmitted to the spectators in a peculiar way: as the film begins, the camera is focused on a close-up of a middle-aged Moroccan man who is looking at the camera.
We hear a voice-over, probably his, reading a text in heavily accented Spanish. As he stares at the camera, this voice explains:

> Soy un inmigrante, alguien que ha tenido que abandonar su propia tierra, su propia casa, y sus seres queridos para sobrevivir. Vengo de Marruecos, pero podría venir de Argelia, de Túnez, de Senegal, de Filipinas o de cualquier otro lugar.

> [I am an immigrant, someone who has had to abandon his own land, his own house, and his dear ones in order to survive. I come from Morocco, but I could come from Algeria, Tunisia, Senegal, the Philippines or any other place.]

As the film progresses, we witness the journey of Hicham, a young Moroccan man who has just arrived in Madrid to be reunited with his cousin Youssef. The story narrates Hicham's progressive disappointment with the reality of Moroccan immigrants' life in a shantytown on the outskirts of Madrid. What makes this film distinct is its inclusion of other immigrants, two other men and a woman, who stare at the camera in silence, while we hear their voices reading a text. These texts become increasingly accusatory as they speak directly to Spaniards, the implicit spectators of the film. The first one, for example, says:

> No se emigra por elección. Emigramos por la imposibilidad de estar en un lugar donde en vez de un puesto de trabajo encontramos solo desocupación, hambre y sobre todo ningún futuro. Pero eso no os interesa. Para vosotros no somos más que extracomunitarios, no somos más que delincuentes, drogadictos, violadores, camellos, asesinos, mentirosos, portadores de enfermedad, putas, ladrones, robatrabajos y moros.

> [One does not emigrate by choice. We emigrate because of the impossibility of being in a place where instead of a job we only find unemployment, hunger and, above all, no future. But you do not care about that. To you we are only non-European, we are only criminals, drug addicts, rapists, drug dealers, assassins, liars, sickness carriers, prostitutes, robbers, job stealers and Moors.]

They also speak of the implicit and explicit violence they confront daily in their lives, of their harsh working and living conditions, and of Spaniards' ignorance. This ignorance is what the film tries to confront. The second speaker, a young man, angrily says: "¿Qué sabéis de nosotros? Nada o casi nada. Con nosotros no habéis hablado. Y si lo habéis hecho, la mayoría de las veces no nos habéis escuchado" ["What do you know about us? Nothing or almost nothing. You have not spoken with us. And if you have, most of the time you did not listen to us"].

The way this testimonial is used in this film seems at first to be very different from the heavy editorial mediation we find in *Dormir al raso, Yo, Mohamed,* or *Todo negro no igual.* After all, the four immigrants who appear, looking at the camera and looking at us as spectators, seem to be *directly speaking to us,* telling us *themselves* how it feels to be an immigrant. However, is this mechanism truly different from the other *testimonios*? Or does it feel different, more "real" and "authentic" because of the visual power of their faces on the screen? After all, we do not know, in the same way we did not know in the other texts, the degree to which "their voices" are mediated, or even scripted, by the editor or the director. It is very possible, indeed, that the texts these immigrants are reading are not at all "theirs," but Lemcke's.[4]

Some sociological studies undertaken in the last few years to study the phenomenon of immigration in Spain operate under the same assumptions as these *testimonio* texts, and they fall into the same traps. Gema Martín Muñoz's *Marroquíes en España* begins by explaining, in a fashion similar to *Yo, Mohamed* and *Todos os llamáis Mohamed,* that Moroccans focalize many of the debates around immigration and integration. Spaniards' perception of them, says Martín Muñoz, is based more on external factors than on the reality of who they are (8). The research for the book *Marroquíes en España* originates in the desire to check that reality:

> detectar lo que verdaderamente ocurre y constatar con conocimiento de causa si, en efecto, esa realidad confirma el imaginario o, si no, contribuir a colocar las cosas en una más justa medida . . . aportando un conocimiento más real sobre ellos mismos.

[to detect what truly happens and verify with field knowledge if, in fact, that reality conforms to the imaginary or, if
not, to contribute to correcting it . . . providing a more real
knowledge about them.] (Martín Muñoz 9)

The assumption at the origin of this work is, thus, that belief
denounced by Clifford and other anthropologists in ethnography's power to have access to an unmediated, transparent
reality. Like the *testimonio* texts, this study also assumes an
unproblematic access to the other's "voice" when it claims
"hemos optado por hablar con ellos, por conocer a través de
ellos" ["we have opted to talk to them, to know through them"]
(Martín Muñoz 9).

The methodology used for this end is that of "ethnographic
semi-structured interviews." Martín Muñoz tries to emphasize
this method's openness and flexibility, in which questions are
organized "according to the discursive logic of the informant,"
in a "relaxed and comfortable atmosphere," with the researcher
"playing a secondary role" (72). The interviews are recorded,
transcribed, analyzed, and categorized, and used in the redaction of the study (Martín Muñoz 73). The study itself, however,
is completely driven by the voice of a narrator, who introduces a
particular topic, such as the first one, "Experience and Memory
of the Country of Origin," and summarizes the answers given
in this regard. The dangers of this selection and editing process
become evident in the narrator's choices about the hierarchy
and organization of the material, by deciding, for example,
which answers are the most representative, and which are asides
or exceptions to a rule. In this first section, for example, the narrator explains:

en todos los casos, la familia se recuerda con añoranza y
cariño, en algunos como un recuerdo "idílico," a pesar de
que varios de los entrevistados admiten haber presenciado o
sufrido la rigidez y castigo de la autoridad paterna.

[in every case, family is remembered with nostalgia and
affection, in some cases as an "idyllic" memory, although
several of those interviewed admit to have witnessed or
suffered the rigidity and punishment of paternal authority.]
(Martín Muñoz 77)

The narrator thus guides our understanding of the collected material, following the general explanation of the topic with quotes from different interviews that support this explanation. The hierarchy of voices thus becomes very clear. The informants' answers are distributed according to the logic of the main narrative, to support it, not to serve as a narrative themselves, but in the form of short quotes, identified as "Interview with a Moroccan man" or "Interview with a Moroccan woman."

César Manzanos Bilbao's *El grito del otro: arqueología de la marginación racial* also assumes the possibility of directly knowing the reality of the other, and having access to the other's voice, by means of ethnographic interviews. The prologue of the project affirms that the social transformations brought about by immigration are analyzed "desde la mirada y el grito del otro" ["from the look and the cry of the other"] (Manzanos Bilbao 13), and that the project pays special attention to methodology "para no construir al otro desde nosotros, sino desde la propia autodefinición" ["so as not to construct the other from our perspective, but from their own self-definition"] (Manzanos Bilbao 14). The prologue also insists on the desirability of giving the other the possibility to speak for himself or herself, but it does not acknowledge, in any way, that there might be difficulties in doing so, or that the answers provided by informants in a traditional ethnographic interview might not correspond exactly to letting them "speak for themselves." The prologue asserts:

> es imprescindible darle la palabra al "otro": nadie mejor que ellos puede sentir y decir cuáles son y cómo se entrecruzan los mecanismos explícitos y sutiles . . . que convierten al otro en un objeto sobre el que se ejerce la discriminación.

> [it is indispensable to give the word to the "other": nobody better than them can feel and explain the subtle and explicit mechanisms that make the other an object of discrimination and what these mechanisms are.] (Manzanos Bilbao 14)

Thus, the project has an already-established, definite goal for those others' words, and that is to have *them* explain the functioning of discrimination for the interviewers. After all, as we have seen in other texts, the "they" is just a way to getting to know what is happening to the "we," as the prologue says quite literally:

Conocer cómo nuestras sociedades piensan, se representan,
perciben o le dan un lugar a los "otros" en el espacio social es
un buen camino para conocer cuáles son las claves de cómo
se está reelaborando el devenir del "nosotros."

[To know how our societies think, represent themselves,
perceive or give a place to the "others" in the social space is
a good way to know which are the keys of what will happen
to the "us."] (Manzanos Bilbao 13)

The novel *Las voces del Estrecho* by Andrés Sorel struggles
with similar issues. As in the other texts, the desire of testimony
and its inherent entrapments lie at the origin of narration. Sorel
explains about his novel: "Yo quería *transmitir el secreto*, la
vida de *esas voces perdidas* en las aguas del estrecho, *rescatar
el silencio* de los naúfragos de las pateras" ["I wanted to *transmit the secret*, the life of *those voices lost* in the waters of the
Strait, *to rescue the silence* of the shipwrecked people"] (Sorel,
"Las voces"; my emphasis). These words by Sorel seem to
claim as possible something that the field of ethnography has
stopped believing it can do: to have direct access to experience
through representation, "claiming transparency of representation and immediacy of experience" (Clifford 2). Sorel's aim
seems almost missionary in his desire to "rescue" the stories of
"those lost voices." When he talks of his desire to "transmit the
secret" of those drowned, we are reminded of Doris Sommer's
reflections about Rigoberta Menchú's secrets. Sommer wonders
if our ardent interest to "know the story" or the "secrets" of an
informant covers a desire to control him or her (Sommer, "No
Secrets" 131). This explanation about the need to rescue these
lost voices is also incorporated into the novel, when, at the end,
after having read the stories of many people who drowned in the
Strait, we find out Abraham's motivation to tell their stories:

Me dijiste: tienes que ir allí, pintar aquello. Tal vez pronto
sea también tarde. *Pintar las voces que ya nadie escucha, a
las que no se da importancia.* Porque hace tiempo que hemos
cegado los ojos y tapiado el corazón. Es el gran silencio, el
no declarado: el que cae sobre las víctimas sin nombre, el de
las voces del Estrecho.

[You told me: you must go there, paint that. Perhaps soon
it would be too late. *Paint the voices that nobody hears*

> *anymore, those nobody cares about.* Because we have shut
> our eyes and covered our hearts for some time. It is the great
> silence, the one not declared: the one that falls upon the
> nameless victims, upon the voices of the Strait.] (Sorel 216)

Giving the silenced or the subaltern a voice, as Spivak has
shown, runs many risks (Spivak 296). As we have already
seen, this desire to tell the stories of others very often includes
a therapeutic aspect for the ethnographers/editors themselves,
who are in search of their own story or voice through that of
their informants.[5] Sorel's description of his plan of action in
order to access the drowned "secrets" seems very much to be a
search for his own sake:

> Me propuse reconstruir la historia de alguno de los ahogados
> . . . las mil y una noches de los desaparecidos en las aguas
> del Estrecho. Imaginaría sus vidas. Visitaría algunos de los
> lugares de las tragedias...Quería *convertir mi angustia en
> testimonio* e identificar a quienes no son ni materia periodís-
> tica: profundizar en sus vidas para que a su vez el lector las
> reconstruya, transforme, enriquezca, *haga suyas.*
>
> [I wanted to reconstruct the story of some of the drowned . . .
> the thousand and one nights of the disappeared in the waters
> of the Strait. I would imagine their lives. I would visit some
> of the places of the tragedies . . . I wanted *to transform my
> anguish into testimony* and identify those who are not even
> journalistic material: go deep into their lives so that in their
> turn the readers could reconstruct them, transform them, en-
> rich them, *make them theirs.*] (Sorel, "Las voces")

Transform my anguish into testimony, make them [the informant's lives] *theirs* [the reader's]: to appropriate immigrants'
suffering and deaths for the purpose of the novel.

Las voces del Estrecho, however, seems at least at one
moment to be aware of the mediation of representation, and
perhaps, of the problematic ethics of the translation and appropriation it performs. In a highly revealing metanarrative
moment, the narrator explains that Abraham, after hearing the
ghosts of the drowned, would paint their stories. Representation
is described in this passage as transformation, not as unmediated transparency:

abría el cuaderno de páginas en blanco y sobre él vertía
sus voces, su lenguaje adaptado al del propio Abraham: le
importaba más el significado que el significante, el relato, el
hilo de las historias escuchadas que la repetición mimética de
lo que le dijeran. Buscaba recrear, transmitir.

[he would open the white-paged notebook and in it he would
pour their voices, their language adapted to that of Abraham's own: he cared more about the meaning than about
the signifier, he cared more about the story, the thread of the
stories heard than about the mimetic repetition of what they
said. He wanted to re-create, to transmit.] (Sorel 80)

The Journalist as Hero

Together with the publication of semi-ethnographic *testimonios*
and the airing of documentaries that attempt to represent immigrants' lives, we have, in several fictional texts, the character
of the journalist or writer who investigates precisely this, what
immigrants' lives are like and how to tell their stories. Through
the character of this journalist, usually a woman, we often have
glimpses of reflection upon the issues raised by *testimonio* texts:
the uneven power relationship between ethnographer or writer
and informant, the problem of wanting the other's "secret," and
the ultimately ethnocentric and egocentric search for "a great
untold story." The character of the investigative journalist is
analyzed in two short stories of the collection *Por la vía de
Tarifa*, in the novel *La aventura de Saïd*, and in the film *Ilegal*.

Although *Por la vía de Tarifa* is a fictional work, it inhabits,
as do most of the texts analyzed in this chapter, the slippery terrain between literature and ethnography, fiction and document.
As such, it includes a series of photographs that document some
iconic instances of the crossing of the Strait of Gibraltar: the
two coasts separated by a few miles of sea, a small boat carrying immigrants, a boat spotted by the Civil Guard, another one
broken against the coastal rocks, dead bodies of immigrants
on the Spanish coast. Its prologue, written by Juan José Téllez
Rubio, emphasizes the testimonial aspect of the book: he talks
about the stories being about "gente de carne y hueso, parábolas
de la vida real, testimonios . . . la franqueza le gana la partida
a la invención . . . se sacrifica lo libresco a favor de lo vital"

["people of flesh and blood, parables of real life, testimonies . . . frankness beats invention . . . the literary is sacrificed for the real"] (Téllez Rubio 10).

The short story "Gabriela" explores precisely this unstable border between the literary and the real. It begins as Gabriela, who is twelve years old, looks at old black-and-white photographs left in a tower in Tarifa. The photographs are those we find in the pages of *Por la vía de Tarifa*: they tell the story of the illegal crossing of the Strait in small boats or *pateras*. Gabriela looks at them from the future: they used to belong to her grandfather, who lived at the end of the twentieth century (García Benito 44). She chooses one and invents a story about it. The invented narrative, which appears next in italics, is the description of a photograph by José Luis Moreno, placed on the page before this short story. It describes the people in the boat, their relationships, how they decided to make the crossing, and how most of them still look at the Moroccan coast while on the verge of arriving in Spain. The short narrative then breaks to a different section, in which we find out that what we have read, is, in fact, a short story written by a character called María, who turns off her computer feeling that her idea of going to the future to talk about the crossing of the Strait is not working after all. While gazing at her daughter, Gabriela, who is two months old, she hears a commotion outside, and, to her surprise, she sees a *patera* that has just arrived on the beach. Getting off it, one by one, are the people she had described in her story. While returning home, she thinks "jamás volveré a titular un cuento con el nombre de mi hija Gabriela" ["I will never use my daughter Gabriela's name as a title for a short story again"] (García Benito 47). In this way, "Gabriela" contains a meta-critical reflection on writing about immigration and its intrinsic "dangers." In this story, the danger is that of the unstable border between reality and fiction and the inherent responsibility that writing about this topic entails: imagining what immigrants' lives are like cannot easily be contained as a purely imaginary activity; it can quickly turn into something very "real."

In the short story entitled "Sa'ra'," the first-person narrator, Luz, tells us about her first assignment as a journalist. She was still a student when these events took place. Her plan was to get first-hand information, to be provided by a recently arrived immigrant, about the crossing of the Strait. This immigrant, Abdellatif, in the Red Cross Hospital with severe headaches and a bandage across his eyes, refuses to talk to anybody. He only repeats one Arabic word that nobody can understand. From her present perspective, she sees her own intentions at the time as profoundly naïve: she thought Abdellatif would undoubtedly trust her and tell her everything, and that she would write a greatly successful story revealing immigrants' suffering, which would contribute to greater justice and a better world (García Benito 51–52). However, neither Luz's daily visits nor her Moroccan sweets and signs of affection make him talk. After a month, Abdellatif's bandage is gone, and Luz sees that he has lost an eye. When he says the word "Sara," Luz thinks he has mistaken her name, but she is intrigued, suspecting there is something she has missed. The night before her deadline, she seems to have found it, because her report is published, although the man who was in the bed next to Abdellatif's in the hospital—we later find out he was a member of the Civil Guard—tells the publisher that what Luz has written is not true. It is only at the end of the story that we find a clue to what happened to Abdellatif in the dictionary's definition of the word *jara*. Originating in the Arabic word *sa'ra'*, it means both an evergreen vegetation common in Spain and a stick used as a weapon, a club (García Benito 54). We conclude from reading this definition that Abdellatif's message-in-a-word was that a Civil Guard had hit him with his *jara* and taken away his eye as a result. The Civil Guard was trying to conceal this, having someone watch Abdellatif while pretending to be a hospital patient in the next bed. We also conclude that this person, who asks the newspapers' director about Luz's journalist status, prevents her from actually graduating and becoming a journalist.

This short story thus highlights some of the dynamics present in the exchanges between informant and journalist/ethnographer: the issue of misguided assumptions about the other, (mis)communication and (mis)translation, what the one who wants to hear the story of the other is actually able to hear and not to hear, to see and not to see (the protagonist's name, Luz, means "light" in Spanish). The story also performs a curious reversal, which is also present in "Gabriela," and in the novel *La aventura de Saïd*. Though Abdellatif was the real victim, whose story we needed to hear, the unearthing of his tale transforms Luz, the brave journalist, into the heroic victim. The story, it turns out, is not that of Abdellatif's tragedy, but that of Luz's attempt to denounce injustice and her punishment at the hands of the Civil Guard for doing so. As she remarks at the beginning of the story, this is the narrative of her failure to achieve her goal to be a real journalist (García Benito 51). The "other," once again, seems to be the excuse to talk the "self."

In the novel *La aventura de Saïd* by Josep Lorman, we have a character very much like Luz in the short story "Sa'ra'": Ana is a twenty-year-old journalism student who is researching the life of Moroccan immigrants in Barcelona. When Ana meets Saïd and Ahmed, two Moroccan immigrants, she tells them she wants to ask them some questions: "que me expliquéis por qué salisteis de Marruecos, vuestra situación aquí, las dificultades con que os habéis encontrado…" ["I want you to explain to me why you left Morocco, your situation here, the difficulties you have encountered . . . "] (Lorman 59). Ana's sense of entitlement in asking these questions and expecting the two men she has just met to answer them corresponds to that controlling disposition of uneven power relationships described by Derrida as "an inquisitorial insistence, an order, a petition . . . To demand the narrative of the other, to exhort it from him like a secretless secret" (qtd. by Sommer, "No Secrets" 131). Saïd's initial reaction to her request—"Que te contemos nuestra vida, vaya" ["Well, you want us to tell you our life"]—ironically acknowledges the "ethnographer/informant" dynamic proposed by Ana: by placing herself in the ethnographer's position, she has made them into "natives," whether they agree or not to the exchange. Furthermore, the narrator's explanation of Ana's interest in Moroccan immigrants falls into the trap of the discourse of "compassion" and missionary "rescue" already observed in Spanish-edited texts about immigration: "Había elegido aquel tema de trabajo por su actualidad y movida por un *íntimo sentimiento de compasión ante el sufrimiento*" ["She had chosen this topic to work on because of its timeliness and moved by an *intimate feeling of compassion before suffering*"] (Lorman 73; my emphasis).

The novel, however, quickly takes Ana's "side" by emphasizing her good qualities, and it does so very effectively by placing this positive evaluation of her behavior in terms of an unquestionable truth imparted by the omniscient narrator:

> Empezaron hablando con cierta prevención, pero poco a poco se fue creando un clima de cordialidad que venció la indiferencia inicial de Saïd. Ana era una persona sensible e inteligente, que sabía conducir el relato de los dos amigos hacia el terreno de la confidencia . . . lo que comenzó como una entrevista de trabajo acabó siendo una reunión de amigos.

> [They began talking with some distrust, but, little by little, a cordial climate, which won over Saïd's initial indifference, was created. Ana was a sensible and intelligent person who knew how to take the story of the two friends to the terrain of the confidential . . . what began as a job interview ended as a getting-together of friends.] (Lorman 59)

Days later, Ana's inherent position as a privileged Spaniard is made clear in a conversation with Saïd, Ahmed, and two more of their friends, Alí and Taïb. Alí and Taïb talk about the injustice of closing the frontiers to immigrants who leave their countries of origin because of poverty and underdevelopment; a direct consequence and responsibility of European colonial rule. Ana's reaction to this conversation is one of naïve surprise:

> Nunca había mirado el hecho colonial desde la óptica que adoptaba Alí . . . De hecho, nunca se había planteado a fondo el problema de los países de origen de los inmigrantes . . . ahora descubría una serie de razones que, como mínimo, hacían dudar de la legitimidad de las medidas que tomaban los gobiernos de la Europa comunitaria.

> [She had never looked at the colonial enterprise from the perspective adopted by Alí . . . In fact, she had never thought deeply about the problem of the immigrants' countries of origin . . . now she discovered a series of reasons that, at least, introduced doubt over the legitimacy of the policies adopted by Europe's governments.] (Lorman 73)

Ana's surprise shows her privileged position: only those privileged enough not to be touched by certain facts can have the luxury of ignoring them.

After Ana comments that it might be "normal" to want to regulate immigrants' entrance to Europe, Alí confronts her over her defense of a normalcy of poverty for certain people and wealth for others. Ana becomes silent, and the narrator explains the situation: "Por fin, se habían repartido los papeles y, de pronto, los personajes se encontraban representando los mundos opuestos a que pertenecían . . . las palabras de Alí habían marcado las diferencias. Ella, quisiera o no, pertenecía al norte" ["Finally, roles had been distributed, and, suddenly, the characters found themselves representing the opposite worlds they belonged to . . . Alí's words had marked the differences. She, whether she wanted it or not, belonged to the north"] (Lorman 74). Interestingly enough, it is only at the moment when Alí openly voices a critical opinion of Ana and the worldview she represents—her "compassion" notwithstanding—that the narrator tells us that a barrier exists between Ana and the Moroccan men. It is Alí, from the narrator's point of view, who has "marked the differences." One could very well think that it was Ana, playing her role of ethnographer searching for data about the men's lives, who has, from the beginning, "marked the differences" between them. Alí's words are furthermore invalidated by Ahmed when he comments to Ana, once they have left the restaurant, that she should not listen to him, that Alí talks too much and he is always questioning an immutable situation that has always existed (Lorman 76).

The novel further establishes Ana's "innocence" by introducing a group that will occupy, without any subtlety, the "villain" position: the skinheads that attack Ana, Ahmed, and Saïd, precisely after leaving the restaurant where Ana's allegiances had been questioned. The skins' attack and subsequent threats to the three of them ensure that, for the rest of the novel, we see Saïd and Ahmed's interests and situations as being the same as Ana's. Right after the attack, in which Ahmed is severely injured, Saïd suggests to Ana that being close to him is only causing her problems, and that maybe they should not see each other anymore. Ana lightly rejects the idea as silly, and she demonstrates her "sensitivity" by staying with Ahmed in the hospital, while Saïd returns home, for fear that the police might arrest him (Lorman 80–81). Ana is so angry at what has happened that she decides to take action, calling a lawyer and, together with the SOS Racism organization, filing a suit against the skins: "no quería quedarse quieta, indiferente, ante tanta violencia impune" ["she did not want to be quiet, indifferent, before such unpunished violence"] (Lorman 84). In fact, from this moment on, Ana not only shares the victim position with Ahmed and Saïd because of the attack, but she actually takes it away from them, since the skins now choose her as their target because of her decision to testify against them. Ana thus becomes the novel's heroine, rejecting her father's suggestion to stay away from the risks associated with the trial, accusing the police of corruption and complicity with the skins, volunteering at SOS Racism, identifying two of the skins in a line-up, and maintaining her accusations against them in the face of the skins' verbal and physical threats.

After opening up the issue of the more subtle—and therefore more pervasive and insidious—racism and construction of otherness implicit in the ethnographic performance of Ana's journalism project, *La aventura de Saïd* chooses to focus on the more "spectacular" and blunt racism of the skinheads. The unfortunate consequence of this focus is that, in the same way that Ana's position of privilege and the inherent violence of her ethnographic performance textually disappear in comparison to the skins' violence, so does the readers' (or the spectators', since this novel was made into a film) sense of shared responsibility for the far more generalized and subtle everyday racism, very often a racism that masks itself, like Ana's, as "compassion" and "good intentions."

The film *Ilegal* by Ignacio Vilar also reflects upon journalists' information-gathering and documentary-making. Vilar incorporates in this film some of the material he had previously treated in documentary form: in particular, his documentary *Polizones* [*Stowaways*], in which he explored the topic of the ships that clandestinely carry illegal immigrants from Africa to Europe. The film constantly reminds us of the mediating role of filmic equipment, showing the images of the ship where immigrants are crammed, for example, never as a reality we have direct access to, but as something we only see through the journalist's camera. The film's opening titles are shown, as well, in the protagonist's small digital camera, interpolated with his recording of the remains of an abandoned *patera* and its passengers' belongings. But what *Ilegal* does especially is to take to its limit the journalist's interest in finding "a great story" at the expense of the subject of that story. As the film begins, Luis and Durán, two Galician journalists from rival networks, are in Morocco trying to find "a great story" connected to the traffic of illegal immigrants across the Strait of Gibraltar. As the result of a misunderstanding through which he takes the place of his colleague, Luis is able to infiltrate a ship on which twenty-one Sub-Saharan immigrants are hidden as stowaways. He records a video of the dreadful conditions of the trip, and, after obtaining it, he happily heads back to Galicia with his prize, where he becomes the target of persecution by both the traffickers' crime organization and the rival network, which had paid a fortune for Durán to obtain access to the ship. Trying to escape this persecution and secure his possession of the video, Luis causes first the death of his assistant at the network then the deaths of the stowaways, who are dumped into the sea by the traffickers once they find out there is a compromising video, and finally the death of the only surviving immigrant who had been able to escape from drowning.

While these tragedies take place, Luis's only preoccupation is his great story. There is a symptomatic scene in this respect at the beginning of the film: in search of information on how African immigrants cross to Europe, Luis and Durán, with the help of María, their African guide, get inside a clandestine Moroccan camp. Luis pays some money to a man in exchange for his story, and when the man begins to tell the story of how he walked across Africa to get to Morocco, Luis interrupts him, saying he has heard that story many times; the story he has paid for is not that one, but the one about the crossing of the Strait of Gibraltar. The immigrants' situation is only interesting to him if he can find an unknown, thrilling angle to take to his station as a *new* story. Moments before, while driving to the camp, Durán had reminded him how the latter's documentary, "The Boats in the Strait of Gibraltar," was aired in prime time and drew a huge audience. Therefore Luis needs *his* story in order to compete with Durán's. The tale, then, is never about the immigrants themselves, but about Luis and Durán's rivalry, which moves from a professional level to an erotic one, as both compete for María's affections, and, later, as Luis tries to convince

himself that Sofía, a private detective hired by Durán's chan-
nel, is actually interested in him and not in his video footage.
What seemed at the beginning to be a film about immigration
quickly becomes a film about "who gets the girl": at the end,
after all the deaths caused by the footage have occurred, the
police have caught the traffickers, and Luis is finally free to air
his video, instead he chooses to throw the tapes into the sea.
He does this as evidence of his love for Sofía, thinking she is
dead. It is because of *her* presumed death (she turns out, however, not to be dead, after all) that, for the first time, he stops
to think about the deaths the tapes have caused and decides to
get rid of them. At the point at which, after all the tragedy that
ensued because of those images, they could have been aired
and served their purpose of denunciation, Luis decides they are
of no use to him anymore. After all, he has already gotten the
girl: the film ends "happily" with their kiss. *Ilegal* thus takes
to the extreme the egocentricity and self-centeredness of the
journalist's ethnographic stance. In addition, we can also see
in *Ilegal* the process by which immigrants are constructed into
subalterns, in order to try to secure the distance between a new,
modern, European Spain and its Third World, underdeveloped,
pre-modern visitors. It is through this distancing mechanism
that, in collective terms, this film becomes a "feel good" movie.
There is a particular scene that accomplishes this: in the middle
of their search for the surviving immigrant, Sofía and Luis are
welcomed to a celebration of Ramadan in the house of Moroccan immigrants. In a reference to Vilar's previous documentary
La aldea, lo antiguo y lo nuevo [*The Village, the Old and the
New*], Sofía, while eating the lamb, remembers the goat feasts
in the Galician village where she grew up. She comments nos-
talgically how that life has disappeared and there is no village
left. Remembering a vanished way of life in the Galician village
that has given way to a Galicia insistently showcased in the
film as modern and up-to-date with the latest advances in every
social and technological realm produces a certain nostalgia
but, more than anything, it produces an irrepressible pride. In
the same way that the novel *La aventura de Saïd* and the film
based on it allow the reader and spectator to identify with Ana
as the personification of a new Catalonia, and a new Spain that
is, in contrast to the Spain of her parents' generation, young,

compassionate, and caring, *Ilegal* invites the spectator to sit comfortably in the space desired by others, and enjoy having gotten the girl. Or, in other words, having gotten the ultimate prize of a place in European modernity.

The Refusal to Speak: "Fátima de los naufragios"

In the texts analyzed in this chapter, the positioning of the Spanish journalist, writer, or sociologist as traditional ethnographer produces the effect of converting their immigrant informants into subalterns, erecting an insurmountable distance between them. This distancing, constitutive of racism, fixes the immigrant as an irremediable other. As Stuart Hall explains,

> racism ... operates by constructing impassable symbolic boundaries between racially constituted categories, and its typically binary system of representation constantly marks and attempts to fix and naturalize the difference between belongingness and otherness. (Hall, "New Ethnicities" 255)

Although not directly using the ethnographic stance, the short story "Fátima de los naufragios" by Lourdes Ortiz also constructs the immigrant as subaltern, at the same time that it explores what happens when that subaltern actually refuses to speak. Thus it breaks the possibility of satisfying the ethnographic desire to know and possess the other and to reinforce, by doing so, that "difference between belongingness and otherness." This short story centers on Fátima, a Moroccan immigrant woman who sits on the beach of a coastal Spanish town gazing at the sea. What characterizes Fátima is her impenetrability, the impossibility, for the town inhabitants, of reading her. She does not speak to anybody; they cannot tell whether she is old or young, nor can they grasp the meaning of her minimal gestures. Her face, the narrator tells us, is a mask, and she is "a statue of pain," motionless, and imperturbable (Ortiz 7–8).

The town, at the beginning, tries to "fix" her, to find a position for her, both literally, by finding her a job or physical place to be, and symbolically, by trying to categorize her as greenhouse worker, maid, crazy, or homeless:

> Hubo quien le ofreció trabajar en los invernaderos, y una
> señora de postín se acercó un día a brindarle un trabajo por

horas . . . los municipales hablaron del asilo y una concejala
emprendedora se acercó una vez a proponerle asistencia social y la sopa del pobre.

[Someone offered her a job in the greenhouses, and an
important lady approached her one day to offer her hourly
work . . . the municipal officials talked of the asylum and an
enterprising town councilor approached her once to offer her
social assistance and the soup for the poor.] (Ortiz 8)

These efforts fail, as her silence reinforces itself. This is a crucial moment in the relationship between the town and Fátima.
Through her silence, she can achieve something impossible by
any other method: a recognition of her dignity and respect: "en-
tendieron el silencio, tan impasible y quieto, como una negativa
que imponía respeto" ["they understood the silence, so impas-
sible and quiet, as a refusal that imposed respect"] (Ortiz 8).
Her silence and immobility become, paradoxically, instruments
for agency: through them, she avoids the town's attempts at
controlling her and fixing her in a stable position of otherness.
Anne Anlin Cheng, taking the example of slavery, explains
how, in extreme conditions, "survival and the management of
grief exceed our vernacular understanding of agency, of what
it means to take control of oneself and one's surroundings"
(Cheng 21).[6] Agency can be achieved through different means:
the refusal to speak becomes, in Fátima's situation, a way of
asserting her own will. She wants to mourn.

Given her silence, the inhabitants of the town proceed to
project their fantasies about who or what she is: for Antonio, the
fisherman, she is crazy, but harmless (Ortiz 8). He thinks she
does not belong to this world anymore: the sea has emptied her
brain, he says, and she has emerged from it as a premonition or
a warning: "demasiados muertos, muchos muertos; el mar se los
traga, pero el mar nos la ha devuelto a ella, para que sepamos
que las cosas no están bien" ["too many dead, so many dead;
the sea swallows them, but the sea has returned her to us, so that
we know that things are not right"] (Ortiz 14). For the tourists,
she is the crazy woman on the beach, the African beggar (even
though she never begs) (8). For Lucas, Antonio's son, she is
a ghost, an apparition or a dream; for Felisa, the bread maker,
she is a saint with healing powers (9–10). Mohamed, the young
survivor of a *patera*'s shipwreck, tells them she is the mother

and wife who came with him in the boat with her husband and young child. He assures them it was impossible for her to save herself from the shipwreck, in the same way that nobody else was able to survive: he did because he had spent years practicing swimming, but Fátima could not have swum the several miles that separated the boat from the coast (11–12). Mohamed explains to them that she seems to be the same woman, but considerably aged and changed: in the boat, she was young, beautiful, and talkative. She never stopped talking and singing lullabies to her child (16). He also tries to speak to her, pressed by the town that hopes to solve the mystery of who she is. But Fátima does not look at him, and she covers her face, maintaining her silence (14). She is to Mohamed an apparition of death, a witch, or a ghost (14).

Fátima's silence also produces in the town strong feelings of empathy and identification. For the women of this fishing village living off the sea, she comes to represent their own anguish as they wait for their husbands, fathers, and sons to return from the water every day. Fátima reminds them of every time they feared the worst and of every time someone did not come back (Ortiz 17–18). María, the mailman's wife, explains it this way:

> cuando la veo allí fija, me dan ganas de ponerme a su lado y ... no sé, quedarme allí quieta a su vera, porque yo sé bien lo que es perder a un padre y a un abuelo, ¡que el mar es muy suyo y muy traicionero! Y no sabe el que no lo ha pasado lo que es el dolor, lo que es la desesperación.

> [When I see her fixed there, I feel like sitting next to her and ... I don't know, staying quiet there with her, because I know very well what it means to lose a father and a grandfather, the sea is very much its own and very treacherous! Nobody who has not gone through that knows what pain is, what desperation is.] (Ortiz 17)

For increasing numbers of people, she also becomes an image of the Virgin: for Angustias, Fátima is the Macarena, the Virgin of Hope of Seville: "tiene la mismita cara de la Macarena, una Macarena tostada por el sol ... es ... la Macarena de los moros; es la madre que perdió a su hijo y aún le espera y reza por él" ["she has the same face as the Macarena, a Macarena tanned by the sun ... she is ... the Macarena of the Moors, the mother who has lost her son and still awaits him and prays for him"] (Ortiz 7). For the fishermen, she is the Virgen del Carmen—the Virgin who protects fishermen from the sea's perils—and *la moreneta*, the informal name of the Virgin of Montserrat, patron saint of Catalonia, who has a dark-skinned complexion (Ortiz 10). Her name, Fátima, harks back both to the prophet Mohamed's sister and to the Portuguese Virgin of Fátima. Through her silence and quiet pose, thus, she becomes the recipient of the town's fears and hopes. Not able to classify her ethnographically because of her refusal to speak and act as an informant, she acquires a mystic and sacred quality for them.[7]

But what her silence and quiet pose while looking at the sea allows *her* to do is the work of mourning for her loss. One day, after four years, a dead male body appears on the beach, and Fátima takes him into her arms, cradles and sings to him. Seeing this, Lucas tells the town that Fatima's son has returned, and everybody runs to the beach to see the miracle. Fátima is again seen as a Virgin; she is Michelangelo's *Piedad*, with Christ cradled in her arms. Antonio, however, explains to everybody that he cannot be her son, who was, by Mohamed's account, much younger, about nine years old. The body, says Marcelino, is probably that of a young man from Sub-Saharan Africa, probably that of a recently drowned immigrant (Ortiz 19). Meanwhile, Fátima keeps singing and crying "sobre el rostro tan redondo y perfecto del Cristo africano" ["over the face so round and perfect of the African Christ"] (20). She kisses him and smiles to him, "la sonrisa de una madre que acaba de escuchar las primeras palabras balbucidas por su hijo . . . una sonrisa suave, complacida" ["the smile of a mother who has just heard the first words babbled by her son . . . a pleased, soft smile"] (Ortiz 20). After a while, Fátima leaves the body on the beach and walks slowly into the sea, while the people of the town cannot do anything but watch, immobilized by the sacred nature of the scene. We can read her decision to drown herself as a continuation of her silence, as her act of will in an extreme situation. So even though we never hear Fátima's voice in this text—if she was to speak, whose voice would that be? Hers? Lourdes Ortiz's?—"Fátima de los naufragios" offers us the possibility of imagining agency through, precisely, the absence of that voice, the refusal to play the ethnographic game of becoming an informant.

The options are not, of course, solely those of either play-ing the role of an informant or refusing to do it. The option chosen by some immigrants who were able and wanted to do so has been one of telling their story themselves. This is the case of *El Diablo de Yudis* by Moroccan Ahmed Daoudi, *Jo també sóc catalana* by Moroccan Najat El Hachmi, *Calella sen saída* by Cameroonian Víctor Omgbá, or *Diario de un ilegal* by Moroccan Rachid Nini. These texts, based on the immigrant experience of their authors in Spain, were written in Spanish (Daoudi's), Catalan (El Hachmi's), Galician (Omgbá's), and Arabic (Nini's). The fact that they were written by immigrants does not mean, however, that they somehow convey a more "authentic" truth about the immigrant experience in Spain than those studied in this chapter. These texts are themselves mediated by other factors, and they do not represent "the immigrant experience" any more—*or any less*—than Spanish "ethnographic" texts. Their analysis, like that of *testimonios*, should always be aware of the entrapments of taking a text to be a transparent medium of representation that gives us direct access to the experience of a homogeneous and commensurable community.

Conclusion

Confronting Ghosts

A thread of profound anxiety runs through the many narratives that chronicle contemporary Spanish responses to Moroccan immigration. This uneasiness was compounded by the fact that this immigration phenomenon began to take place precisely at the time when Spain, after officially being accepted as a member of the EU, was attempting to highlight its "Europeaness" both domestically and abroad. Perceived as a contemporary "return of the Moors," the arrival of Moroccan workers over the last twenty years has obligated Spain to confront old ghosts related to its own national, regional, racial, and cultural identities. Moroccans today are received differently from other immigrant groups precisely because of these old ghosts: throughout the last 1,300 years, tellings and retellings of the stories of past encounters with "the Moors" have shaped the very way Spain has constituted itself as a nation. The inherent slippage between past and present that fuels this perception is captured in the naming itself: Moroccans, in the everyday language of today's Spain, are "Moors." And Moors, as the retellings of Spanish narratives of national identity demonstrate, are precisely that chimera of an ancient enemy against which Spain has formed itself as a nation. Much effort has been spent in constructing "the Moor" as the ultimate horizon of difference, the "them" against which the Spanish "us" has constituted itself. However, as the texts studied in this book demonstrate, there is an inherent ambivalence and difficulty that results from attempting to place the Moroccan immigrant as "Moor" in a stable category of otherness. Neither in the space of medieval Spain nor in the contemporary context are the boundaries between ones and others definitely traced. While insisting on the problem of the Moor, *Morisco,* or Moroccan difference, Spaniards are in fact attempting to reassure themselves of the existence of that difference: the problem is not that they are different, but that *they are not different enough.*

Consequently, the social and cultural responses to this "return of the Moor" have been deeply ambivalent. Even in "sympathetic" or presumably "welcoming" texts explicitly produced with the intention of denouncing the mistreatment that immigrants undergo, there is a profound need to maintain a distance from them. This distance is produced through repetitive strategies of separation and demarcation of fixed identity positions. Thus, for example, the recurrent accounts in the news media of immigrants' crossing of the Strait of Gibraltar, like the mock "*Desembarcos*" performed yearly in the festivals of Moors and Christians, visually and conceptually reinforce the idea of the "Moors" as invaders and the Spaniards as invaded. The immigrants aboard the *pateras*, like the Moors aboard the mock medieval vessels, are rendered visible and fixed as foreign trespassers in the moment of their arrival on the coast of a territory that does not belong to them. This indexical connection to the invading medieval Moor is rampant in contemporary responses to Moroccan immigration: present in social confrontations and violent collective attacks against Moroccan workers, in Spanish politicians' comments, in fictional works and ethnographic testimonies, it constitutes one of the most recurrent tropes by which the significance of current Moroccan immigration is explained.

Another distancing mechanism by which the fears, anxieties, and hopes generated by the present are projected into the past is that of the construction of the Moor as part of an idealized *convivencia* and multiculturalism "*avant la lettre*" situated in medieval al-Andalus. This imaginary Moor has little to do with the real lives of Berbers and Arabs in medieval al-Andalus or Moroccans today. These fictional representations have, however, an immense popular appeal, and they have multiplied in the Spanish culture industry coinciding with the numerical increase of Moroccan immigrants in Spain in the last twenty years. In the context of the new Europe, Spain is presented in these texts as an experienced partner in the practice of multiculturalism. At the same time that these representations of benign and cultured medieval Moors produce their particular appeal because they are characters fixed in a safe past, contemporary immigrants are also presented, in another series of texts, as subjects impossible to integrate into modern, secular European Spain because, precisely, of their irremediable belonging to the past. This is the case in certain social debates, such as those that emerge around the use of the Muslim headscarf in schools, or in the repetitive depiction in films and novels of stories about an impossible relationship between an immigrant man and a Spanish woman. In these instances, the figure of the immigrant is transformed into that of the Moor who is anti-modern, conservative, and oppressive to women.

The ethnographic performance through the use of the *testimonio* genre is another mechanism by which immigrants are placed at a safe distance of otherness. While ostensibly attempting to give a voice to those who do not have one, these texts actually construct immigrants as voiceless subalterns. This mode of representation has a profound appeal, as demonstrated by the high number of books and articles published and the many documentaries aired that use it. By focusing on rescuing and replacing immigrants' *voices*, texts such as *Dormir al raso*, *Yo, Mohamed*, *Todo negro no igual*, *Todos os llamáis Mohamed*, *Las voces del Estrecho*, or *El grito del otro* share with other types of social texts a deep concern for language related to older debates about language use within Spain. The preoccupation about immigrants being able to speak their stories is not far from a preoccupation about which language they will use to do so. As the controversies over immigrants' use of Catalan or Castilian in Catalonia show, immigrants intersect with prior debates about Spanish transnational, national, and regional identities and sense of self. Moroccan immigrants, in particular, as we have seen, awaken some of the most sensitive issues that Spain as a nation has had to solve: its own regional, ethnic, cultural, religious, and linguistic internal heterogeneity, the management of its internal others, and its position of "difference" and inferiority in a more developed and modernized Europe.

Through their responses to the present manifestation of the "Moor" as the Moroccan other, Spaniards are attempting to untangle some of these questions. Trying to reassure themselves of their stable geopolitical position in Europe, they perform through these social and cultural texts the position of self-assured hosts who, in welcoming a guest to their homes, affirm their own primary rights of ownership, occupation, and belonging:

> To dare say welcome is perhaps to insinuate that one is at home here, that one knows what it means to be at home, and that at home one receives, invites, or offers hospitality, thus appropriating a space for oneself, a space to *welcome* the other, or, worse, *welcoming* the other in order to appropriate for oneself a place and then speak the language of hospitality. (Derrida, *Adieu* 15–16; emphasis in original)

In the Spanish/Moroccan case, the ambivalence of the guest/host positions is never solved, but continuously negotiated at every encounter. Stuart Hall has insisted on the concept of identity as a never-completed process, without closure, always in construction, and always needing the other: "As a process it operates across difference, it entails discursive work, the binding and marking of symbolic boundaries, the production of 'frontier-effects.' It requires what is left outside, its constitutive outside, to consolidate the process" (Hall, "Introduction" 2–3). In their present encounter with the "Moor," this time in the context of the new Europe, Spaniards are once more engaging in their own constitutive process of identity formation, trying to solve unsolved questions, and attempting to come to terms with their own ghosts.

Notes

Introduction
European Immigration,
New Racism, and the Case of Spain

1. For an explanation of the difficulties in terminology one encounters when dealing with the subject of the Muslims in Spain, see Harvey, *Islamic Spain* 1–5.

2. Moroccans were, until very recently, the largest immigrant national group in Spain: according to statistics of the INE (National Institute of Statistics), in 2001 there were 234,937 residents from Morocco, followed by those of Ecuador, with 84,699 residents, and the UK, with 80,183. The latest published statistics, from 2003, show a significant increase in the number of residents from Ecuador, who now occupy first place with 390,119 residents, followed by 378,787 from Morocco, 244,570 from Colombia, and 161,398 from the UK. The total of foreign residents has also increased considerably. In 2001 there were 1,109,060, constituting 2.7 percent of the total population. In 2003, there were 2,672,596, or 6.26 percent of the total population (España, *España en cifras*).

3. It is important to note that there exists a variety of efforts to undermine this barrier between Morocco and Spain and to counter the effects of widespread racism toward Moroccan immigrants. These range from the work of NGOs such as SOS Racismo, to the attempts by José Luis Rodríguez Zapatero to improve political relationships with Morocco and implement some of the demands made by immigrant organizations, to the cultural exchanges facilitated by several organizations and programs.

4. These conditions had a precedent in those adopted in medieval times by both Muslims and Christians. The degree to which medieval Spain can be characterized as a time of religious "tolerance" and *convivencia*, in the sense of *peaceful* coexistence, is a very controversial issue. Américo Castro, in his *España en su historia: cristianos, moros y judíos*, argued that Spanish cultural identity arose in the Middle Ages from the combination of Muslim, Jewish, and Christian elements (14–16), and that the three religions coexisted, without too many confrontations, until the Christian persecutions of Jews at the end of the fourteenth century (203). In his account of tolerance (he actually uses this term, *tolerancia,* more than the famous "*convivencia*"), he emphasizes that this was a completely Islamic tradition, and that, when the Christians practiced it, they did so in imitation of the Muslims (199, 202, 203). He emphatically clarifies: "La tolerancia española fue islámica y no cristiana" ["Spanish tolerance was Islamic, not Christian"] (202). His thesis were famously contested by Sánchez Albornoz, in a series of long-lasting disputes whose endurance and bitterness demonstrate the high stakes at play in the subject of Islam and Judaism's place in Spain. More recently, historians, literary critics, and politicians have revived this debate, especially in reference to the often-idealized image of al-Andalus. In regards to this, it is important to differentiate two basic positions: one is that of the right-wing critics of the concept of *convivencia*, who object to this characterization of medieval Spain by reviving Sánchez Albornoz's ideas of an essential, Christian Spanishness never "contaminated" by Judaism and Islam, such as César Vidal and Serafín Fanjul. The other is that of historians like Mercedes García Arenal, who criticize, for example, María Rosa Menocal's *The Ornament of the World: How Muslims, Jews and Christians Created a Culture of Tolerance in Medieval Spain* for its anachronistic use of modern concepts of religious tolerance and equal rights, but recognize the much better status of Christians and Jews in Islamic lands than the one of Muslims and Jews in Christian lands, and the importance of their mutual influences in shaping the high Islamic civilization of al-Andalus (García Arenal 803). As García Arenal points out in her review of Menocal's book, in reference to the concept of religious tolerance:

> [Menocal] is drawing a myth, a beautiful myth, which, as myths do, proposes a model. The fact that it is a positive and attractive model (even perhaps a necessary one in these hard times of the "Clash of Civilizations") should not obscure the fact that al-Andalus and Christian Spain were, like all multiple (multiethnic, multireligious) societies, fraught with tension and conflict, very often violent internal conflict, even warfare, which did not preclude mutual influences. (803)

5. For more nuances on the meaning of this term and its problems, see Harvey, *Muslims* 2–6.

6. For many *Moriscos*, passing afforded them the opportunity to stay in Spain or to return to it after their expulsion, as Ricote does in the second part of *Don Quijote*. As Barbara Fuchs explains, the frontier between Spain and the Muslim world was a porous one, crossed by exiles, deserters, corsairs, captives, and renegades. Some of the renegades were Christian captives who had been forced to convert to Islam, but many others converted voluntarily for a variety of reasons. The Spanish garrisons in North Africa were a particularly vulnerable frontier position: many soldiers deserted these outposts and crossed over to Islam. In this context, conversion and passing brought considerable social and economic advantages. Some renegades, and some expelled *Moriscos*, became corsairs and were very successful as such, passing as Christian Spaniards: with their knowledge of the Spanish territory and of the Castilian language, they could easily trick their victims (Fuchs, *Passing* 10–14). Another instance of *Moriscos'* passing was through the opportunity offered by the rescue of Christian Spaniards who had been taken captive by corsairs. The following instruction given by the Crown to the religious orders in charge of redeeming those captives shows the extent of the *Moriscos'* success:

"watch with great vigilance that the captives you redeem are not Moriscos expelled from this kingdom" (Friedman 147, qtd. in Fuchs, *Mimesis* 153, *Passing* 15). Passing also occurred the other way around: when renegades were taken captive by Christian corsairs, they had to hide their Christian origin, or else they would be brought to the Inquisition. Many thus passed as Muslims in origin and were successful at doing so, unless they were denounced by their shipmates (Fuchs, *Passing* 15). In the context of the Alpujarras rebellion, the second volume of Pérez de Hita's *Guerras civiles de Granada* describes other instances of passing between the two camps (Fuchs, *Mimesis* 55). As Fuchs explores in both *Mimesis* and *Passing*, these instances of passing among Christians and Muslims show the fluidity between Christian and Muslim identity and the vulnerability of the notion of an essential, purely Christian "Spanishness." For more on passing among Christians and *Moriscos*, see also Burshatin, "Written on the Body" and "Playing the Moor."

7. Another crucial "problem" with the *Moriscos* was their presumed lack of political allegiance to the Spanish state. Especially during the Alpujarras uprising, they were seen as a potential fifth column in a Muslim naval attack on the Spanish coasts. For the dismantling of this myth as well as the myth of the unanimity of opinion regarding their expulsion, see Márquez Villanueva, "El problema"; Haliczer. For more on the *Moriscos*, see Caro Baroja; Harvey, *Muslims in Spain*; Meyerson, *The Muslims*. For a thorough discussion of the Granada context in which the *plomos* controversy took place, see Coleman, *Creating* 188–201; Fuchs, *Mimesis* 101–11.

8. This contrast can be attributed to the different ideological aims of these types of texts. The play *Las famosas asturianas* [*The Famous Asturians*] (1612), by Lope de Vega, beautifully articulates what is at stake in these attributions of masculinity. In it, the chastity of Alfonso II de Asturias (760–842) is identified with impotency and military weakness, and the Moors' sexual potency with fierceness in battle. This Moorish aggressive masculinity accounts for their conquest of Spain. By the end of the play, however, the Christians show their true virility by defeating the Moors. With the advance of the Reconquest, thus, the gender dynamics are reversed, positing the defeated Muslims as weak and feminine. For the feminization of the oriental man as a convention, see Edward Said.

Chapter One
Difference Within and Without: Negotiating European, National, and Regional Identities in Spain

1. Elena Delgado points exactly at this problem:

> the constant invocations to "Europeanness," modernity and normalcy present in the political and cultural discourse predominant in the Spanish state are not accompanied by a rigorous

intellectual interrogation of those terms. What is being alluded
to and what is elided/concealed when one refers to "Europe" and
"modernity"? And why are we not even considering the possibility of studying those two signifiers as ideologically charged
constructions, rather than as unquestionable axioms? (Delgado,
"Settled" 124)

2. Eduardo Subirats sees Spain's enthusiasm for Europe as excessively
sudden and superficial, without a real exchange of ideas or a critical reception of European thought. Instead, he argues, Spaniards uncritically
embraced their heightened consuming power and the commercial promises of "sudden happiness" (Subirats 82–83).

3. This was, however, precisely the idea of Europe that was promoted
for the construction of the European Single Market in 1992 (Ang 22), an
idea that misses key European experiences such as decolonization, migration, and globalization, and is inherently linked to nineteenth-century
imperial myth-formation (Nederveen Pieterse 4–5). This notion of "Europeanness" is underpinned by the effort at ignoring the complicity between
Western modernity and rationality and racial terror: modernity "includes
a rational 'concept' of emancipation . . . but, at the same time, it develops
an irrational myth, a justification for genocidal violence" (Dussel 66). As
Gilroy indicates, the rational and universalist claims of the Enlightenment
project, which define Europe's modernity and were, in theory, valid for
all humanity, contain a very particular and restrictively defined notion of
humanity (Gilroy 43).

4. Barbara Fuchs shows how at the end of the sixteenth century and the
beginning of the seventeenth, Spain's efforts at racializing and othering
conversos and *Moriscos*, and the exacerbation of anti-Moorish rhetoric in
Spain, coincide with the construction of the Black Legend, in which Spain
is stigmatized not only as cruel and barbaric, but also as the racial other
of Europe (Fuchs, "The Spanish Race"). This chronological coincidence
reinforces one of the main ideas of this chapter: that Spain sees its belonging to Europe as directly connected with its efforts to separate itself from
the Moorish and Jewish elements of its national identity.

5. Exoticism proved to be a highly successful formula of self-market-
ing for tourist purposes. As Pi-Sunyer notes, during Franco's regime,
Spain's similarity to other Mediterranean regions was countered by
stressing the exotic (237). It is not surprising then that the Spanish tourist
slogan of the 1960s was "*Spain is different.*" The intention of the slogan,
as Kelly indicates, was "to attract tourists to a 'exotic' destination, with
interesting local customs and traditions *differing from the European
norm*" (Kelly 30; my emphasis). The formula worked, and from the early
1950s tourism in Spain experienced a boom of unprecedented size, rapid-
ity, and duration. The 4 million visitors to Spain in 1959 became 34 million by 1973, 40 million by the late 1970s and early 1980s, and 54 million
by 1989 (Pi-Sunyer 237).

6. This double bind in which Spain both Orientalizes and is Orientalized itself complicates Edward Said's concept of Orientalism. Said defines the limits of his project, explaining that he will focus on the British and French cases because "[u]nlike the Americans, the French and the British–less so the Germans, Russians, Spanish, Portuguese, Italians, and Swiss–have had a long tradition of what I shall be calling *Orientalism*" (1). Aijaz Ahmad argues that by exclusively using the British and French cases as representatives of a "European mentality," Said reproduces the essentialism of the West and Europe he is trying to undo in relationship to the Orient (Ahmad 183). A growing group of critics within Hispanism is currently working on remedying, in Kirsty Hooper's words, "the dual absence . . . of Spain from interdisciplinary studies of Orient and Empire, and of Orient and Empire from literary and cultural studies of Spain" (Hooper 172).

7. Torrecilla mentions some exceptions to these acknowledgments of Spain's links with the Moors only out of spite or against a seemingly impossible quest to attain European status. In the eighteenth century, Juan Pablo Forner argues in his *Oración apologética* that medieval Spanish Muslims were the precursors of modern scientists. Therefore, he maintains that it is precisely through the scientific and cultural contributions of al-Andalus that Spain belongs to Europe. Along this same line of thought, writers like Faustino de Borbón, the count of Campomanes, and the Jesuits Juan Andrés and Francisco Javier Llampillas also posit Spain's Muslim past as an antecedent of the European Enlightenment (Torrecilla, *España exótica* 99).

8. The army knew this very well and complained about a treaty that highlighted Spain's international weakness. In this way, a military newspaper grumbled: "por débiles tenemos que contentarnos con las migas de un festín que debiera ser para nosotros solos" ["Because of our weakness we have to be content with the breadcrumbs of a feast that should have been only ours"] and "hemos vendido nuestra progenitura por un plato de lentejas" ["We have sold our inheritance rights for a plate of lentils"] (qtd. in Balfour, *Abrazo* 37).

9. For more on Spanish colonialism in Africa, and its connections to the Spanish Civil War, see Martin-Márquez's forthcoming *Disorientations: Spanish Colonialism in Africa and the Performance of Identity*. See also Balfour, *Abrazo mortal* [*Deadly Embrace*], and Madariaga.

10. It is from this point of view that García Morente goes to enormous lengths to justify Spain's "national character" in terms of Christian homogeneity: "la nacionalidad . . . consiste . . . en la homogeneidad de esencia . . . ser español es actuar 'a la española,' de modo homogéneo a como actuaron nuestros padres y abuelos . . . nación es . . . unidad fundamental de estilo en todos los actos colectivos" ["Nationality . . . consists of . . . homogeneity of essence . . . to be Spaniard is to act 'Spanish,' in a manner homogeneous with the way our parents and grandparents acted . . . Nation is . . . a fundamental unity of style in all collective acts"] (39–40). And this national essence, or national style, is best represented, says García Morente, by the figure of the Christian knight (48), "un hombre que representa las más íntimas aspiraciones del alma española . . . el diseño ideal e individual de lo que en el fondo de su alma todo español quisiera ser" ["a man who represents the most intimate aspirations of the Spanish soul . . . the ideal and individual design of that which at the bottom of his soul every Spaniard wishes to be"] (García Morente 56). The homogeneity and unity of the Spanish nation consists, thus, of Catholicism: "todo lo demás puede considerarse como contingente o accidental. El catolicismo, empero, es consustancial con la idea misma de la hispanidad" ["everything else can be considered contingent or accidental. Catholicism, however, is identical to the idea of the Hispanic world itself"] (186): "entre la nación española y la religión católica hay una profunda y esencial identidad" ["between the Spanish nation and the Catholic religion there is a profound and essential identity"] (García Morente 188).

11. For a critical assessment of the transition to democracy and what he calls its "Europeist cult," see Subirats. Cristina Moreiras Menor also critiques this period as a moment in which Spain's common project is "'venderse' a Europa para llegar a formar parte de ella, no sin antes venderse a sí misma para olvidar ese pasado nefando que todavía pesa sobre ella" ["to sell herself to Europe in order to achieve membership into it, having first sold herself to forget that shameful past that still weighs on her"] (Moreiras Menor 74–75).

12. It is important to note also that an estimated 1.4 million people, mostly from Andalusia, Murcia, and Castile, migrated to Catalonia and settled there between 1950 and 1975 (Woolard 30). This internal migration, which is briefly discussed in the following section of this chapter, was due to the same economic conditions as Spaniards' migration to Europe in these same years.

13. This controversial 1985 law was replaced in 2000 by the *Ley Orgánica* 4/2000, which broadened immigrants' rights: it recognized their equality with Spaniards, their rights to education for minors, emergency medical care, and basic social services, and it devised a mechanism through which immigrants who had been in Spain for two years could legalize their situation. However, after the Popular Party won the general elections by absolute majority in 2000, it introduced reforms that severely restricted these rights. The *Ley Orgánica* 8/2000 deprived immigrants of their rights to assembly, association, public demonstration, syndication, and strike, it raised from two to five the years required to obtain a residency permit, and established a deportation procedure. The latest legal development was the institution of an extraordinary process of legalization by the newly elected Socialist Party in December 2004.

14. In a much earlier article, originally published in *El furgón de cola* in 1967 and quoted in *España y sus Ejidos*, Goytisolo sees this pattern already occurring in the 1960s, when most Spaniards experienced the economic boom of the so-called "years of development":

Con la excitación y las prisas del último comensal llegado al banquete, los españoles procuran atrapar como pueden y se esfuerzan en alcanzar en unos meses el nivel técnico y social que los pueblos europeos han conquistado pacientemente . . . Gracias al turismo y a la emigración, han descubierto los valores de las sociedades más avanzadas y los cultivan con celo de neófito.

[With the excitement and hurry of the last to arrive at the banquet, the Spaniards try to grab what they can, and they make an effort to try in a few months to reach the technical and social level that the European peoples have patiently conquered . . . Thanks to tourism and emigration, they have discovered the values of more advanced societies and they cultivate them with the eagerness of neophytes.] (Goytisolo, *España* 33)

15. Although this idea currently competes with that of Spain as a modern European nation, represented by spaces such as the new Guggenheim Museum in Bilbao.

16. Some films and documentaries that have Spanish emigration to Europe as their main subject matter are *Españolas en París* [*Spanish Women in Paris*] (Robert Bodegas, 1971), *Vente a Alemania, Pepe* [*Come to Germany, Pepe*] (Pedro Lazaga, 1971), *De aquí y de allí: testimonios de mujeres españolas emigrantes en Francia* [*From Here and from There: Testimonies of Emigrant Spanish Women in France*] (Serge Gordey and Saïd Smihi, 1990), *El tren de la memoria* [*The Train of Memory*] (Marta Arribas and Ana Pérez, 2005) and *Un Franco, 14 pesetas* [*One Franc, 14 pesetas*] (Carlos Iglesias, 2006).

17. Another famous controversy was that of the new mosque of Granada. While local mosques had been functioning in already-existing buildings, a 20-year-long dispute ensued over the construction of its first modern mosque building, the *Mezquita Mayor* of the Albaicín, which was completed and inaugurated in July 2003. For the history of this controversy, see Coleman, "The Persistence."

18. Brad Epps teases out some of these dynamics between Catalonia and Spain, both haunted by Africa, in the correspondence between Miguel de Unamuno and Joan Maragall. See Epps, "Between."

19. The alarmist and arguably racist (because of its essentialism and fixed notion of group behavior) claim of the higher fertility rate of Spanish-speaking migrants as opposed to that of "Catalans" is still widely used today by anthropologists and sociolinguists. See Strubell, Woolard, Pujolar i Cos, and O'Donnell.

20. For more on the relationship between Catalans and Spanish immigrants in the 1960s, including a discussion of the complexities at play when defining what it means to be "Catalan," see Jacqueline Hall, Woolard, and Vilarós.

21. What is not often acknowledged in this type of statistics is the existence of Spanish-speaking families in Catalonia who are *not* the poor immigrants from Andalusia and Murcia (disdainfully called *xarnegos*). Their existence and potentially enormous influence was pointed out by Badia in 1969, who considered *them* a threat: "the greatest 'threat' to the language came from the Spanish-speaking upper classes, who might set an example of a Spanish-speaking educated and economically well-off sector" (Pujolar i Cos 146). Sociolinguistic studies also participate in the fear of miscegenation that is analyzed in more detail in chapter 4. For example, in a famous study done in 1981, Strubell argued that the language predominantly used in "mixed" families would probably decide the future of Catalan. From surveys of children of these marriages, he concluded that the Catalan-speaking population was decreasing. These results, of course, caused great concern, in a sense raising a red flag about the "danger" of marrying "immigrants" (speakers of Castilian). However, as Pujolar i Cos explains, "the evidence that this [Catalan's decline] was due to tendencies in mixed marriages was inconclusive, mainly because the category 'mixed' was ascribed according to the parents' places of birth and not according to their family language" (148). Again, what is at stake here is an essentialist, isolated understanding of identity, in which the possibility that the "Catalan" spouse could have been the one already speaking Castilian is not contemplated. For another example of a study in which mixed marriages appear as the culprit for either "recruitment" or "defection" of Catalan speakers, see O'Donnell.

22. A paradigmatic example of this was the declaration of Fernández-Miranda, the Immigration General Secretary under the Partido Popular government, who said in March of 2001 that it was "convenient" for immigrants to be Catholic, the religion of the majority of Spaniards, in order to integrate themselves into Spanish society ("Fernández-Miranda").

Chapter Two
Ghostly Returns: The "Loss" of Spain, the Invading "Moor," and the Contemporary Moroccan Immigrant

1. Some scholars of Hispanism have already noted the possibilities offered by what has been called "Hauntology studies" to reflect on issues of memory, the refusal to confront the traumas of the past (Labanyi, "History" 65) and the status of heterogeneous cultural processes (Labanyi, "Introduction" 3) in contemporary Spain. I am referring especially to the collection of essays *Disremembering the Dictatorship: The Politics of Memory in the Spanish Transition to Democracy*, edited by Joan Ramon Resina, and to the essays of Jo Labanyi, both in the aforementioned book and in the introduction to her edited collection of essays *Constructing Identity in Contemporary Spain*.

2. In the same way that we might question the allusion to Spain as al-Andalus in the video found in Leganés, we must also question the Spanish use of this same concept in contexts such as the war in Iraq: the Spanish military base that came under attack in the spring of 2004 in Nayaf carried the name of al-Andalus, something probably perceived as bizarre or just plain macabre by many Muslims, and probably thought of as conciliatory by the Spanish military.

3. As reproduced in the recording of the lecture posted in *El País Digital* on 22 Sept. 2004.

4. The opposite view was held by Américo Castro, who argued that Spanish cultural identity arose in the Middle Ages from the combination of Muslim, Jewish, and Christian elements (Castro 14–16). See note 4 of the introduction.

5. The central role of North African figures in the development of Early Christianity (St. Athanasius, St. Augustine, St. Anthony) reminds us of how religious and cultural identity are historically contingent, as opposed to eternally constant.

6. The Vandals, when they settled in southern Spain, were the ones who crossed to North Africa, which is why the Arabs called Muslim Spain "Andalus," a slightly distorted form of the tribal name "Vandals" (Makki 5).

7. The Mozarabs maintained their religion, but they were highly influenced by the advanced Arab culture that surrounded them, speaking Arabic, wearing Arab clothing, etc.

8. There is speculation about the place of residence of the author of this important chronicle. While Wolf (*Conquerors* 26) proposes the Cordoban court, Collins believes he probably lived in Toledo (16–17), as does Díaz y Díaz (315). López Pereira suggests Murcia (15–16).

9. A fascinating passage of the chronicle reveals the interconnectedness of the Christian and Muslim points of view in these first years of the conquest. This "Christian" chronicle, written in Latin probably by a churchman, speaks of the actions of "un sarraceno llamado Yahía dictador terrible, que . . . llevado de su duro carácter, persigue a los sarracenos y a los moros de España . . . y devuelve muchas cosas a los cristianos" (*Crónica* 91); "a Saracen by the name of Yahya . . . was a cruel and terrible despot…With bitter deceit, he stirred up the Saracens and Moors of Spain by confiscating property that they were holding for the sake of peace and restoring many things to the Christians" (Wolf, *Conquerors* 141). López Pereira indicates in his corresponding footnote that this passage is probably based on an Arab source, which would explain why he speaks ill of a governor who favored Christians and persecuted Muslims (91). This passage, however, can also be explained through Wolf's argument that the chronicle does not highlight religious difference between Islam and Christianity but political developments that affected the stability of the kingdom (Wolf, *Conquerors* 33).

10. In the years following AD 711, and throughout the Peninsula, Christian clerics were busy reprimanding Christians for unorthodoxy and contagion from Jewish practices, while not mentioning the subject of

Islam as a separate religion that could possibly threaten Christianity. The chronicle mentions several cases of Christian heresy: a man who claimed to be the Messiah in AD 721, a Sabellian heretic in AD 744, and Christians in Seville who celebrated Easter on the wrong date, for whose education a book was written in AD 750 (Wolf, "Christians" 88–89).

11. The chronicle's description of "Spain's disgraces" uses the highly formulaic conventions of the rhetoric of lament that was repeated over the centuries by Christian chroniclers to explain Spain's "loss": "¡¿Quién podrá, pues, narrar tan grandes peligros?! ¡¿Quién podrá enumerar desastres tan lamentables?! Pues aunque todos sus miembros se convirtiesen en lengua, no podría de ninguna manera la naturaleza humana referir la ruina de España ni tantos y tan grandes males como ésta soportó" (*Crónica* 73); "Who can relate such perils? Who can enumerate such grievous disasters? Even if every limb were transformed into a tongue, it would be beyond human capability to express the ruin of Spain and its many and great evils" (Wolf, *Conquerors* 133). Alfonso el Sabio's *Historia de España* uses the same rhetoric, amplifying it for didactic purposes (see Impey): "¿Qual mal o qual tempestad non passo Espanna? . . . ¿Quien me darie agua que toda mi cabeça fuesse ende bannada, e a mios oios fuentes que siempre manassen llagrimas por que llorasse el llanniesse la perdida et la muerte de los de Espanna et la mezquindad et ell aterramiento de los godos?" ["Which evil or tempest did Spain not suffer? . . . Who would give me water for my whole head to be bathed in, and fountains for my eyes to always shed tears to cry and lament the loss and the death of those from Spain and the disgrace and panic of the Goths?"] (Alfonso 313).

12. As commented in chapter 1, Josep María Navarro has found in his study of Spanish school textbooks that the conquering Muslims are consistently characterized as invading, non-European foreigners who produced a rupture of Spain from European history (Navarro 124–27).

13. Israel Burshatin's article builds its argument in contrast with Menéndez Pidal's view of the sexual misdeed as the central element of the story. Burshatin shows how Menéndez Pidal and other critics emphasize this element in order to trace a Christian origin for the legend—the (Germanic) Gothic Ermanarich cycle. In contrast to the rape, Rodrigo's intrusion into the House of Hercules was regarded as an "oriental" element in the narrative, with "oriental" signifying ahistorical, fanciful, and purely fictive (Burshatin, "Narratives" 14–16). Instead of analyzing the ideological implications of this dismissal of Muslim sources as purely "fictional" next to "reliable" Christian sources, Burshatin examines this episode in relation to hagiographic narrative tradition, thus reinscribing it as a Christian one. Even though Burshatin's argument is compelling, we must wonder why most critics are so eager to find the Christian connections of the legend, instead of investigating the interconnectedness of Muslim, Mozarab, and Christian sources.

14. As I pointed out in the introduction, in Reconquest medieval texts and in texts from later contexts, the sexual dynamics are reversed, and Muslims appear as effeminate or homosexual, to underscore their (fantasized or true) defeat at "masculine" Christian hands.

15. Not all Republican romances reproduced this image of the Moor. Some of them pointed out how Moroccan soldiers were actually victims of a deception that would take them to their deaths. See "El moro engañado" ["The deceived Moor"] by Emilio Prados, or the anonymous "Si yo el árabe supiera . . ." ["If I knew Arabic . . ."].

16. One of the most compelling and troubling explorations of this image of the Moor as Spain's sexual predator is Juan Goytisolo's *Reivindicación del conde don Julián*. This novel, a classic of twentieth-century Spanish literature, imagines a Moorish re-invasion of Spain through Arab sexual violence, self-consciously taking up and parodying the representation of Spain as a virginal Christian land and woman who will be destroyed by the invasion. For a critical assessment of this novel, see Jo Labanyi (*Myth and History*) and Brad Epps (*Significant Violence*), who argue that it problematically repeats the violence it attempts to subvert.

17. Freud states: "[I]t may happen that a man who has experienced some frightful accident—a railway collision, for instance—leaves the scene of the event apparently uninjured. In the course of the next few weeks, however, he develops a number of severe physical and motor symptoms which can only be traced back to his shock . . . he now has a 'traumatic neurosis' . . . the time that has passed between the accident and the first appearance of the symptoms is described as the 'incubation period'" (Freud, *Moses* 67).

18. Caruth thus finds latency to be "[t]he central Freudian insight into trauma . . . the impact of the traumatic event lies precisely in its belatedness, in its refusal to be simply located, in its insistent appearance outside the boundaries of any single place or time" (9).

19. Kaplan and Wang's volume, *Trauma and Cinema: Cross-Cultural Explorations* is based on this assumption that "cultures too can be traumatized . . . traces of traumatic events leave their mark on cultures" (Kaplan and Wang 16). See also Kaplan, "Melodrama" and "Trauma."

20. Images of "invasion" are also employed when discussing the presence of immigrant children in Spanish schools. While many schools in different parts of Spain are involved in promoting their integration into Spanish society and actually see the cultural diversity these children bring as an asset, many individuals still see them as a threat that needs to be contained. Pilar Urmeneta, director of the "Santa María" public school in Lavapiés, Madrid, explained to a journalist: "nosotros no tenemos ese problema. Por ahora, nos estamos librando de la entrada de inmigrantes, pero hay otros centros que se están llenando. Eso es porque entre ellos se juntan y acaban yendo todos al mismo colegio. Pero se están extendiendo, y ya están llegando al nuestro" ["We do not have that problem. For now, we are liberating ourselves from the entrance of immigrants, but there are other centers that are getting filled. That is because they get together among themselves and end up all going to the same school. But they are extending, and they are already reaching our school"] (Peregil).

21. For a more detailed account of the particular situation of El Ejido and the confrontations that took place there, see Francisco Checa's *El Ejido: la ciudad-cortijo,* Juan Goytisolo's *España y sus Ejidos,* and, from the controversial perspective of the Spanish neighbors of this town, Mikel Azurmendi's *Estampas de El Ejido.* See also Yeon-Soo Kim's discussion of the photographic exhibition *Inmigrantes, El Egido,* by Rick Dávila. Kim shows how this series of portraits of Arab immigrants, taken shortly after the riots, has a lot of good intentions but ultimately fails at promoting their inclusion in the "Spanish family." The portraits, explains Kim, appear decontextualized from the racial violence that originated them, at the same time that their subjects are stripped of any sort of agency (Kim 189–203).

22. This nostalgia for a lost al-Andalus in which Muslims were the victors and owners of most of Spain is often invoked in writings about Muslims *written by Spaniards.* With this, I do not mean to say that this nostalgia does not exist in the Arab world or in the minds of "real" (as opposed to fictional) immigrants. What I want to stress is that this ventriloquism of Muslim immigrants by Spaniards tells us more about the anxieties of those Spaniards producing the texts than about the preoccupations of real immigrants. Nostalgia for an idealized al-Andalus characterized as the site of peaceful co-existence of Arabs, Christians, and Jews (which is a different nostalgia from the one felt by the characters of *Las voces,* who are said to miss their *power* over Christians) exists across national, ethnic, and religious barriers. See, for example, Denise Filios's essay, in which she analyzes the nostalgic idealization of al-Andalus by María Rosa Menocal, Amin Maalouf, and Rachid Nini, and Lisa Abend's essay on how Spain's Muslim converts have made this idealized image of al-Andalus their "spiritual home." See also note 4 of the introduction.

23. Not all social and cultural texts regarding the topic of immigration do this, however. In a forthcoming essay, I analyze the short story "La quema de los barcos" by Miloudi Chaghmoum, which serves as an example of the construction of a radically different past and present, in which clear "essential" or ethnic differences between Spaniards and Moroccans cannot be easily traced. This understanding of identity inexorably challenges the still pervasive belief in national cultures existing in isolation from one another, and needing to protect themselves against "invading foreigners" (Flesler). Susan Martin-Márquez finds a similar thrust in the work of artists such as Miquel Barceló and José Luis Guerín (Martin-Márquez, "Constructing").

Chapter Three
Playing Guest and Host: Moors and Christians, Moroccans and Spaniards in Historical Novels and Festive Reenactments

1. An earlier version of this section was co-authored with Adrián Pérez Melgosa, and published in article form in *Journal of Spanish Cultural Studies*. I thank Adrián for allowing me to use part of that material here.

2. For an analysis of the festivals in Villena and Castalla (also in Alicante) see Harris. For Andalusian examples, see Baumann and Driessen.

3. Baumann describes an exception to this pervasive pattern of Christian victory. In Alcalá la Real, Jaén, where the festivals had not been celebrated since 1833, they were revived a few years ago with a conciliatory ending. The festivals there do not end with the conversion of the defeated Moors but "in a dance of friendship between the two as a sign of coexistence and peace between the two cultures" (324). We can relate this innovation to the effort of introducing the concept of "reconciliation" with Muslims and Jews connected to the official commemoration of the 500th anniversary of 1492.

4. In his essay, "Cara y cruz del moro en nuestra literatura," Goytisolo analyzes precisely this phenomenon of the fascination with an exotized past image of the Moor in contrast to the rejection of "real" Muslims. See note 9. Alarcón's already-mentioned *Diario de un testigo de la Guerra de África* is an excellent example of the simultaneously explicit idealization and derision of the "Moor." For Alarcón, so powerful is the idealized image of maurophilic literature that he considers those fictional Moors to be more "real" than the "real" Moroccans he is fighting the war against. Thus, he says of a Moroccan prisoner: "Era un verdadero moro, esto es, un moro de novela" ["He was a real Moor, that is, a literary Moor"] (Alarcón 207).

5. The presence of Moroccan immigrants in Valencia, as in other Communities, began in the mid-1980s. More than 80 percent of them are employed in agriculture, especially in the province of Valencia, while in Alicante and Castellón, 15 percent work in the fishing industry. In the coastal towns of Alicante, where most of the festivals take place, 35 percent of Moroccan immigrants practice commercial activities connected to tourism (Zapata de la Vega 185–89).

6. For more on passing between Muslims and Christians, see the introduction.

7. The apparent current insistence of the festivals on this equation of Spanishness with Christianity is also an attempt to affirm both a religious and cultural homogeneity that has never been representative of Spain and is even less so today. At the same time that the "Moors" are no longer "somewhere else," large numbers of Spaniards no longer declare themselves to be practicing Catholics. As Rosa Montero recalls, "in 1970 the overwhelming majority of Spaniards regarded themselves as practicing Catholics (87 per cent), while in 1991 the figure had fallen to less than half the population (49 per cent)" (316).

8. For the last twenty years Spain has experienced a boom in the historical novel. Some examples of the great number of special collections dedicated to this genre are *Narrativas históricas* by Edhasa, with more than one hundred titles, *Selección de la historia* by Planeta, divided into seven different types of historical narrative, and *Grandes éxitos de la novela histórica* by Salvat, with massive distribution through street vendors (Romera Castillo 11). The topic of "convivencia" and the often-idealized portrait of al-Andalus has become a genre in its own right. A case in point is that of Magdalena Lasala. After the publication and success of *Moras y cristianas*, she has published *La estirpe de la mariposa* (1999); *Abderramán III, el gran califa de al-Andalus* (2001); *Almanzor* (2002); *Walläda La Omeya, la última princesa del esplendor andalusí* (2003); *Boabdil: tragedia del último rey de Granada* (2004); *Doña Jimena, la gran desconocida en la historia del Cid* (2006); and *Zaida, la pasión del rey* (2007). All of them have had several re-editions and translations.

9. In this sense, these novels can be linked to the literary tradition of "maurofilia," or maurophilic literature of the late sixteenth century, in which there is an idealized portrayal of the imaginary Moors of the past at the same time that their contemporary, "real" counterparts were in fact being deprived of their culture and religion. This tradition includes *El Abencerraje* [*The Abencerraje*] (1561), *Las guerras civiles de Granada* I and II [*The Civil Wars of Granada*] by Pérez de Hita (1595 and 1597), and the short novel *Oxmín y Daraja*, included in Mateo Alemán's *Guzmán de Alfarache* (1599). See Carrasco-Urgoiti, *El moro de Granada*; Goytisolo, "Cara y cruz"; Burshatin, "Power"; and Fuchs's forthcoming book *Exotic Nation*.

10. Although, as described in the introduction in the case of the *Moriscos*, a point was reached when conversion to Christianity was not enough. As explained by Fuchs, *Moriscos* suffered "the root contradiction of Spanish religious proselytism in a climate of quasi-racial intolerance: 'New' or converted Christians remain ostracized by Old Christians, who are untainted by a Moorish or Jewish past" (Fuchs, *Mimesis* 176). As explained in the introduction, this process of increasing suspicion against *Moriscos* culminated in a series of expulsions (from Granada in 1569–70, from Valencia and then from the rest of Aragon and Castile in 1609–14). In contrast to earlier expulsions, such as the expulsion of the Jews in 1492, and previous expulsions of *Mudéjares* (Muslims under Christian rule) who did not want to convert to Christianity throughout the sixteenth century, the expulsion of *Moriscos* was not based on religion (since they were, at least nominally, Christian), but on cultural, ethnic traits, now seen as non-Spaniard. See Root; Fuchs, *Mimesis*; Márquez Villanueva, "El problema"; and Coleman, *Creating*.

11. This description coincides with Américo Castro's conceptualization of medieval Spain as "el resultado de la combinación de una actitud de sumisión y maravilla frente a un enemigo superior, y del esfuerzo por superar esa inferioridad" ["the result of the combination of an attitude of submission and awe before a superior enemy, and the effort of trying to overcome that inferiority"] (Castro 49).

12. Américo Castro uses bathing as a measure to calculate the enormous Muslim influence on the whole of the Peninsula. It seems that most small towns in Castile had a public bath in the thirteenth century. This practice began to dwindle with time among Christians, and since 1526 it was prohibited among *Moriscos* (Castro 82–83).

Chapter Four
Impossible Love: The Presumed Incompatibility of Islam and (European) Spain

1. The "newness" of the concept of "new racism" has been questioned by Robert Miles, who criticizes its lack of extensive historical contextualization. He argues that

> the distinction between "old" and "new" racism, in itself, presumes a unilinear evolution: by definition, it periodises different forms of racism as characterizing successively different conjunctures. In the absence of supporting historical evidence, it is more valid to conceptualize the distinction as a difference of form and content rather than as chronological. (40–41)

Miles agrees with Taguieff's characterization of Barker's distinction between an old and a new racism analytically by referring to a *racisme inégalitaire* and a *racisme différentialiste*, "thereby avoiding the implication that the contemporary racism is *by definition* a new or "post-modern" phenomenon" (Miles 41). For a more detailed critique of Barker's argument, see Miles and Brown 61–64.

2. Shih denounces this culturalism that melts into culture the ethnic, historical, political, and national. As a global extension of the concept of American multiculturalism, "each nation is supposed to represent one reified culture, with a set of recognizable traits" (Shih 22–23).

3. Regarding the debates about the New European Constitution, the Pope congratulated former Prime Minister José María Aznar for his efforts to introduce an explicit mention of the "Christian roots" of Europe ("Juan Pablo II").

4. For a thorough discussion of films related to the topic of immigration, see Santaolalla, *Los "otros."* For the specific topic of Moroccans in Spanish film, see also López García, "El cine." For an overview of the topic of immigration in film, see Urioste. For an analysis of *Flores de otro mundo, Poniente,* and *Extranjeras* as films directed by women, see Ballesteros, "Embracing."

5. In her classic study, *Foundational Fictions: The National Romances of Latin America*, Doris Sommer explains the enduring appeal of the erotic rhetoric in Latin American nation-building novels of the nineteenth century. Her book aims "[t]o show the inextricability of politics from fiction in the history of nation-building" (5) through love stories that allegorize the different components of the nation. As in the group of films analyzed in this essay, she finds in these novels a consistent rhetoric of love used to justify specific political projects for the nation. Putting aside the obvious differences between nineteenth century Latin America and contemporary Spain, there is a disturbing resemblance between these two groups of fictions. If Sommer's novels offer "the pretty lies of national romance . . . [as] strategies to contain the racial, regional, economic, and gender conflicts that threatened the development of new Latin American nations," in an effort "to hegemonize a culture in formation" (Sommer, *Foundational* 29), the impossible, unhappy romances of Spanish immigration films respond to a comparable effort of presenting an imaginary hegemonizing picture of contemporary Spain, in which difference is always something that is outside the self and that can be easily broken with.

6. A good example of this persistence is described by director Claire Denis: she explains how the "excitement" of an interracial heterosexual romance was sought by the producers of her film, *Chocolat*: "I was . . . strongly advised to construct an affair between Protée, the male black servant in the film, and the white woman. The producers saw this outcome as good box office" (Denis 67).

7. For a more extensive analysis of *Bwana*, see Santaolalla, "Close encounters." For both *Bwana* and *Las cartas de Alou*, see Molina Gavilán and Di Salvo; and Ballesteros, "Xenofobia."

8. Regular jurors were luminaries like Juan Marsé, Ricardo Muñoz Suay, Jaime Gil de Biedma, and Beatriz de Moura. Sometimes others like José Cela, Fernando Fernán-Gómez, and Jorge Edwards joined. Winners included Ana Rossetti, and it introduced such authors as Almudena Grandes and Eduardo Mendicutti.

9. From the Spanish perspective, the category of "Moor" automatically collapses different nationalities. Part of the general European discourse about the threat of Muslim immigrants is, precisely, this collapsing of internal differences. In this essay I place together films whose male immigrant protagonists have different national origins because I am analyzing *Spanish* responses to immigration (as opposed to the way immigrants might represent themselves). It is because Jalil is assimilated into the category of "Moor" that it is useful to compare the construction of his character to Saïd's, for example, the Moroccan character in *Susanna*.

10. For an extensive analysis of this film, see del Pino; Kim; Martín-Cabrera; Martínez-Carazo, "*Flores*"; and Nair, "In Modernity's Wake."

11. Another earlier Spanish film genre that contains points of contact (and important divergences) with the racial/romantic dynamics present in immigration films is the Francoist *folklórica* musical, where, in most cases, a gypsy, lower-class female protagonist becomes romantically involved with a non-gypsy, higher-class male. See Labanyi, "Race"; Vernon; Woods; del Pino.

12. Something similar occurs in Rick Dávila's portraits of Arab immigrants, analyzed by Yeon-Soo Kim. As she explains, in the museum exhibition they were part of, these portraits were placed side by side with photographs of Spaniards, with the good intention of dignifying the immigrants, while including them in "the Spanish family." The other photographs, however, showed a very particular image of Spaniards. They contained, as explained by Kim, seniors vacationing, a festival of pornography, a bachelorette party, and young people who "flaunt their individualities through appearance and the idiosyncratic decoration of their environments" (Kim 201). The consequence is that, in comparison,

> the immigrants look more self-contained than the subjects of the other photographs who appear to be eccentric, outlandish, and unconventional . . . the principal distinction between the immigrants and the Spanish natives captured in the exhibition's photographs in the midst of vacations, parties, and at leisure is that the first group looks backward while the second group is presented as self-made and self-fashioning. (Kim 201–02)

As in the texts studied in this chapter, the resulting message of the exhibition analyzed by Kim is the equation of Arabs with backwardness and Spaniards with modernity.

13. *Hijab* isn't really a garment in particular, as implied by the articles in *El País*, but the act of covering. Fátima Mernissi explains the concept of *hijab* as three-dimensional: "[t]he first is a visual dimension: hiding from view. The root of the verb *hajaba* means to 'hide'. The second dimension is spatial: to separate, to mark a boundary, establish a threshold. Lastly, the third dimension is ethical: it relates to the question of prohibition . . . A space hidden by *hijab* 'is a forbidden space'" (Mernissi, *Women's Rebellion* 51–52; also Mernissi, *Women and Islam* 93–94). For a history of the origin of *hijab* in Islam, see Mernissi, *Women and Islam* 85–101.

14. James Mill could say, in the nineteenth century, that "Among rude people the women are generally degraded, among civilized people they are exalted" (qtd. in Enloe 48). Enloe untangles the contradictions between this discourse and real practices of domination and female subordination in the Western world when she explains how, in the British case,

> British officials passed legislation in India improving women's inheritance rights (1874, 1929, 1937), prohibiting widow-burning (1829) and allowing widow remarriage (1856), all in the name of advancing civilization. At the same time, Victorian values allowed these British officials to enact laws which imposed prison sentences on wives who refused to fulfill their sexual obligations to their husbands and imposed a system of prostitution that provided Indian women to sexually service British soldiers

stationed in India. The riddle of two such contradictory sets of colonial policies comes unravelled if one sees British masculinized imperialism not as a crusade to abolish male domination of women but to establish European male rule over the men of Asian and African societies. (Enloe 49)

This idea would also permeate Spanish discourses about Moroccans at the beginning of the twentieth century. The treatment of women by Moroccan males would be one of the justifications of the need for European intervention in Morocco.

15. McClintock has shown how in "Algeria Unveiled," "[s]o eager is Fanon to deny the colonial rescue fantasy that he refuses to grant the veil any prior role in the gender dynamics of Algerian society. Having refused the colonial's desire to invest the veil with an essentialist meaning (the sign of women's servitude), he bends over backward to insist on the veil's semiotic innocence in Algerian society before colonization" (McClintock 97).

16. *La Vanguardia's* question was "¿Aprueba la decisión de permitir a la niña marroquí Fátima El Idrissi asistir a clase con pañuelo?" ["Do you approve the decision to allow the Moroccan girl Fátima El Idrissi to attend school with the scarf?"] 30.62 percent of the answers were "Yes" (537 votes), and 68.19 percent were "No" (1,196 votes). *El País's* question was "¿Considera acertado permitir sin condiciones el uso del pañuelo en la escuela?" ["Do you consider it correct to allow without conditions the use of the scarf in schools?"]. Of 4,279 answers, 47 percent were affirmative and 51 percent negative. For more on the politics of the veil in Spain, see Nair, "Moor-Veiled-Matters."

Chapter Five
Testimonies of Immigrant Life: Fact, Fiction, and the Ethnographic Performance

1. A film that could also be included in this category of semi-*testimonio* is Helena Taberna's *Extranjeras* [*Foreign Women*] (2002). For María Pilar Rodríguez, this film breaks the conventions of the documentary with "an innovative ethic, ideological, and formal positioning," in which the director does not intervene with commentary, letting the spectators establish a direct relationship with the film's protagonists, the immigrant women themselves. See also Ballesteros, "Embracing." Cristina Martínez-Carazo ("Cine") adopts a more critical stance, arguing that relationships of unequal power, and the Spanish director, representative of the hegemonic group, are inevitably present even though the director "minimizes" her presence and voice on screen. For more on this film, see the production company's Web site, <http://www.lamiaproducciones.com/extranjeras>.

2. This was the vision of the early, celebratory critical receptions of Latin American *testimonio*, seen as a vehicle for the "real," "authentic" voice of the subaltern, who was finally heard. For these critics, a *testimonio* was motivated by the informant's intentionality and urgency to communicate a situation of repression, poverty, and injustice to a wider public. The journalist or anthropologist was thus seen as someone *needed* by the informant in order to achieve this aim. The important aspect of these exchanges was, then, not their power imbalance but their collaborative nature, or, in John Beverley's words, the narrator and interlocutor's "articulation together in a common program or front" (Beverley 33). The different vocabulary choices of Skłodowska and Beverley, reflective of their differing critical readings of *testimonio*, should be noted: the first refers to the exchange as one between "informant" and "editor"; the second as one between "narrator" and "interlocutor."

3. For a comparison of *Dormir al raso* with migration testimonies of the Mexican/US frontier, see Martín Rodríguez.

4. In her analysis of the short story "Cailcedrat" by Nieves García Benito, based on a press photograph of a dead African immigrant by Ildefonso Sena, Yeon-Soo Kim proposes that the short story "allows the reader to look at immigration from the perspective of immigrants who normally do not have proper channels to voice their views and to tell their stories" (203), in a reciprocal engagement (209) in which an African perspective is incorporated (Kim 220). As I have argued in this chapter, however, this terrain becomes very slippery in works that are conceived, produced, and consumed by and for Spaniards. Is an African voice present, as asserted, or is there a Spanish one that, with the same good intentions as those of other writers, ventriloquizes the African point of view?

5. Marco Kunz arrives at a similar conclusion in his analysis of Spanish literary works about immigration: "predomina el patetismo de la conmiseración con las víctimas necesitadas de ayuda, compasión puramente literaria . . . que muy probablemente les sirve a los inmigrantes mucho menos que a las conciencias atormentadas de los escritores y lectores españoles" ["The pathos of pity for the victims in need of help predominates, purely literary compassion . . . that probably is a lot less useful to the immigrants than to the tormented consciences of Spanish writers and readers"] (Kunz 134). Irene Andrés-Suárez, on the other hand, does not question the feasibility of "rescuing" the immigrants' experience, and she finds in *Las voces del Estrecho* the presence of a "polyphony of voices" (Andrés-Suárez 261–66).

6. Cheng is remarking on Paul Gilroy's analysis of Frederick Douglass's work in *The Black Atlantic*. For slaves, says Gilroy, death becomes a choice, an act of will, rebellion, and self-assertion in a desperate situation devoid of will. Thus, Death as agency can be found as a motif in much African-American writing (see Gilroy 60–65; Cheng 20–21).

7. This does not mean that a true communication has been established between Fátima and the town. She is, until the end, inscrutable to them, and the town's perceptions of her, the only ones we are aware of, are strictly unidirectional. In this sense, I do not agree with Cornejo-Parriego's celebratory assessment of the story as an example of a hybrid, new identity for the town and for Spain through contact with immigrants.

Works Cited

Abend, Lisa. "Spain's New Muslims: A Historical Romance." *In the Light of Medieval Spain: Islam, the West and the Relevance of History.* Ed. Simon R. Doubleday and David Coleman. New York: Palgrave Macmillan, forthcoming 2008.

"Acuerdo de Cooperación entre el Estado Español y la Comisión Islámica de España." <http://www.webislam.com/?idt=175>.

Ahmad, Aijaz. "*Orientalism* and After: Ambivalence and Metropolitan Location in the Work of Edward Said." *In Theory: Classes, Nations, Literatures.* London and New York: Verso, 1992: 159–219.

Ahmed, Sarah. *Strange Encounters: Embodied Others in Post-Coloniality.* London and New York: Routledge, 2000.

Alameda, Sol. "Entrevista: José Chamizo defensor del pueblo andaluz." *El País Digital* 5 Jan. 2002. <http://www.elpais.com>.

Alarcón, Pedro Antonio de. *Diario de un testigo de la Guerra de África.* Sevilla: Fundación José Manuel Lara, 2005.

Alfonso X el Sabio. *Primera crónica general de España.* Ed. Ramón Menéndez Pidal. *Nueva Biblioteca de Autores españoles* 5. Madrid: Bailly-Bailliere e hijos, 1906.

Anderson, Benedict. *Imagined Communities: Reflections on the Origin and Spread of Nationalism.* London: Verso, 1983.

Andrés-Suárez, Irene. "*Las voces del Estrecho* de Andrés Sorel." *La inmigración en la literatura española contemporánea.* By Irene Andrés-Suárez, Marco Kunz, and Inés d'Ors. Madrid: Verbum, 2002. 257–78.

Ang, Ien. "Hegemony-in-Trouble: Nostalgia and the Ideology of the Impossible in European Cinema." *Screening Europe: Image and Identity in Contemporary European Cinema.* Ed. Duncan Petrie. London: British Film Institute, 1992. 21–31.

"arabista estima que el error de traducir cristianos por sionistas en el cartel de Alcoi es 'intencionado,' Un." *El País Digital* 8 Apr. 2004. <http://www.elpais.com>.

Asad, Talal. "Muslims and European Identity: Can Europe Represent Islam?" *Cultural Encounters: Representing "Otherness."* Ed. Elizabeth Hallam and Brian V. Street. London and New York: Routledge, 2000. 11–27.

Asociación de San Jorge de Alcoy. *Nostra Festa.* Alcoy, Alicante: Gráficas Ciudad, 1982. 7 vols.

219

Works Cited

Azurmendi, Mikel. *Estampas de El Ejido: un reportaje sobre la integración del inmigrante.* Madrid: Taurus, 2001.

Balibar, Étienne, "Is There a 'Neo-Racism'?" *Race, Nation, Class: Ambiguous Identities.* Ed. Étienne Balibar and Immanuel Wallerstein. London and New York: Verso, 1991. 17–28.

Balfour, Sebástian. *Abrazo mortal: de la guerra colonial a la Guerra Civil en España y Marruecos (1909–1939).* Barcelona: Península, 2002.

——. "The Loss of Empire, Regenerationism, and the Forging of a Myth of National Identity." *Spanish Cultural Studies: An Introduction.* Ed. Jo Labanyi and Helen Graham. Oxford and New York: Oxford UP, 1995. 25–31.

Ballard, Roger. "Islam and the Construction of Europe." *Muslims in the Margin: Political Responses to the Presence of Islam in Western Europe.* Ed. W. A. R. Shadid and P. S. Van Koningsveld. Kampen, Neth.: Kok Pharos, 1996. 15–51.

Ballesteros, Isolina. "Embracing the Other: The Feminization of Spanish Immigration Cinema." *Studies in Hispanic Cinemas* 2.1 (2005): 3–14.

——. "Xenofobia y racismo en España: la inmigración Africana en *Las cartas de Alou* (1990) de Montxo Armendáriz y *Bwana* (1996) de Imanol Uribe." *Cine (Ins)urgente: textos fílmicos y contextos culturales de la España posfranquista.* Madrid: Fundamentos, 2001. 205–32.

Barker, Martin. *The New Racism: Conservatives and the Ideology of the Tribe.* London: Junction, 1981.

Baumann, Roland. *The Moors and Christians of Válor: Folklore and Conflict in the Alpujarra (Andalusia).* Diss. Tulane U, 1995. Ann Arbor: UMI, 2002.

Beneyto, José María. *Tragedia y razón: Europa en el pensamiento español del siglo XX.* Madrid: Taurus, 1999.

Bernabeu Rico, José Luis. *Significados sociales de las fiestas de moros y cristianos.* Alicante: Universidad Nacional de Educación a Distancia, 1981.

Beverley, John. "The Margin at the Center." Gugelberger, *Real* 23–41.

Bhabha, Homi K. *The Location of Culture.* New York: Routledge, 1994.

Blackburn, Robin. *The Making of New World Slavery: From the Baroque to the Modern, 1492–1800.* London: Verso, 1996.

Blackmore, Josiah, and Gregory S. Hutcheson, eds. *Queer Iberia: Sexualities, Cultures, and Crossings from the Middle Ages to the Renaissance.* Durham and London: Duke UP, 1999.

Blommaert, Jan, and Jef Verschueren. *Debating Diversity*. London: Routledge, 1998.

Brinker-Gabler, Gisela, and Sidonie Smith. "Gender, Nation, and Immigration in the New Europe." *Writing New Identities: Gender, Nation, and Immigration in Contemporary Europe*. Ed. Brinker-Gabler and Smith. Minneapolis and London: U of Minnesota P, 1997. 1–27.

Burshatin, Israel. "Narratives of Reconquest: Rodrigo, Pelayo, and the Saints." *Saints and Their Authors: Studies in Medieval Hagiography in Honor of John K. Walsh*. Ed. Alan Deyermond. Madison: Hispanic Seminary of Medieval Studies, 1990. 13–26.

———. "Playing the Moor: Parody and Performance in Lope de Vega's *El Primer Fajardo*." *PMLA* 107 (1992): 566–81.

———. "Power, Discourse, and Metaphor in the *Abencerraje*." *MLN* 99.2 (1984): 195–213.

———. "The Moor in the Text: Metaphor, Emblem, and Silence." *"Race," Writing and Difference*. Ed. Henry Louis Gates, Jr. Chicago and London: U of Chicago P, 1986. 117–37.

———. "Written on the Body: Slave or Hermaphrodite in Sixteenth-Century Spain." *Queer Iberia: Sexualities, Cultures, and Crossings from the Middle Ages to the Renaissance*. Ed. Josia Blackmore and Gregory S. Hutcheson. Durham and London: Duke UP, 1999. 420–54.

Bwana. Dir. Imanol Uribe. Aurum, 1996.

Cabello, Encarna. *La cazadora*. Melilla: Ciudad de Melilla, Consejería de Cultura, 1995.

Caro Baroja, Julio. *Los moriscos del reino de Granada*. Madrid: Istmo, 1976.

Carr, Matthew. "Spain: Racism at the Frontier." *Race and Class* 32 (1991): 93–97.

Carrasco Urgoiti, María Soledad. *El moro de Granada en la literatura (del siglo XV al XX)*. Madrid: Revista de Occidente, 1956.

———. *El moro retador y el moro amigo (Estudios sobre fiestas y comedias de moros y cristianos)*. Granada: Universidad de Granada, 1996.

cartas de Alou, Las. Dir. Montxo Armendáriz. Manga Films, 1990.

Caruth, Cathy, ed. *Trauma: Explorations in Memory*. Baltimore and London: Johns Hopkins UP, 1995.

Castro, Américo. *España en su historia: cristianos, moros y judíos*. Barcelona: Crítica, 1983.

Cembrero, Ignacio. "Cartas de la desesperanza." *El País* 30 July 2000: 8.

Cesarini, David, and Mary Fulbrook. *Citizenship, Nationality and Migration in Europe*. London and New York: Routledge, 1996.

Chakor, Mohamed. "Prejuicios hispano-marroquíes: el moro en el imaginario español." *Actas del encuentro España-Marruecos: diálogo y convivencia*. Tetuán: Publicaciones de la Asociación Tetuán-Asmir, 1999. 115–28.

Charnon-Deutsch, Lou. *The Spanish Gypsy: The History of a European Obsession*. University Park, PA: Pennsylvania State UP, 2004.

———. "Exoticism and the Politics of Difference in Late Nineteenth-Century Spanish Periodicals." *Culture and Gender in Nineteenth-Century Spain*. Ed. Charnon-Deutsch and Jo Labanyi. Oxford: Clarendon, 1995. 250–70.

Checa, Francisco, et al. *El Ejido: la ciudad-cortijo. Claves económicas del conflicto étnico*. Barcelona: Icaria Antrazyt, 2001.

Cheng, Anne Anlin. *The Melancholy of Race*. Oxford: Oxford UP, 2000.

Chow, Rey. *The Protestant Ethnic and the Spirit of Capitalism*. New York: Columbia UP, 2002.

Clifford, James. Introduction. *Writing Culture: The Poetics and Politics of Ethnography*. Ed. Clifford and George E. Marcus. Berkeley and Los Angeles: U of California P, 1986. 1–26.

Coleman, David. *Creating Christian Granada: Society and Religious Culture in an Old-World Frontier City, 1492–1600*. Ithaca: Cornell UP, 2003.

———. "The Persistence of the Past in the Albaicín: Granada's New Mosque and the Question of Historic Relevance." *In the Light of Medieval Spain: Islam, the West and the Relevance of History*. Ed. Simon R. Doubleday and David Coleman. New York: Palgrave Macmillan, forthcoming 2008.

Colmeiro, José F. "Exorcising Exoticism: *Carmen* and the Construction of Oriental Spain." *Comparative Literature* 54.2 (2002): 127–44.

Collins, Roger. *The Arab Conquest of Spain (710–797)*. Oxford: Blackwell, 1989.

Conde, Don José Antonio. *Historia de la dominación de los árabes en España, sacada de varios manuscritos y memorias arábigas*. Valladolid: Maxtor, 2001. (First ed. Madrid: Marín y Companía, 1874).

Constenla, T., and A. Torregrosa. "Vecinos de El Ejido atacan a los inmigrantes y destrozan sus locales." *El País Digital* 7 Feb. 2000. <http://www.elpais.com>.

Corkill, David. "Race, Immigration and Multiculturalism in Spain." *Contemporary Spanish Cultural Studies*. Ed. Barry Jordan and Rikki Morgan-Tamosunas. London: Arnold, 2000. 48–57.

Cornejo-Parriego, Rosalía. "Espacios híbridos, íconos mestizos: imaginando la España global." *Letras Peninsulares* 15.3 (2002–03): 515–31.

Covarrubias, Sebastián de. *Tesoro de la lengua castellana o española*. Ed. Martín de Riquer. Barcelona: Horta, 1943. (Rpt. Barcelona: Alta Fulla, 1998.)

Crónica mozárabe de 754. Ed. José Eduardo López Pereira. Zaragoza: Anubar, 1980.

Culla i Clarà, Joan B. "Inmigración y responsabilidades." *El País Digital* 2 Mar. 2001. <http://www.elpais.com>.

Daoudi, Ahmed. *El Diablo de Yudis*. Madrid: Vosa, 1994.

De la Serna, Alfonso. *Al Sur de Tarifa: Marruecos-España: un malentendido histórico*. Madrid: Marcial Pons, 2001.

del Corral, Pedro. *Crónica del rey don Rodrigo postrimero rey de los godos (Crónica sarracina)*. Vols. 1 and 2. Ed. James Donald Fogelquist. Madrid: Castaglia, 2001.

Delgado, Elena L. "La nación deseada: Europeización, diferencia y la utopia de (las) España(s)." *From Stateless Nations to Postnational Spain*. Ed. Antonio Cortijo, Silvia Bermúdez, and Timothy McGovern. Boulder: Society of Spanish and Spanish-American Studies, 2002. 207–21.

———. "Settled in Normal: Narratives of a Prozaic (Spanish) Nation.'" *Arizona Journal of Hispanic Cultural Studies* 7 (2003): 117–32.

del Pino, José Manuel. "Morena oscura: la reconfiguración del pueblo español en *Flores de otro mundo* (1999) de Icíar Bollaín." (Paper presented at the 2000 MLA Convention.)

Denis, Claire. "The Film Makers Panel." *Screening Europe: Image and Identity in Contemporary European Cinema*. Ed. Duncan Petrie. London: British Film Institute, 1992.

Derrida, Jacques. *Adieu to Emmanuel Levinas*. Stanford: Stanford UP, 1999.

———. "Différance." *Margins of Philosophy*. Chicago: U of Chicago P, 1982. 1–27.

———. *Specters of Marx: The State of the Debt, the Work of Mourning, and the New International*. New York and London: Routledge, 1994.

Deyermond, Alan. "The Death and Rebirth of Visigothic Spain in the *Estoria de España.*" *Revista Canadiense de Estudios Hispánicos* 9.3 (1985): 345–67.

Díaz, Beatriz. *Todo negro no igual: voces de emigrantes en el barrio bilbaíno de San Francisco.* Barcelona: Virus, 1997.

Díaz y Díaz, Manuel. "La historiografía hispana desde la invasion árabe hasta el año mil." *Storiografia altomedievale.* Spoleto: Centro italiano di studi sull Alto Medioevo, 1970. 313–43

Dopico Black, Georgina. "Ghostly Remains: Valencia, 1609." *Arizona Journal of Hispanic Cultural Studies* 7 (2003): 91–100.

Driessen, Henk. "Mock Battles between Moors and Christians: Playing the Confrontation of Crescent with Cross in Spain's South." *Ethnologia Europaea* 15.2 (1985): 105–15.

Dussel, Enrique. "Eurocentrism and Modernity." *Boundary 2* 20.3 (1993): 65–76.

El Hachmi, Najat. *Jo també sóc catalana.* Barcelona: Columna, 2004.

En construcción. Dir. José Luis Guerín. Ovídeo TV, 2001.

Enloe, Cynthia. *Bananas, Beaches and Bases: Making Feminist Sense of International Politics.* Berkeley: U of California P, 1990.

"Entrevista: Antonio Chavarrías." *Susanna* DVD extras, 2003.

Epps, Brad. "Between Europe and Africa: Modernity, Race, and Nationality in the Correspondence of Miguel de Unamuno and Joan Maragall." *Anales de la Literatura Española Contemporánea* 30.1–2 (2005): 97–132.

———. *Significant Violence: Oppression and Resistance in the Narratives of Juan Goytisolo, 1970–1990.* Oxford: Clarendon, 1996.

España, Instituto Nacional de Estadística. *Censo de Población y Viviendas 2001.* <http://www.ine.es/censo2001/pobcen01menu.htm>.

———. *España en cifras 2003–2004.* <http://www.ine.es/prodyser/pubweb/espcif/espcif0304.htm>.

Extranjeras. Dir. Helena Taberna. Lamia Producciones, 2003.

Fanjul, Serafín. *La quimera de al-Andalus.* Madrid: Siglo XXI, 2004.

———. *Al-Andalus contra España: la forja del mito.* Madrid: Siglo XXI, 2002.

"Fernández-Miranda dice que es más fácil integrar a católicos practicantes." *El País Digital* 12 Mar. 2001. <http://www.elpais.com>.

Filios, Denise. "Expulsion from Paradise: Exiled Intellectuals and Andalusian Tolerance." *In the Light of Medieval Spain: Islam, the West and the Relevance of History.* Ed. Simon R. Doubleday and David Coleman. New York: Palgrave Macmillan, forthcoming 2008.

Flesler, Daniela. "Contemporary Moroccan Immigration and Its Ghosts." *In the Light of Medieval Spain: Islam, the West and the Relevance of History.* Ed. Simon R. Doubleday and David Coleman. New York: Palgrave Macmillan, forthcoming 2008.

Fletcher, Richard. *Moorish Spain.* Berkeley and Los Angeles: U of California P, 1992.

Flores de otro mundo. Dir. Icíar Bollaín. Alta Films, 1999.

Freud, Sigmund. *Beyond the Pleasure Principle. The Standard Edition of the Complete Works of Sigmund Freud* (SE). Vol. 18. London: Hogarth and the Institute of Psycho-Analysis, 1955.

———. *Moses and Monotheism. The Standard Edition of the Complete Works of Sigmund Freud* (SE). Vol. 23. London: Hogarth and the Institute of Psycho-Analysis, 1955.

———. "Psycho-Analysis and War Neuroses." *The Standard Edition of the Complete Works of Sigmund Freud* (SE) Vol. 17. London: Hogarth and the Institute of Psycho-Analysis, 1955. 207–10.

———. "The Uncanny." *The Standard Edition of the Complete Works of Sigmund Freud* (SE). Vol. 17. London: Hogarth and the Institute of Psycho-Analysis, 1955. 219–56.

Fuchs, Barbara. *Exotic Nation: Maurophilia and the Conflictive Construction of Spain,* forthcoming.

———. *Mimesis and Empire: The New World, Islam, and European Identities.* Cambridge: Cambridge UP, 2001.

———. *Passing for Spain. Cervantes and the Fictions of Identity.* Urbana-Champaign and Chicago: U of Illinois P, 2003.

———. "The Spanish Race." *Rereading the Black Legend: The Discourses of Racism in the Renaissance Empires.* Ed. Margaret Greer, Walter Mignolo, and Maureen Quilligan. Chicago: U of Chicago P, 2007.

Gabilondo, Joseba. "Uncanny Identity: Violence, Gaze, and Desire in Contemporary Basque Cinema." *Constructing Identity in Contemporary Spain: Theoretical Debates and Cultural Practices.* Ed. Jo Labanyi. New York and London: Oxford UP, 2002. 262–79.

———. "Jon Juaristi: Compulsive Archaeology and the Basque Nationalist Primal Scene." *Revista Internacional de Estudios Vascos* 43.2 (1998): 539–54.

Gadea, Lucía. "Alcoi retira 15.000 carteles que por error aludían en árabe a unas fiestas de moros y 'sionistas.'" *El País Digital* 7 Apr. 2004. <http://www.elpais.com>.

Galaz, Mabel. "Una niña marroquí está sin escolarizar porque su padre la obliga a llevar el chador." *El País Digital* 15 Feb. 2002. <http://www.elpais.com>.

Galdós, Benito Pérez. *Aita Tettauen*. Madrid: Akal, 2004.

García Arenal, Mercedes. Rev. of *The Ornament of the World: How Muslims, Jews and Christians Created a Culture of Tolerance in Medieval Spain*. By María Rosa Menocal. *Speculum* 79 (2004): 801–04.

García Benito, Nieves. *Por la vía de Tarifa*. Madrid: Calambur, 1999.

García Morente, Manuel. *Idea de la Hispanidad*. Madrid: Espasa-Calpe, 1961.

Gilroy, Paul. *The Black Atlantic: Modernity and Double Consciousness*. Cambridge, MA: Harvard UP, 1993.

Gingras, Gerald L. "Virtue and Vice: Historical Explanation in Alfonso X's *Primera crónica general*." *Thought* 60.239 (1985): 430–38.

Gordon, Avery. *Ghostly Matters: Haunting and the Sociological Imagination*. Minneapolis and London: U of Minnesota P, 1997.

Goytisolo, Juan. "Cara y cruz del moro en nuestra literatura." *Crónicas sarracinas*. Madrid: Alfaguara, 1998. 9–30.

———. *España y sus Ejidos*. Madrid: Hijos de Muley Rubio, 2003.

Goytisolo, Juan, and Sami Naïr. *El peaje de la vida: integración o rechazo de la emigración en España*. Madrid: Aguilar, 2000.

Graham, Helen, and Antonio Sánchez. "The Politics of 1992." *Spanish Cultural Studies*. Ed. Jo Labanyi and Graham. Oxford and New York: Oxford UP, 1995. 406–18.

Gubbins, Paul, and Mike Holt. Introduction. *Beyond Boundaries: Language and Identity in Contemporary Europe*. Ed. Gubbins and Holt. Clevedon, Engl., Buffalo, NY, Toronto, and Sydney: Multilingual Matters, 2002. 1–10.

Gugelberger, Georg M., ed. *The Real Thing: Testimonial Discourse and Latin America*. Durham: Duke UP, 1996.

———. "Introduction: Institutionalization of Transgression: Testimonial Discourse and Beyond." Gugelberger, *Real* 1–19.

Guss, David M. *The Festive State: Race, Ethnicity, and Nationalism in Cultural Performance*. Berkeley: U of California P, 2000.

Haliczer, Stephen. "The Moriscos: Loyal Subjects of His Catholic Majesty Philip III." *Christians, Muslims, and Jews in Medieval and Early Modern Spain*. Ed. Mark D. Meyerson and Edward D. English. Notre Dame, IN: U of Notre Dame P, 1999.

Hall, Jacqueline. "Immigration et nationalisme en Catalogne." *Perspectiva Social* 14 (1979): 93–136.

Hall, Stuart. "Introduction: Who Needs 'Identity'?" *Questions of Cultural Identity*. Ed. Stuart Hall and Paul du Gay. London: Sage, 1996. 1–17.

———. "New Ethnicities." *"Race," Culture and Difference*. Ed. James Donald and Ali Rattansi. London: Sage, 1992. 252–59.

Harrington, Thomas. "Rapping on the Cast(i)le Gates: Nationalism and Culture-Planning in Contemporary Spain." *Ideologies of Hispanism*. Ed. Mabel Moraña. Nashville: Vanderbilt UP, 2005. 107–37.

Harris, Max. "Muhammad and the Virgin: Folk Dramatizations of Battles between Moors and Christians in Modern Spain." *Drama Review* 38.1 (1994): 45–61.

Harvey, L. P. *Islamic Spain: 1250 to 1500*. Chicago: U of Chicago P, 1992.

———. *Muslims in Spain: 1500 to 1614*. Chicago: U of Chicago P, 2005.

Herbert, Jean Loup. Prólogo. *El Islam en las aulas: contenidos, silencios, enseñanza*. Ed. Josep María Navarro. Barcelona: Icaria Antrazyt, 1997. 11–13.

Hermida, José. "La catedral compostelana retira una imagen de Santiago 'Matamoros.'" *El País Digital* 2 May 2004. <http://www.elpais.com>.

Hobsbawm, Eric, and Terence Ranger, eds. *The Invention of Tradition*. Cambridge: Cambridge UP, 1983.

Hooper, Kirsty. "Reading Spain's 'African Vocation': The Figure of the Moorish Priest in Three *fin de siglo* Novels (1890–1907)." *Revista de Estudios Hispánicos* 40 (2006): 171–95.

Iglesias, Carmen. "España desde fuera." *España: reflexiones sobre el ser de España*. Madrid: Real Academia de la Historia, 1998. 377–428.

Ilegal. Dir. Ignacio Vilar. Laurenfilm, 2003.

Impey, Olga Tudorica. "Del duello de los godos de Espanna': la retórica del llanto y su motivación." *Romance Quarterly* 33 (1986): 295–307

Irisarri, Ángeles de. *El viaje de la reina*. Barcelona: Emecé, 1997.

Irisarri, Ángeles de, and Magdalena Lasala. *Moras y cristianas*. Barcelona: Emecé, 1998.

Izquierdo, Antonio. *La inmigración inesperada: la población extranjera en España (1991–1995)*. Madrid: Trotta, 1996.

Jackson, Stevi. "Women and Heterosexual Love: Complicity, Resistance and Change." *Romance Revisited*. Ed. L. Pearce and J. Stacey. New York and London: New York UP, 1995. 49–62.

Jordan, Barry. "How Spanish Is It? Spanish Cinema and National Identity." *Contemporary Spanish Cultural Studies*. Ed. Barry Jordan and Rikki Morgan-Tamosunas. London: Arnold, 2000. 68–78.

"Juan Pablo II felicita a Aznar por su empeño en que Europa reconozca sus raíces cristianas." *El País Digital* 23 Jan. 2004. <http://www.elpais.com>.

Kabbani, Rana. *Europe's Myths of Orient*. Bloomington: Indiana UP, 1986.

Kanneh, Kadiatu. "Feminism and the Colonial Body." *The Post-Colonial Studies Reader*. Ed. Bill Ashcroft, Gareth Griffiths, and Helen Tiffin. London: Routledge, 1995. 346–48.

Kaplan, E. Ann. "Trauma, Aging and Melodrama (with reference to Tracey Moffat's *Night Cries*)." *Feminist Locations*. Ed. M. DeKoven. New Brunswick, NJ: Rutgers UP, 2001. 304–28.

———."Melodrama, Cinema and Trauma." *Screen* 42.2 (2001): 201–05.

Kaplan, E. Ann, and Ban Wang, eds. *Trauma and Cinema: Cross-Cultural Explorations*. Hong Kong: Hong Kong UP, 2004.

Keating, Michael. "The Minority Nations of Spain and European Integration: A New Framework for Autonomy?" *Journal of Spanish Cultural Studies* 1.1 (2000): 29–42.

———. *State and Regional Nationalism: Territorial Politics and the European State*. London: Harvester, 1988.

Kelly, Dorothy. "Selling Spanish 'Otherness' since the 1960s." *Contemporary Spanish Cultural Studies*. Ed. Barry Jordan and Rikki Morgan-Tamosunas. London: Arnold, 2000. 29–37.

Kim, Yeon-Soo. *The Family Album: Histories, Subjectivities, and Immigration in Contemporary Spanish Culture*. Lewisburg, PA: Bucknell UP, 2005.

Kinder, Marsha. *Blood Cinema*. Berkeley: U of California P, 1993.

King, Russell, ed. *The Mediterranean Passage: Migration and New Cultural Encounters in Southern Europe*. Liverpool: Liverpool UP, 2001.

Kunz, Marco. "La inmigración en la literatura española contemporánea: un panorama crítico." *La inmigración en la literatura española contemporánea*. By Irene Andrés-Suárez, Kunz, and Inés d'Ors, Madrid: Verbum, 2002. 109–36.

Kushner, Tony. "The Spice of Life? Ethnic Difference, Politics and Culture in Modern Britain." *Citizenship, Nationality and Migration in Europe.* Ed. David Cesarini and Mary Fulbrook. New York and London: Routledge, 1996. 125–45.

La Capra, Dominick. *Writing History, Writing Trauma.* Baltimore and London: Johns Hopkins UP, 2001.

Labanyi, Jo. "History and Hauntology; or, What Does One Do with the Ghosts of the Past? Reflections on Spanish Film and Fiction of the Post-Franco Period." *Disremembering the Dictatorship: The Politics of Memory in the Spanish Transition to Democracy.* Ed. Joan Ramón Resina. Amsterdam and Atlanta: Rodopi, 2000. 65–82.

———. "Internalisations of Empire: Colonial Ambivalence and the Early Francoist Missionary Film." *Discourse* 23.1 (2001): 25–42.

———. "Introduction: Engaging with Ghosts; or, Theorizing Culture in Modern Spain." *Constructing Identity in Contemporary Spain.* Ed. Jo Labanyi. Oxford: Oxford UP, 2002. 1–14.

———. *Myth and History in the Contemporary Spanish Novel.* Cambridge: Cambridge UP, 1989.

———. "Race, Gender and Disavowal in Spanish Cinema of the Early Franco Period: The Missionary Film and the Folkloric Musical." *Screen* 38.3 (1997): 215–31.

Labanyi, Jo, and Helen Graham, eds. *Spanish Cultural Studies: An Introduction.* Oxford and New York: Oxford UP, 1995.

Lezra, Jacques. "'La mora encantada': Covarrubias in the Soul of Spain." *Journal of Spanish Cultural Studies* 1.1 (2000): 5–27.

Libertarias. Dir. Vicente Aranda. Academy Pictures, 1996.

López García, Bernabé. "El cine y las relaciones hispano-marroquíes: de la imagen del 'protegido' a la del inmigrado." *Relaciones entre España y Marruecos en el siglo XX.* Coord. José U. Martínez Carreras. Madrid: Asociación española de Africanistas, 2000.

———, et al. *Inmigración magrebí en España: el retorno de los moriscos.* Madrid: Maphre, 1993.

López Pereira, José Eduardo. *Estudio crítico sobre la Crónica mozárabe de 754.* Zaragoza: Anubar, 1980.

Lorman, Josep. *La aventura de Saïd.* Madrid: SM, 2002.

Lowe, Lisa. *Critical Terrains: French and British Orientalisms.* Ithaca and London: Cornell UP, 1991.

Lucas, Javier de. *Puertas que se cierran: Europa como fortaleza.* Barcelona: Icaria, 1996.

Lynch, John. *The Hispanic World in Crisis and Change: 1598–1700.* Cambridge: Blackwell, 1992.

Madariaga, María Rosa de. *Los moros que trajo Franco . . . la intervención de tropas coloniales en la Guerra Civil.* Barcelona: Martínez Roca, 2002.

Makki, Mahmoud. "The Political History of Al-Andalus (92/711–897/1492)." *The Legacy of Muslim Spain.* Vol. 1. Ed. Salma Khadra Jayyusi. Leiden, Neth.: Brill, 1994. 3–87.

Manzanos Bilbao, César. *El grito del otro: arqueología de la marginación racial.* Madrid: Tecnos, 1999.

Mar Molinero, Clare. "The Politics of Language: Spain's Minority Languages." *Spanish Cultural Studies: An Introduction.* Ed. Jo Labanyi and Helen Graham. Oxford and New York: Oxford UP, 1995. 336–42.

Mariscal, George. *Contradictory Subjects: Quevedo, Cervantes, and Seventeenth Century Spanish Culture.* Cornell: Cornell UP, 1991.

———. "The Role of Spain in Contemporary Race Theory." *Arizona Journal of Hispanic Cultural Studies* 2 (1998): 7–22.

Márquez Villanueva, Francisco. "El problema historiográfico de los moriscos." *Bulletin Hispanique* 86 (1984): 61–135.

———. "La voluntad de leyenda de Miguel de Luna." *Nueva Revista de Filología Hispánica* 30.2 (1981): 391–93.

———. *Santiago: trayectoria de un mito.* Barcelona: Bellaterra, 2004.

Martín, Miguel. *El colonialismo español en Marruecos (1860–1956).* París: Ruedo Ibérico, 1973.

Martín-Cabrera, Luis. "Postcolonial Memories and Racial Violence in *Flores de otro mundo.*" *Journal of Spanish Cultural Studies* 3.1 (2002): 43–55.

Martín Corrales, Eloy. *La imagen del magrebí en España: una perspectiva histórica siglos XVI–XX.* Barcelona: Bellaterra, 2002.

Martin-Márquez, Susan. "A World of Difference in Home-making: The Films of Icíar Bollaín." *Women's Narrative and Film in Twentieth-Century Spain.* Ed. Ofelia Ferrán and Kathleen M. Glenn. New York: Routledge, 2002. 256–72.

———. "Constructing *Convivencia*: Miquel Barceló, José Luis Guerín, and Spanish-African Solidarity." Ed. Benita Sampedro and Simon Doubleday. *Border Interrogations. Crossing and Questioning Spanish Frontiers.* Oxford: Berghahn Books, forthcoming 2008.

———. *Disorientations: Spanish Colonialism in Africa and the Performance of Identity.* New Haven: Yale UP, forthcoming 2008.

———. "Here's Spain Looking at You": Shifting Perspectives on North African Otherness in Galdós and Fortuny." *Arizona Journal of Hispanic Cultural Studies* 5 (2001): 1–18.

———. "Hibridez y modernidad en la obra de Marià Fortuny: el desnudo desorientado y los retratos de Carmen." *Arizona Journal of Hispanic Cultural Studies* 7 (2003): 83–90.

Martín Muñoz, Gema. *Marroquíes en España: estudio sobre su integración*. Madrid: Fundación Repsol YPF, 2003.

Martín-Rodríguez, Manuel M. "Aztlán y Al-Andalus: la idea del retorno en dos literaturas inmigrantes." *La Palabra y el Hombre* 120 (2001): 29–38.

Martínez-Carazo, Cristina. "Cine e inmigración: Madrid como espacio de encuentro/desencuentro y su representación en *Extranjeras* de Helena Taberna." *Hispanic Research Journal: Iberian and Latin American Studies* 6.3 (2005): 265–75.

———. "*Flores de otro mundo*: la pluralidad cultural como propuesta." *Letras Peninsulares* 15.2 (2002): 377–90.

McClintock, Anne. "'No longer in a Future Heaven': Gender, Race and Nationalism." *Dangerous Liaisons: Gender, Nation and Postcolonial Perspectives*. Ed. McClintock, Aamir Mufti, and Ella Shohat. Minneapolis: U of Minnesota P, 1997. 89–112.

Menéndez Pidal, Ramón. *Floresta de leyendas heroicas españolas: Rodrigo, el último godo*. Vol. 3. Madrid: La lectura, 1927.

Menéndez y Pelayo, Marcelino. *Historia de los heterodoxos españoles*. Vol. 2. Madrid: Librería católica de San José, 1880.

Menocal, María Rosa. *The Ornament of the World: How Muslims, Jews and Christians Created a Culture of Tolerance in Medieval Spain*. New York: Little, 2002.

Mernissi, Fátima. *Beyond the Veil: Male-Female Dynamics in a Modern Muslim Society*. Cambridge, MA: Schenkman, 1975.

———. *Women and Islam: An Historical and Theological Enquiry*. Oxford: Blackwell, 1991.

———. *Women's Rebellion and Islamic Memory*. London and Atlantic Highlands, NJ: Zed, 1996.

Meyerson, Mark D. *The Muslims of Valencia in the Age of Fernando and Isabel: Between Coexistence and Crusade*. Berkeley: U of California P, 1990.

———. Introduction. *Christians, Muslims, and Jews in Medieval and Early Modern Spain: Interaction and Cultural Change*. Ed. Mark D. Meyerson and Edward D. English. Notre Dame, IN: U of Notre Dame P, 1999. xi–xxi.

Mezquita NO! Dir. Alberto Aranda and Guillermo Cruz. Manga Films, 2005.

Miles, Robert. "The Articulation of Racism and Nationalism: Reflections on European History." *Racism and Migration in Western Europe.* Ed. John Solomos and John Wrench. Oxford and Providence: Berg, 1993. 35–52.

Miles, Robert, and Malcolm Brown. *Racism.* New York: Routledge, 2003.

"Ministro Aparicio compara el uso del pañuelo islámico con la ablación, El." *El País Digital* 16 Feb. 2002. <http://www.elpais.com>.

Mirrer, Louise. *Women, Jews, and Muslims in the texts of Reconquest Castile.* Ann Arbor: U of Michigan P, 1996.

Mohanty, Chandra Talpade. "Under Western Eyes: Feminist Scholarship and Colonial Discourses." *The Post-Colonial Studies Reader.* Ed. Bill Ashcroft, Gareth Griffiths, and Helen Tiffin. London and New York: Routledge, 1999. 259–63.

Molina Gavilán, Yolanda, and Thomas J. Di Salvo. "Policing Spanish/European Borders: Xenophobia and Racism in Contemporary Spanish Cinema." *Ciberletras* 5 (2001). <http://www.lehman.cuny.edu/ciberletras>.

Montero, Rosa. "Political Transition and Cultural Democracy: Coping with the Speed of Change." *Spanish Cultural Studies: An Introduction.* Ed. Jo Labanyi and Helen Graham. Oxford and New York: Oxford UP, 1995. 315–20.

Morán, María Luz. "Cultural Policy and European Identity in Spain." *Spain and EC Membership Evaluated.* Ed. Amparo Almarcha Barbado. New York: Printer's Press, 1993. 285–92.

Moreiras Menor, Cristina. *Cultura herida: literatura y cine en la España democrática.* Madrid: Libertarias, 2002.

Moreno Torregrosa, Pasqual, and Mohamed El Gheryb. *Dormir al raso.* Prol. Manuel Vásquez Montalban and Mahdi Elmandjara. Madrid: VOSA, 1994.

Morgan, Susan. *Place Matters: Gendered Geography in Victorian Women's Travel Books about Southeast Asia.* New Brunswick, NJ: Rutgers UP, 1996.

Murphy, Brendan, Cristina Díaz-Varela, and Salvatore Colucello. "Transformation of the State in Western Europe: Regionalism in Catalonia and Northern Italy." *Beyond Boundaries: Language and Identity in Contemporary Europe.* Ed. Paul Gubbins and Mike Holt. Clevedon, Engl., Buffalo, NY, Toronto, and Sydney: Multilingual Matters, 2002. 73–90.

"Muslims in Western Europe." *The Economist* 10 Aug. 2002: 22.

Nair, Parvati. "In Modernity's Wake: Transculturality, Deterritorialization and the Question of Community in Icíar Bollaín's *Flores de otro mundo.*" *Post Script: Essays in Film and the Humanities* 21.2 (2002): 38–49.

————. "Moor-Veiled-Matters: The Hijab as Troubling Interrogative of the Relation between the West and Islam." *New Formations* 51 (2003–04): 39–49.

Naïr, Sami. "Cinco ideas falsas sobre la inmigración en España." *El País Digital* 16 May 2002. <http://www.elpais.com>.

Navarro, Josep María, ed. *El Islam en las aulas: contenidos, silencios, enseñanza*. Barcelona: Icaria Antrazyt, 1997.

Nederveen Pieterse, Jan. "Fictions of Europe." *Race and Class* 32 (1991): 3–10.

Newman, Michael. "The Language Ideologies of New Immigrants in Barcelona to Spanish and Catalan: Perspectives on the Linguistic Future." Unpublished Fulbright Fellowship proposal.

Niehoff, Susan C. "The Unity of Lope's *El último godo*." *Kentucky Romance Quarterly* 29.3 (1982): 261–72.

Nini, Rachid. *Diario de un ilegal*. Madrid: Ediciones del Oriente y del Mediterráneo, 2002.

"número de alumnas marroquíes en la escuela cae en picado al llegar a la secundaria, El." *El País Digital* 16 Feb. 2002. <http://www.elpais.com>.

Núñez Ruiz, Rafael. "Catalanismo, inmigración y asociacionismo cultural 'andaluz' y flamenco en Cataluña entre los años 60 y 90: los procesos identitarios de la nueva cultura popular urbana." *Flamenco y nacionalismo: aportaciones para una sociología política del flamenco. Actas del I y II Seminario Teórico sobre arte, mentalidad e identidad colectiva. Sevilla, 1995, 1997*. Seville: U of Seville, 1998. 267–87.

O'Donnell, Paul E. "'It Depends Who I Marry': Linguistic Recruitment and Defection in Barcelona." *Catalan Review* 9.2 (1995): 163–71.

Omgbá, Víctor. *Calella sen saída*. Vigo: Galaxia, 2001.

Ormazabal, M., and I. Camacho. "La suave avalancha migratoria." *El País Digital* 27 Apr. 2001. <http://www.elpais.com>.

Ortiz, Lourdes. "Fátima de los naufragios." *Fátima de los naufragios: relatos de tierra y mar*. Barcelona: Planeta, 1998. 7–22.

Páez, Marcelo. "Entrevista a Isabel Gardela, directora de *Tomándote*." <http://www.otrocampo.com/festivales/lacinemafe01/isabelgardela.html>.

Pearce, Lynne, and Jackie Stacey, eds. *Romance Revisited*. New York and London: New York UP, 1995.

Peregil, Francisco. "100.000 niños extranjeros se incorporan al sistema educativo español en el curso 2001–2002." *El País Digital* 25 May 2002. <http://www.elpais.com>.

Perry, Kathryn. "The Heart of Whiteness: White Subjectivity and Inter-racial Relationships." Pearce and Stacey 171–84.

Pi-Sunyer, O. "Tourism in Catalonia." *Tourism in Spain. Critical Issues.* Ed. M. Barke, J. Towner, and M.T. Newton. Wallingford, Oxon, UK: Cab International, 1996. 231–64.

Poniente. Dir. Chus Gutiérrez. Amboto Audiovisual, 2002.

Prats, Juan Manuel. "Ordenan la escolarización sin condiciones de la niña marroquí que quiere llevar velo." *La Vanguardia Online* 16 Feb. 2002. <http://www.lavanguardia.es>.

Pratt, Mary Louise. *Imperial Eyes: Travel Writing and Transculturation.* London and New York: Routledge, 1992.

Pujolar i Cos, Joan. "Immigration in Catalonia: The Politics of Sociolin-guistic Research." *Catalan Review* 9.2 (1995): 141–62.

Regás, Rosa. "Introducción: un milagro de la vida cotidiana." Irisarri and Lasala 9–13.

Resina, Joan Ramon, ed. *Disremembering the Dictatorship: The Politics of Memory in the Spanish Transition to Democracy.* Amsterdam: Rodopi, 2000.

Ridao, José María. "El islam como coartada." *El País Digital* 27 Mar. 2002. <http://www.elpais.com>.

Rodríguez, María Pilar. "Extranjeras." <http://www.lamiaproducciones.com/extranjeras/textompilar.htm>.

Romera Castillo, José. "El pasado, prehistoria literaria del presente." *La novela histórica a finales del siglo XX.* Ed. José Romera Castillo, Francisco Gutiérrez Carbajo, and Mario García-Page. Madrid: Visor, 1996.

Root, Deborah. "Speaking Christian: Orthodoxy and Difference in Sixteenth-Century Spain." *Representations* 23 (1988): 118–34.

Saavedra Fajardo, Diego de. *Corona gótica, castellana y austríaca, en Obras de don Diego Saavedra Fajardo.* Biblioteca de autores españoles 25. Madrid: Imprenta de los sucesores de Hernando, 1920.

Saïd. Dir. Llorenç Soler. Centre Promotor de la Imatge, Barcelona, 1998.

Said, Edward W. *Orientalism.* New York: Pantheon, 1978.

Sánchez, Esther, and Ana López Escudero. "La niña marroquí de El Es-corial podrá ir a un colegio público, pero sin pañuelo." *El País Digital* 16 Feb. 2002. <http://www.elpais.com>.

Sánchez Albornoz, Claudio. *Ensayos sobre historia de España.* Madrid: Siglo XXI, 1973.

————. *El Islam de España y el Occidente.* Madrid: Espasa-Calpe, 1974.

Santaolalla, Isabel. *Los "otros": etnicidad y "raza" en el cine español contemporáneo.* Zaragoza: Prensas Universitarias de Zaragoza and Ocho y Medio, 2005.

————. "Ethnic and Racial Configurations in Contemporary Spanish Culture." *Constructing Identity in Contemporary Spain: Theoretical Debates and Cultural Practice.* Ed. Jo Labanyi. Oxford: Oxford UP, 2002. 55–71.

————. "Close Encounters: Racial Otherness in Imanol Uribe's *Bwana.*" *Bulletin of Hispanic Studies* 76 (1999): 111–22.

Santonja, Gonzalo, ed. *Romancero de la Guerra Civil.* Series 1. Madrid: Visor, 1984.

Sassen, Saskia. *Guests and Aliens.* New York: New Press, 1999.

Schmidt-Nowara, Chris. "'This Rotting Corpse': Spain between the Black Atlantic and the Black Legend." *Arizona Journal of Hispanic Cultural Studies* 5 (2001): 149–60.

Sherzer, Dina. "Race Matters and Matters of Race: Interracial Relationships in Colonial and Postcolonial Films." *Cinema, Colonialism, Postcolonialism: Perspectives from the French and Francophone World.* Ed. Sherzer. Austin: U of Texas P, 1996. 229–48.

Shih, Shu-Mei. "Global Literature and the Technologies of Recognition." *PMLA* 119.1 (2004): 16–30.

Shohat, Ella, and Robert Stam. *Unthinking Eurocentrism: Multiculturalism and the Media.* London: Routledge, 1994.

Silverman, Kaja. *Male Subjectivity at the Margins.* New York and London: Routledge, 1992.

Sklodowska, Elzbieta. "Spanish American Testimonial Novel: Some Afterthoughts." Gugelberger, *Real* 84–100.

Smith, Colin. *Christians and Moors in Spain.* Vol. 1. Warminster, Engl.: Aris & Phillips, 1988.

Socolovsky, Jerome. "Muslim Cartoon Rioting Affects Spanish Rituals." *NPR.* 15 Feb. 2006.

Solé Tura, Jordi. "Vargas Llosa y la salvación de Cataluña." *El País Digital* 14 Mar. 2001. <http://www.elpais.com>.

Solomos, John, and John Wrench, eds. *Racism and Migration in Western Europe.* Oxford and Providence: Berg, 1993.

Sommer, Doris. *Foundational Fictions: The National Romances of Latin America.* Berkeley and Los Angeles: U of California P, 1991.

Sommer, Doris. "No Secrets." Gugelberger, *Real* 130–57.

Sorel, Andrés. *Las voces del Estrecho*. Barcelona: Muchnik, 2000.

———. "Las voces del Estrecho." *El otro país de este mundo* 3 (2002). <http://www.nodo50.org/elotropais/n3/sorel.htm>.

Soysal, Yasemin Nuhoglu. "Changing Citizenship in Europe: Remarks on Postnational Membership and the National State." *Citizenship, Nationality and Migration in Europe*. Ed. David Cesarini and Mary Fulbrook. New York and London: Routledge, 1996. 17–29.

Spivak, Gayatri Chakravorty. "Can the Subaltern Speak?" *Marxism and the Interpretation of Culture*. Ed. Cary Nelson and Lawrence Grossberg. Urbana and Chicago: U of Illinois P, 1988. 271–313.

Strubell, Miquel. *Llengua i població a Catalunya*. Barcelona: la Magrana, 1981.

Subirats, Eduardo. *Después de la lluvia: sobre la ambigua modernidad española*. Madrid: Temas de Hoy, 1993.

Susanna. Dir. Antonio Chavarrías. Oberón Cinematográfica, 1996.

Taguieff, Pierre-André. "The New Cultural Racism in France." *Telos* 83 (1990): 109–22.

Téllez Rubio, Juan José. "Esto había que contarlo." *Por la vía de Tarifa*. By Nieves García Benito. Madrid: Calambur, 2000. 9–10.

Todos os llamáis Mohamed. Dir. Maximiliano Lemcke González. Maximiliano Lemcke González, 1997.

Tomándote. Dir. Isabel Gardela. Kilimanjaro Productions, 2000.

Torrecilla, Jesús. *España exótica: la formación de la imagen española moderna*. Boulder: Society of Spanish and Spanish-American Studies, 2004.

———. *El tiempo y los márgenes: Europa como utopía y como amenaza en la literatura española*. Chapel Hill: U of North Carolina P, 1996.

Torres, Rafael. *Yo, Mohamed: historias de inmigrantes en un país de emigrantes*. Madrid: Temas de Hoy, 1995.

Unamuno, Miguel de. "Sobre la europeización (Arbitrariedades)." *Obras completas 3*. Madrid: Escelicer, 1968. 925–39.

Urioste, Carmen. "Migración y racismo en el cine español." *Monographic Review / Revista Monográfica* 15 (2000): 44–59.

Vargas Llosa, Mario. "Salvemos a Cataluña." *El País Digital* 5 Mar. 2001. <http://www.elpais.com>.

Vega Carpio, Lope Félix de. *El último godo. Obras escogidas.* Vol. 3. Ed. Federico Carlos Sainz de Robles. Madrid: Aguilar, 1964. 635–65.

Vernon, Kathleen. "Culture and Cinema to 1975." *The Cambridge Companion to Modern Spanish Culture.* Ed. David T. Gies. Cambridge: Cambridge UP, 1999. 248–66.

Vidal, César. *España frente al Islam: de Mahoma a Ben Laden.* Madrid: La esfera de los libros, 2004.

Vilarós, Teresa. "The Passing of the *Xarnego*-Immigrant: Post-Nationalism and the Ideologies of Assimilation in Catalonia." *Arizona Journal of Hispanic Cultural Studies* 7 (2003): 229–46.

White, Hayden. *Tropics of Discourse: Essays in Cultural Criticism.* Baltimore and London: Johns Hopkins UP, 1978.

Williams, Raymond. *Marxism and Literature.* Oxford: Oxford UP, 1977.

Wolf, Kenneth Baxter. "Christian Views of Islam in Early Medieval Spain." *Medieval Christian Perceptions of Islam.* Ed. John Victor Tolan. New York and London: Garland, 1996. 85–108.

———. *Conquerors and Chroniclers of Early Medieval Spain.* Liverpool: Liverpool UP, 1999. (1st ed. 1990.)

Woods, Eva M. *White Gypsies: Racing for Modernity in Spanish Folkloric Musical Films, 1923–1954.* Minneapolis: U of Minnesota P, forthcoming 2008.

Woolard, Kathryn. *Doubletalk: Bilingualism and the Politics of Ethnicity in Catalonia.* Stanford: Stanford UP, 1989.

Young, Robert J. C. *Postcolonialism: An Historical Introduction.* Oxford: Blackwell, 2001.

Zapata de la Vega, Javier. "Marroquíes en el País Valenciano." *Atlas de la inmigración magrebí en España.* Ed. Bernabé López García. Madrid: Universidad Autónoma de Madrid, 1996. 185–90.

Index

About the Author

Daniela Flesler, State University of New York, Stony Brook, specializes in contemporary Spanish literary and cultural studies, with a focus on transnationalism, immigration, and the construction of national identities. She has published essays in *Revista de Estudios Hispánicos, Arizona Journal of Hispanic Cultural Studies, Journal of Spanish Cultural Studies, Studies in Hispanic Cinemas, Dieciocho,* and *Bulletin of Spanish Studies.*